Against All Odds

*One Man's Story of a Life
He Should Not Have Survived*

R.A. Lang

London | New York

Published by Clink Street Publishing 2014

Copyright © R.A. Lang 2014

First edition.

The author asserts the moral right under the Copyright, Designs and Patents Act 1988 to be identified as the author of this work.

All rights reserved. No part of this publication may be reproduced, stored in a retrieval system or transmitted, in any form or by any means without the prior consent of the author, nor be otherwise circulated in any form of binding or cover other than that which it is published and without a similar condition being imposed on the subsequent purchaser.

ISBN: 978-1-909477-20-9
Ebook: 978-1-909477-21-6

Author's Note

Dear reader,

I just wanted to share my life experiences with the rest of the world to describe the *real* world. The *real* world is something that has to be felt and experienced, rather than seen on television, the Internet or read in newspapers.

For legal reasons, I have not mentioned any companies, projects, or people's names throughout my story, or the name of the Caribbean island. They, if they read my story, will know whom they are. The good guys' names are real by personal requests, the bad guys' names have been changed.

I sincerely hope you enjoy what you are about to read and the journey I am about to take you on, spanning over twenty-four countries. You'll be shocked, horrified and amused, but nevertheless, what I have recorded is factual and exactly how events took place. Some drastic events from chapter 20 onwards!

Lawrence Koster has written a screenplay from chapter 20 for a two hour Hollywood movie due to events I should not have survived, but as you will read, I am not the type to give up easily. Enjoy … and thank you!

"Anyone can read a map, but it's the choice of which path one follows that makes the difference." R. A. Lang 2014.

Acknowledgements

Ward G in Morriston Hospital, Swansea for their Pancreatic Centre of Excellence that saved my life in May 2012, which allowed me to publish my memoirs.

¤¤¤

Sonja, her mother Trudy and father Hans, Myrthe, Pete, Fluer, Koos, Rob & Marion, Eugene, Baard and René from the Café Koepoort in Delft, Holland for all their inspirational support and friendship while I worked in Holland. We'll be friends forever.

¤¤¤

Jo and Richard, proprietors of the Pilot, Mumbles, Swansea, for their warm welcome and excellent selection of real ales, in addition to their own ales. They inspired me to complete my memoirs after many years left dormant.

¤¤¤

Susan and Chris of the Bella Wine Bar, Boutique and Café, Qawra, Malta for their support and encouragement while I rewrote my manuscript adding more detail to the previously published version by Friesen Press.

¤¤¤

Tracy, owner of Soul Solutions Spa, Qawra, Malta, for her revitalising holistic therapy and reflexology, which replenished my energy to continue working.

¤¤¤

Mark and Vanessa of Images snack bar and restaurant, Qawra, Malta for their traditional British cuisine and live sports channels making a home from home for all British and other European visitors.

Contents

Chapter 1 – How It Began..1
Chapter 2 – South Africa..11
Chapter 3 – Back to Wales...30
Chapter 4 – Islamic Republic of Iran..35
Chapter 5 – Kingdom of Saudi Arabia...51
Chapter 6 – Phuket Fishing Tournament...77
Chapter 7 – First Time in Venezuela...82
Chapter 8 – Help from Swansea..100
Chapter 9 – Pakistan...107
Chapter 10 – Second Time in Venezuela..113
Chapter 11 – First Time in Qatar...127
Chapter 12 – Third Time in Venezuela...129
Chapter 13 – Libya to Nigeria..143
Chapter 14 – France..151
Chapter 15 – Tunisia...154
Chapter 16 – South Korea, China, Japan, Singapore, Indonesia, Dubai, Qatar.......158
Chapter 17 – Thailand..174
Chapter 18 – Malaysia..184
Chapter 19 – Second Time in Qatar..191
Chapter 20 – Ghana, Togo, Benin and Nigeria......................................199
Chapter 21 – Caribbean...225
Chapter 22 – Kazakhstan..236
Chapter 23 – Back to the Caribbean...275

Chapter 24 – Return to Nigeria 297
Chapter 25 – Hospitalised 325
Chapter 26 – The Netherlands 339
Chapter 27 – Kurdistan 351
Chapter 28 – Malta 356

Chapter 1
How It Began

It all began in 1978, when I moved back to Wales at the age of sixteen to complete my apprenticeship as a plater in a heavy engineering fabrication shop. The fabrication shop was called Bercon Engineering, and it was located in a small, Welsh village called Penclawdd, which was better known for its cockle factories than its fabrication shops.

There were still remnants of foundations where anti-aircraft guns had helped defend the steel works in Llanelli just across the estuary during the Second World War.

Penclawdd wasn't the easiest place to work for someone who had completely lost his Welsh accent after seven years living outside London, in Hindhead, Surrey. My accent caused quite a bit of hostility, which was eventually overcome. I'd travel the twenty-five minute trip every day on a little moped. This was fine in the summer months, but during the cold winter months my hands and knees would be numb by the time I arrived.

My apprenticeship was to last for four years, and I had to spend every Wednesday in the West Glamorgan Institute for Higher Education for the theoretical part. Because my apprenticeship was long before the days of health and safety codes, the workshop left a lot to be desired. There weren't any machine guards, eye shields, or any other safety measures installed.

The only thing we could do was complain to our union representative when we needed to pay our dues on Friday nights once a month. The union representative would eventually visit the office, but nothing was ever done to improve things.

As an apprentice, the usual jokes were played on me, and I was rather gullible for the first couple of years. I needed to arrive earlier in the mornings than the tradesmen so I could go outside to the red diesel tank and fill twenty-two litre cans. I would use those to refuel the old-fashioned, very unhealthy, diesel salamander heaters in the workshop. These were dangerous, and they often blew back in my face when I lit them.

We'd all huddle around the heaters, holding our damp coveralls near the heat to dry them as much as we could before wearing them. Our gloves would often be wet from the day before, and also frozen in the winter. Meanwhile, I got burnt regularly when I picked up hot steel without realising my gloves had holes in them.

They didn't like to issue new gloves until the old pair was in a really bad condition. The same went for respirators and facemasks. I often become ill when welding galvanised steel because I couldn't avoid breathing in the zinc fumes from inside my welding head shield. We called it chemical flu.

We didn't have any welding curtains or screens either, so we regularly experienced 'arc eye' symptoms. Arc eye occurred when the powerful, ultraviolet light entered the corner of passing workers' eyes as another worker was striking an arc to start welding.

The light caused the membranes protecting the surface of the eyes to dissolve, exposing thousands of nerve endings. It felt like grains of sand in the eyes until the membrane had time to grow back, which sometimes took a couple of days.

Sometimes, the arc eye symptoms were so bad that I couldn't open my eyes, which meant going to work the next day was impossible, so I'd have to lose a day's pay. It helped to put slices of cold cucumber over my affected eyes and stay in a dark room, out of any sunlight.

I suffered many accidents, mostly caused by my own clumsiness and sometimes the clumsiness of others.

Our office secretary hated the sight of blood. When I needed to report an accident and ask to go to hospital, I had to enter her office with my smashed fingertip or broken thumb behind my back so she wouldn't faint.

I visited Singleton Hospital, Swansea, regularly to have sparks and fillings removed from my eyes. The other workers underwent the same procedures.

Creating patterns to cut out the necessary steel shapes was a natural skill I developed, and I was soon given more and more complicated fabrications to do, which I enjoyed.

I became fluent in parallel line development, triangulation, and the common central sphere, and sometimes I used all three methods to develop the more complex patterns. Soon, word got around so I started to get job offers from other fabrication shops in West Glamorgan. Nevertheless, I was comfortable continuing on in the sweatshop until I had at least completed my apprenticeship.

For the first two years, everything seemed to progress in a normal way. I got filthy at the fabrication shop by day, and I played with cars by night, like most of my friends at that age.

I also enjoyed underage drinking at the bottom of the lane near our house in the Woodman Inn in Blackpill, and playing the motorbike touch game while riding through the streets of Mumbles at high speed, all the while trying to avoid getting caught by the police.

In March of 1981, things took a dramatic change for the

worse. Something happened that changed the rest of my life.

I had been meddling with an old vacuum cleaner motor in our old, wooden garage, which had been left standing after my father had built a new garage near the entrance of our drive. The old garage was just for me, and I enjoyed pottering around in it. I had built up quite a comprehensive collection of tools by that time, and a friend of mine spent a lot of time with me repairing cars for extra income. Each week, I'd collect my pay and go into John Hall Tools on the Kingsway in Swansea to buy another tool.

I decided I needed something to sharpen tools with, so I got hold of a nine inch grinding disk, which was made in Germany. We used them in the fabrication shop to grind steel. Not once did I take a moment to consider the motor speed of the old vacuum cleaner with regards to the safe working speed limit of the grinding disk I was mounting on it.

On March 30, 1981, my father returned home with our young Rottweiler after taking her to dog training class at nine o'clock in the evening. By a quarter past nine, my father lay dead on the living room carpet, surrounded by a huge pool of blood. He asked to see the machine working, so I went into the kitchen, plugged it into the wall socket, and switched the motor on.

With 240 volts running up my arms from my fingers touching the bare terminals, and the disk running at twenty thousand ramps per minute, the disk was uncontrollable. It was similar to a gyroscope, keeping the motor too ridged to move or throw.

After what seemed like only a few seconds, there was a loud bang, a sting in the corner of my left eye, and a torrent of blood shooting out from my father's chest. He stood there, clutching his heart with both hands for one or two seconds before collapsing into the entrance of the living room.

Though I was stunned, I went to see to my father, but there wasn't anything that could be done for him. He was lying face down on the living room carpet, and when my mother tried to turn him over, we could see that the carpet below his chest was totally saturated in a pool of blood. The blood seeped about two feet from his body.

I remember my mother keeping her cool. She dialled 999 and calmly asked for an ambulance before giving them our address and other relevant information. I picked up a flashlight and waited at the top of the drive so the ambulance could see where to stop without wasting time looking for the house name.

It only felt like three or four minutes before the sounds of sirens grew closer. I was surprised to see two of them. I hadn't heard my mother request a second ambulance for me. I hurried back to the house with the paramedics and showed them where my father lay motionless.

By the look on the first paramedic's face, it was clear what he was thinking. He slowly shook his head from side to side. The other paramedic moved me back into the kitchen where he had better light to attend to me.

The slight sting I had felt when the accident happened was from fragments of the broken grinding disk penetrating deep into the skin at the corner of my eye, just missing my tear duct.

After what had happened to my father, I wasn't aware of the blood running down the front of my face, nor did it matter. I watched as my father was strapped to a stretcher and taken to the first ambulance. Shortly after I had been temporarily dressed, I was taken to the second.

In those days, Swansea Hospital had a casualty area, and it was just a few minutes down the Mumbles Road.

My father and I were taken to separate rooms, so I couldn't see anything that was being done to him. I was waiting to be treated, and a nurse was sitting near me, quietly by the wall.

After what felt like hours, but was probably just minutes, my sister came in, looked at me, leaned in close to my face, and said, "Dad's dead." Just two words, which I will keep hearing for the rest of my life.

I tried to jump up and see for myself, but the nurse prevented me from doing so. A couple of other nurses rushed in to hold me down, which added to my stress, frustration and helplessness.

After a while, I was taken to a treatment room where as many fragments as possible were removed from my eye before they stitched it up. My father's brother had arrived by that time, together with police officers who wanted a statement while I was being treated. A nurse asked the police to leave because it was not an appropriate time. I was a mess and on a lot of tranquillisers, medication that I ended up taking every night for the following two years. It took several more years for the rest of the fragments to work their way out from my eye area.

The funeral was held in Bishopston Church, which was very close to my father's birthplace. It was one of the biggest funerals held at the church because my father knew many people through his job, and people came from all over the United Kingdom to pay their respects, including my workmates.

Just two weeks after the funeral, I was advised to return back to work in order to occupy my mind with other thoughts. I was required to use the very same grinding disks that had killed my father just three weeks before. In fact, everything I saw that revolved reminded me of the disk that exploded, and this continued for several more months.

I kept my mind occupied with as many distractions as possible. I continued to work in the fabrication shop by day and spent all my spare time working in the garage at the top of the garden until very late at night making wrought iron work. My daily working hours averaged twelve to sixteen and sometimes longer, but at the age of eighteen, this wasn't a bad thing.

My mother would wake up and see the garage light was still on so she'd cut the power for a few seconds as a signal that enough was enough. I enjoyed making gates, railings, balustrading etc. for people, plus it was an additional source of income.

I'd make time to take our Rottweiler for walks across the long beach at Oxwich Bay, around Clyne Valley or Clyne Gardens or anywhere else where she could run freely without the danger from passing traffic, but she mostly walked close to my side. She always insisted on sitting in the front seat of my car when we'd drive somewhere. If the seat was already occupied, she'd force her way to the front until she was sitting upright on their lap with her head out of the window.

Eventually, I completed my four year apprenticeship and settled into a life of work, but I was far from satisfied. I knew there had to be more to my life than a set routine, and I began thinking about ways to change things. My father had never been happy with my chosen career, even embarrassed by it, so I decided to change my career to better suit his wishes.

I had heard about a new course at my local college, Welding Inspection, so I immediately enrolled for the September start. While taking the course, I signed up for another course: Radiograph Interpretation of Welded Joints.

The two courses complemented each other and took up four evenings per week. I attended them after working in the fabrication shop during the day. I figured taking the two courses were the easiest way to change my career path and the choice later paid off.

Whilst attending my night classes, I met a great mix of fellow Welshmen, each with the same enthusiasm to improve their knowledge and gain a better understanding of inspection techniques, which would hopefully enhance their career chances.

It was at these classes I made a new friend, Dai, who arranged a job for me with the engineering company he worked for in Port

Talbot. That turned out to be a great move and I made many new friends from Neath, Port Talbot and the Welsh valleys. We'd be assigned new build, repair and maintenance tasks in the local Port Talbot and other steel works, which we all enjoyed doing.

Until I joined the company, the welding shop comprised mainly welders, fabricators and riggers with a main bias towards civil engineering works. As I was the first plater to work there, the company was able to take on different kinds of contracts, which involved the fabrication of piping, as I was able to develop the patterns for it. This also became a new interest for the rest of the workers, who were all keen to help whenever the need arose, and we all had a great team spirit.

Nobody seemed to complain about the varying conditions we worked in, as we'd receive additional money for the conditions which we had to endure. Some of the conditions included working outside in the pouring rain and working chest deep in oil in the cellars of the steel works. Some of the conditions allowed us to go home as soon as the job was complete, which was especially favourable during the summer months.

On such occasions, I'd hurry home, clean up and go down to Oxwich Bay to help out with a friend's water ski school. On some of the warm summer evenings, we'd choose to sleep on the beach to avoid the morning rush and traffic jams returning back early to continue with the ski school.

On my birthday in July of 1984 I was busy opening my usual birthday cards when I heard the postman make his daily delivery through the letterbox. I picked up the letters and found one addressed to myself. When I opened the letter, it wasn't a birthday greeting at all, but a letter that could better be described as shock and horror.

It was from an ex-girlfriend who had petitioned against me as being the father of her child. The girl was a cook who worked just across the road in the University's halls of residence. I hadn't seen her since the previous Christmas and she was claiming to be five months pregnant. Okay, I thought, then she has stated a time in her petition when I had already left her, so she needed to account for two missing months somewhere.

She was the type who desperately wanted a baby, which was the main reason for leaving her. I wasn't in a position to commit myself to eighteen years of maintenance fees, especially when it was so clear that I wasn't the father.

She wasn't having any of it so it was off to get legal support. It was terribly embarrassing answering all the necessary questions from a female lawyer with regard to how many times a week was I seeing her and how many times a night I needed to satisfy the girl. I must admit, my lawyer looked quite impressed when I mentioned figures like three times a night, seven nights a week, but nonetheless the timing was clear that I wasn't the father so the odds were at least in my favour. After several months of worry had passed by, with the exchange of legal letters and the need to prove the dates I'd left the girl, it fortunately came to nothing.

During this period an Auntie had died and left a Thai Buddha made out of cast brass, which sat on a hand-carved wooden stand. I was later to learn that it was an original antique Thai Buddha aged over three hundred years.

Many years later, I was to learn the true significance of why this Buddha had found its way to me. I was to return it back to the country it had originated, in person, and hand it to a monk who'd play a significant part later in my life.

Chapter 2
South Africa

I had a South African friend who had a double glazing business in Swansea. He met me regularly for a few beers after work. He always told me about his time in South Africa and how good life was when he was living in Cape Town. It sounded like such a wonderful place, and I became even more eager to restructure my future and get away from the United Kingdom for a while.

I was twenty-seven years old, and becoming increasingly frustrated with my day to day routine. In May of 1989, I read in a London newspaper that there was going to be a seminar held in a London hotel regarding emigration to South Africa.

I didn't need to waste time thinking about it. I decided to attend, compiled my first curriculum vitae, and headed to the seminar. At the seminar, there were representatives from South African banks, immigration officials, and representatives from the South African Embassy. It was there I met a man who had a business partner based in Johannesburg who specialised in recruitment. I handed him my CV and he wasted no time in faxing it over to him.

Just a week later, I was flying to Johannesburg to start my very first overseas contract as a welding inspector, representing the client on the first offshore gas platform to be built in the country.
After rushing around having the usual inoculations, buying

suitcases and choosing what to pack, I was ready for my long-awaited adventure to finally begin.

The long-haul flight began in London, Heathrow, and went to Amsterdam and on to Nairobi before landing in Johannesburg. The day I left Swansea was a terrible day filled with torrential rain. I got soaked walking from my mother's car to the coach station along with my mother.

I was both excited and also nervous, not knowing what was in store for me the other end, who would meet me, and where I'd be staying. Emotions were running high and I felt a little choked up when it was time to bid my mother goodbye. I managed to put on my bravest face and made the exchange as brief as I could before boarding the coach.

I waved her goodbye from my window seat and began thinking about the journey ahead. I figured that I wouldn't see her for at least a year and a new empty feeling began in my stomach. The coach eventually pulled out of the Swansea Quadrant bus station a few minutes later and headed towards the junction with Oystermouth Road.

Much to my amazement, there, waiting at the junction in the torrential rain without an umbrella, stood my mother. She gave me one last wave farewell before the coach pulled out onto the main road and headed towards London.

You could see by the look in her eyes that she was excited about her only son's first journey overseas, but she was also saddened to see him leaving with little idea when she would next hear from him or see him again.

It wasn't until several years later that my mother explained to me what she had found when she arrived back at her empty house. As she entered, she could smell a fresh, earth-like aroma, the type one smelt in a forest after it had been raining. She walked into the lounge, only to see a blanket of mist completely covering the blue carpet. In fact, the mist was so dense that one couldn't tell what colour the carpet actually was.

My flights hadn't been organised very well. I boarded the flight to Amsterdam in London Heathrow on time, but it only allowed a brief thirty minute gap before my next flight to Kenya took off, so it was a really hurry in Schiphol airport. Safely onboard my KLM flight, I could finally relax, knowing that I'd made it. My KLM flight finally reached African soil in Nairobi where some passengers got off and others joined the flight. We were invited to get off the flight to stretch our legs, which I took full advantage of.

I walked into Nairobi's airport for a look around, and I was quite surprised to see how expensive it was. I figured that, because Kenya was a popular tourist destination, the prices were deliberately high to milk the tourists of their last remaining holiday money.

Upon arriving in Johannesburg later the same day at around five o'clock in the afternoon, I was met by a representative from the company I would be working for. I was expecting to be handed my domestic flight tickets to Cape Town, but to my surprise, I was instead handed three maps, some car keys, four hotel booking vouchers, and instructions that Cape Town was, "In that direction, straight down the N1 highway."

Although Johannesburg is the commercial centre of the country, it is not one of the three capital cities in South Africa.

The company rep helped me with my luggage and drove the car to the hotel, the Travel Lodge. He helped me carry my luggage to my hotel room because it would not be very safe left back in the car. After that, in true South African style he showed me the way to the bar.

Tired from not getting any sleep on the flight, my first South

African beer hit me hard. The second was easier ... so was the third ... and the fourth. Eventually the rep had to leave me to meet his wife.

I proceeded to drink a few more beers to ensure a good night's sleep before going to the restaurant and then heading for bed. I slept very well that night, and I got up early the next morning to leave at six o'clock while the roads were still quiet for the second leg of my journey.

I had no idea at that time that the South Africans had placed bets on whether I'd make the trip without getting lost. I pulled out of the Travel Lodge and arrived at a crossroads. *Right*, I thought, *no signs saying Cape Town, or N1, or "Andy this way"?* When the lights changed to green, I pulled away and suddenly felt as though I was going in the wrong direction.

I made a U-turn to retrace my steps, but then I made another U-turn and went back the way I originally went. Ultimately, I pulled over to the side of the road to think about it. Luckily, there was a group of local road workers doing some repairs, so I shouted out, "Which way to Cape Town?" They all burst out laughing and all pointed me in the right direction, so I more confidently continued on my journey.

My fuel tank was full when I left, but I was warned not to pass a fuel station without filling up because they were strategically spaced far apart along the N1; if you missed a station, you would run out of fuel before getting to the next one. Sure enough, it was almost three hours later before I saw my first fuel station. I was running low, so I pulled over and filled my tank to the top.

After ten hours of driving down the N1 through the Orange Free State with hardly a bend in the road I arrived at my second hotel. The place was called Bloemfontein.

The Republic of South Africa has three capitals: Pretoria, Cape Town, and Bloemfontein. Pretoria was the home of the executive branch of government, Cape Town held the assembly, and Bloemfontein housed the Supreme Court.

The N1 went straight through the middle of the city, and I found the hotel right alongside the road. It was dark by then, so I had no desire to explore the place. Instead, I checked in, ate, and went straight to bed. There weren't any bills to pay because my company had arranged to pick up the bills from all four hotels.

After another early start and seven hours of driving, I could finally see the awe-inspiring sight of Table Mountain, albeit far in the distance. It was a hot day, and due to the shimmering effect on the road in front of me, I couldn't see too far ahead. Still, Table Mountain stood out on the horizon. Throughout the entire trip, I don't think I drove around a single bend.

As I got nearer to Cape Town, the dual carriageway I was on began featuring some planted flowers. The flowers divided up the two sides of the road. I drove along them for several miles before I entered the city itself, which felt quite welcoming.

The only time I managed to get lost was after I pulled over in Cape Town to ask directions to the Plein Park Travel Lodge Hotel. A friendly local police officer explained that I was just a couple of 'robots' away, so off I drove looking for robots.

I drove around for almost an hour looking for robots before I pulled over again and asked another police officer where the robots were. He realised I was from out of town, and he explained that 'robots' were traffic lights. When I thanked him, he told me to buy a donkey. In fact, everyone I met in South Africa told me to buy a donkey until I learnt that 'bia dankie' meant thank you in Afrikaans.

The next day, I made it to the site office in Saldanha Bay, which was only an hour from Cape Town driving north along the coast on the R27. After being introduced to the project team and checking out the job site, it was time to settle in to my new role.

After work, I followed a new colleague to the Saldanha Bay Hotel, which had also been reserved for me. After checking in, we went to their usual bar. The place which they frequented after work was in a place called The North Western Hotel in a nearby village called Vredenburg.

It was by chance that I met a local South African motorbike police officer called Guy Stokes. He soon became a great new friend and introduced me to a new South African way of life.

Guy helped me find a bungalow to rent in Vredenburg, not far from where he lived. After I was in the country for just a month, Guy came around to my bungalow on a Saturday morning and invited me to join him in target practice. I thought it sounded like fun, so off I went. I was thinking of black and white paper targets with sandbags behind them; how wrong I was!

Guy handed me his standard, police-issue, 9mm CZ semi-automatic and explained that he'd use his unlicensed, Russian, 9mm semi-automatic Tokarev. I innocently asked Guy what targets we would be shooting at, and he replied, "Anyone holding a stone, pitchfork, machete, or anything else in his or her hands!"

I thought: *hang on, I was in Swansea just a month ago, and now I am getting involved in an African tribal riot on a Saturday morning.* Guy said I shouldn't wait for someone to throw anything. Rather, he encouraged me to fire as many rounds into them as I could before they hit the ground.

I thought he was a madman until he explained that the South African police often made an example of a few aggressive rioters so the rest would run away and live to fight another day.

He explained that they saved a lot of lives by doing it this way, that they were preventing a bloody massacre. I've often wondered why they didn't just throw some gas canisters and be done with it instead of resorting to a more permanent solution. Fortunately, no shots needed to be fired.

The following weekend, Guy pulled up again and told me that he wanted me to see Saldanha Naval Base where he was a member. The place was simply amazing. We got through the security gate using Guy's pass, and then we went straight to the officers' mess. I was well received by the officers and made to feel totally at home and given a guided tour of the facility, which they were obviously very proud of.

It was clear how proud they were of their set up. The design of their barbecue was quite unique: it was made from a big sea buoy that had been mounted on a huge ship's propeller bearing. It had a chimney fitted to its top and large handles to its sides so it could be rotated according to the wind direction.

Every Saturday morning, they used one of the naval boats to troll Saldanha Bay for barracuda, which some like to call snook. Later, they cooked them on the barbecue whilst continually basting them with a mixture of margarine and apricot jam, and drank copious amounts of Castle or Amstel beer.

The beer was subsidised. At 10p per beer, we drank loads of the stuff whilst eating barracuda and watching the Northern Transvaal playing the Western Province at rugby.

The officers' mess was a large room with a variety of indoor games arranged around to use up some of its immense space. There were several snooker and pool tables, dartboards, carpet skittles and many other games to occupy their spare time, but it was the barbeque and rugby matches which drew most of the attention.

I got on so well with the officers that, after a few months, they made me an honorary member of the naval base. They explained that I was the first in the history of the South African Navy to be made an honorary member without having any naval history in my family.

I've still got my black South African Navy beret, which they presented to me, and I can only assume my name is still on their honorary member board in gold lettering at the entrance of their officers' mess.

It wasn't long before my senior management learnt of my naval base hideaway, and they asked me if I could get them in so they could take advantage of the eighteen-hole golf course with beautiful views over the Atlantic Ocean. I spoke to the officers, and they thought it would be a great social event to pit themselves against the project management staff in a games night.

It took a few weeks to arrange because everyone's car license plate number had to be given to the naval base security office and visitor passes had to be printed. Sadly, I couldn't enjoy the event I had worked so hard to organise because they had put me on nightshift duty the night of the party.

On the night of the party, the officers were all asking my management where I was and what time I would arrive until they were told they wanted me on night shift duty that night. This infuriated my friends at the naval base; they couldn't believe how selfish and idiotic my co-workers were to do that to me after so many arrangements had been made.

As a result, the naval base banned everyone from my management team from visiting the officers' mess again. They seemed to give me an even bigger welcome after that night, and I miss them all to this day.

I was still renting the small, two-bedroom bungalow in Vredenburg, but because I had rented the house unfurnished, it was hard going sleeping on the floor. Because Guy took up so much of my free time, I couldn't furnish it as quickly as I needed to.

I eventually met a local lady in the nearby supermarket who offered to help me partially furnish the place, starting with all the usual essentials. She also dropped her maid off at the bungalow once a week to clean until I was able to find my own maid.

Eventually, I bought some furniture, sofa, bed, kitchen utensils etc. and rented a cable TV. This made all the difference. Also, because the little bungalow had a barbecue built outside the kitchen, I was able to invite friends around on the weekends.

All was going well. I continued to work shifts: one week working days, the next week working nights. I still hadn't got around to fitting any curtains in the living room of the bungalow, however, so it wasn't long before it was noticed.

I'd only had my TV and cable decoder a week when I returned home from work one morning to find that my little place had been trashed. Local thieves had entered through the back of the house via the kitchen window, which was completely hidden to anyone passing by.

They stole just about everything I had that could fit through the window, but they couldn't get my rented TV through the window. What they couldn't take, they smashed. The most annoying thing they did was urinating over all my vegetables in the drawer at the bottom of the small, second-hand fridge I'd bought.

I called Guy as soon as I saw the devastation, and he wasted no time calling his police colleagues who came over a short time later. Several police officers arrived, and as they looked around, the policeman in charge told me it had been the work of locals who lived close by in a township. After all, they had only taken what they could carry on them.

He also pointed out that they were too stupid to open my back door, which had its key in the lock. If everything had a funny side, this had to be it.

Guy told me he would get me a dog to guard the house while I was out working and the very next day he arrived with a twelve-week-old Rottweiler puppy. The dog was very nervous in the beginning, like most Rottweiler puppies away from their mother for the first time. She quickly sensed that I was a dog lover, especially Rottweilers, so I was no longer alone anymore and had a new interest to take on daily exercise along the beach in Vredenburg and everywhere else I went.

The police had recommended that I get window grills fitted all around the house. Guy was quick to help me yet again and notified the owner, who was more than happy to oblige. The very next day, a pickup truck arrived, and a local wrought ironworker took all the measurements around the house. He was ashamed that a foreigner had had such a bad experience in his country, and he made very nice wrought iron window grills for the bungalow.

I could appreciate his workmanship because I had made people gates, railings, balustrading, and other iron works when I was in Swansea for extra income. I was always interested to see how others did the same kind of work.

His name was Peter. Once he'd finished fitting his handiwork onto all the window frames around the house, we sat outside with a couple of cold beers and chatted. He asked me if I had a maid. I told him I hadn't been lucky because everyone I tried stole minuscule things from me, which was annoying.

He recommended that his sister, Elizabeth, be my maid. She wasn't working, so it seemed the perfect solution. Later the same day, he brought her over to present her to me. She arrived dressed in a newly purchased maid's outfit, which certainly impressed me. I heartily welcomed Elizabeth who became a wonderful little companion to warm up my loneliness while home.

Elizabeth was as honest as the day was long, and she kept the little bungalow immaculately clean. Because it was so sparsely furnished, there wasn't actually much to keep clean. I didn't have a vacuum cleaner or a washing machine, but that didn't matter to Elizabeth.

She had all day, and she paced herself as she swept the carpet and hand washed my clothes. She seemed happy. Elizabeth was extremely honest and if she ever found money in my pockets, she'd put it on the table for me.

The grass in the front of my garden badly needed cutting, so she asked whether her grandfather could take care of my garden for me. *Great,* I thought. The next day, I arrived home to see an old man sitting down on the grass using my front door mat, cutting my grass by hand with what looked like sheep shears. The grass didn't seem to grow very fast, so he'd spend all day, every day snipping away at it.

He liked to smoke marijuana, which made him sleepy. When Elizabeth couldn't see him working, she'd go out and find him sleeping under a big rubber tree in the corner of the back garden. She'd angrily kick him to wake him up and get him back to work. I felt quite sorry for the old man, but Elizabeth made a better boss than I did, and she wouldn't allow him to snooze while I was paying for his services.

Elizabeth was always preparing meals for me with whatever she could find available. Meatballs were a regular preparation, even though that meant chopping up my prized fillet steak sometimes.
We developed a nice routine. Elizabeth would light the barbecue an hour before I was due home, and it was ready to use as I arrived. She'd hear my car pull into the short drive, which was her cue to throw a rib-eye steak on the grill.

By the time I had entered and taken my shoes off, she knew it was time to turn my steak, and then, after I'd had a wash and freshened up, the steak was ready to be placed on a plate together with the maize meal she'd prepared. In South Africa, they called it *mealy pup*, and it was often served with homemade tomato and onion sauce.

I insisted that she ate with me because she looked a little on the skinny side. Therefore, her steak would go on the grill well before mine as she liked hers well done.

Our meals together weren't without their surprises. I didn't have a table, so we had to sit on the little, scruffy sofa I'd bought. We ate off our laps. The first time we ate together, I sat on the sofa and little Elizabeth automatically sat on the carpet beside me.

I asked her what she was doing down there and told her to sit on the sofa, but she answered, "Master, if any of your South African friends call around and see me eating with you, it wouldn't look good for you!"

I thought, *first, I'm not involved, and have no intention of getting involved, with the apartheid*, which was still in full force in South Africa; and *second*, Master *is not my name*.

I explained to Elizabeth that apartheid didn't exist where I came from, and it would never exist inside my house either. She began to call me Andy after that, and the atmosphere changed dramatically. It was so nice having the little angel in the house and that was how it remained.

At that time, I was engaged to get married to a girl back in Swansea called Rita. Rita was becoming increasingly interested in staying with me in South Africa due to the lifestyle I told her about in my letters. I explained to Guy that she was interested in joining me, and he asked whether I would still be required to work nights. "Yes," I said to him. Guy recommended that I buy a sidearm, just in case I was broken into a second time, as it wouldn't be good that the robbers find a white girl alone in the house.

With that in mind, Guy took me to a local gun dealer, and after a short time, I settled for a small, CZ 7.62mm semi-automatic. It fitted well into my small hands, much better than the 9mm guns I also picked up, and it held fourteen rounds in its clip.

The sequence required for the purchase of a gun by a foreigner was to first buy a gun and then take the receipt to the local police station along with a passport.

The police took my fingerprints and a number of other pieces of information before sending my passport to Pretoria, where a gun license could be stapled in the back of it.

A week later, my passport was returned to me with my license, and off I went back to the gun dealer to collect my gun. As part of the requirements, I had to buy a gun safe and have it securely bolted to a wall in a discreet location inside the bungalow. Guy advised me to use the fitted wall cupboard in my bedroom, so that's where we installed it.

Three weeks later, my fiancée arrived, but this was not such a good move. She became increasingly homesick, and it was a long way from home for her first overseas visit.

There were many times when she did enjoy herself, however. Guy's wife used to pick her up in the daytime, and she introduced her to all the other local ladies. Due to the reduced intensity of the project, we began getting long weekends every two weeks. We'd leave work on Friday lunchtime, and we'd start again on Monday lunchtime. This was great because there was a mass exodus to Cape Town every long weekend for a change of scenery. We stayed in the Ritz Hotel in Seapoint, which was just behind a mountain they called the Lion's Head due to its appearance.

The hotel offered an amazing buffet breakfast and had a revolving restaurant on its roof. In the restaurant, someone was always playing a white grand piano. I always walked the wrong way when returning from the restroom because the table had moved, which was very disorienting.

The stays at the hotel didn't improve her homesickness, though. One night back at my house, Rita felt terribly homesick and decided to walk home to Swansea. I knew she wouldn't get far before getting into trouble, so I stopped her.

Just two days before Christmas, I caught her trying to walk out the front door not once, but three times. Eventually, she punched me in the mouth, cleanly snapping the root of my front tooth. All the dentists were on holiday for the week, so I couldn't eat anything. I just had to wait while my front tooth dangled painfully in my mouth.

In February of 1990, my mother came to visit me. She'd never flown further than Greece before, so it took a lot of persuasion to get her to come. The weekend she arrived, we stayed in Cape Town before driving along the N2 through the Garden Route and the wilderness to Port Elizabeth.

The first place I wanted to show her was the massive Sunday market held in Seapoint. It was located in the national stadium's car park near the Lion's Head. As I drove out of the hotel, I couldn't understand why all the roads were so deserted in Cape Town.

On the way back, we found out why. It was February 22nd, and the day Nelson Mandela was freed after twenty-two years in captivity. We were foolishly waiting at a red light when it all started.

Thousands of Africans rushed through the streets and totally surrounded my car. I put my semi-automatic in the car door in case of trouble, not that it would have helped. It was the first time my mother realised I was carrying a gun. Instead, as I beeped the car horn and waved at all the mob, they moved out of our way and let us drive on, right through the middle of them all. They didn't give us any trouble at all.

The following day, we drove east towards a place called George to spend a few days at the popular Victoria Bay. Every day, we'd see the narrow-gauge Apple Express steam train from Port Elizabeth to Loerie going past on the cliff above us. Bristol Carriage & Wagon in the United Kingdom manufactured a number of its original coaches in 1905. By 1924, however, those coaches were taken out of service.

George was a very nice place, and it was home to the crocodile and ostrich farms, not to mention the huge Kango Caves, which we also visited. It was at one of the ostrich farms that I had the opportunity to ride one around the enclosure. Some Japanese tourists watched on with great interest, taking many photos. The South African holding the ostrich advised me to hook my legs around the bird's body, hold onto its short little wings and lean right back to avoid sliding forward, which would have been dangerous if I'd slid off in front of the bird.

With a slap on the bird's rear end I was off and trotting around the small enclosure with a worker running behind me to slap the poor bird again if it stopped.

While dining in the hotel's restaurant on our last night, I was busy with my usual oyster starter when my teeth crunched down on something hard. I put my finders into my mouth and took out a small tear shaped pearl.

We left George the next day and headed to Port Elizabeth, which was also known as the friendly city, where we spent a couple more nights. Whilst there, we drove northeast one day to the Addo elephant park.

After four hours of driving around without seeing an elephant anywhere, we found all forty-seven of them at a watering hole. By sitting on my car's door I managed to take some really nice photos of a mother with its baby, which I eventually had blown up and framed. There was increasing interest from a nearby bull elephant that had started to open its ears in a threatening manner, so we pressed on. On the way back we drove over a green mamba snake.

We worked our way back the same direction we'd come from, and we spent a couple more nights in George until we arrived back in Cape Town. From there we went directly to my bungalow in Vredenburg. Just a couple of days later, my mother's three week visit was over so it was sadly time for her to travel back to Swansea.

By March, my fiancée couldn't shake off her homesickness any longer. The only solution was to get her a flight back to Wales.

She flew back, and I've never seen her again to this day. Nevertheless, I've heard stories that she's doing well for herself so that's nice to know, as she was terrific company.

Just a couple of weeks later, on a warm evening, I was rushing to start my nightshift with my driver's side window fully open. Someone walking at the side of the road, maybe drunk, but definitely angry, threw a broken beer bottle at my car. It all happened so fast: all I could do was put my hand up just in time to stop the bottle from hitting me in the face.

With the combined speed I was driving and the force of the throw, the bottle severed my entire thumb, which was left dangling by a small piece of skin. I wasn't sure where the local hospital was, so I got myself to the office where the contractor's nightshift inspector would be waiting.

His name was Ben. He was a Scottish man who was very much the old school type. He immediately stopped what he was doing and drove me straight to hospital. By the time we arrived, my blood had saturated my shirt and jeans so as we entered the hospital, the night nurse rushed me straight into a treatment room.

In an instant, a doctor joined us. I was still holding my thumb together against my right hand. Infection had already set in, and the pain was rising fast. It was difficult for me to let go of my thumb because areas of the blood, which had dried, had set like glue.

I put my confidence in the doctor while he lowered my arm down and slowly separated my left hand from my thumb to begin his assessment. Without needing time to think, he said, "It's lost. We just need to cut this small piece of skin remaining and stitch you up the best we can."

I couldn't accept this. I asked him to do whatever he could to save my thumb. He said, "There's nothing left to save. All nerves, tendons, everything has been completely severed." And then he repeated his words: "There isn't anything left to save."

Again, I asked him to at least try. I told him my right hand would be useless without a thumb, so he agreed. He stated, "I'll do my best, but it'll probably be a waste of time."

The doctor was a general practitioner, not a surgeon, and he spent five and a half long hours doing all he could before stitching my skin back together. He had to keep injecting more and more painkillers into me, but they did nothing to stop the burning sensation I was feeling from the infection in my thumb.

He wrote a prescription for a course of antibiotics and a few other drugs, and he told me to clean the area and change the dressing daily until I returned to have the stitches removed.

I couldn't clean my wound myself because doing so required two hands to slowly unwrap the blood soaked bandage. Luckily, the two local barmaids from the North Western Hotel took turns in helping me.

The two girls, Julie and Dalmaine, decided who would visit me each day and for the following two weeks, they were always on time, never missing a day. The wound was badly infected, and the pain prevented me from sleeping.

Sometimes, I had to stop the girls from pulling on the bandage when trying to separate it from the dried blood because the pain was too great and there was the constant risk of opening the wound. Instead, they gently dampened the blood with warm sterile water until it was soft enough to pull the bandage free.

I kept off any kind of alcohol with the hope that the antibiotics would succeed against the infection. Ultimately, my choice paid off. Eventually, back at the hospital, the stitches were removed even though the doctor didn't have any confidence that I would ever be able to use, feel, or move my thumb again.

So, with the confidence that I still had my thumb attached and on the mend I continued to work out my contract as usual and enjoy the South African lifestyle. The man from the gun shop told me about his friend who'd had a similar accident and was able to feel and use his thumb as normal. He advised me to keep dipping my hand in a bowl of hot water and try squeezing a tennis ball as often as I could. This I continued for months, and it really seemed to be doing something. My original twelve month contract was nearing completion, as was the project in Saldanha Bay.

Preparations were being made to move the entire project management team to Mosel Bay where the gas plant would be constructed to receive the gas imported from our newly, soon-to-be-installed offshore platform. It had almost been twelve months since I'd left the UK and I was starting to think of returning home, with the plan that my next overseas trip would be longer with some rotational leaves built in.

I began to advertise among my colleagues in my office the items I'd bought to make my rental bungalow home but they offered me ridiculous amounts for my items. Rather than sell everything off for such low prices I decided to give everything to little Elizabeth who had at least been a great support and a lovely little friend to. Poor little Elizabeth cried when I told her she needed to arrange some transport to empty my bungalow and take it all home with her as I was leaving South Africa. She partly understood my reasons but still didn't fully understand, as my work was not over.

She called her brother who'd introduced me to her months earlier and he came to see how much he needed to move. It was really nice to see him again and we had a barbeque, which Elizabeth had become very good at.

Eighteen months later, after spending every opportunity trying to bend my frozen thumb joint using my left hand it began to move slightly. A few months later, I could feel the tip of it tingling, but only slightly. I continued bending and stretching my thumb for another two years until full feeling had returned. In the end, I could move it without any help from my other hand. My thumb was fine again.

Chapter 3
Back to Wales

I returned back to Swansea in June of 1990, after recovering from a very hospitable twelve months in South Africa. It wasn't too long before I secured a short contract for a three-month shutdown on a nuclear power station in Dungeness, New Romney, Kent.

New Romney was a really nice place to be, and so was the pub I stayed in whilst working there. The shutdown crew was from North Yorkshire, and were a real mix of characters. They were great to work with, and they all knew their roles. I was still a little new to the business, but I had learnt enough from South Africa to hold my own, plus I knew what was required of me.

Because I was the quality assurance engineer, I was the only person taking care of the quality for the shutdown. I also needed to work late every night to keep up with the progress and large amount of paperwork. I had contractors for site coverage, inspection, heat treatment services etc., but in the end, the responsibility fell on my shoulders.

We had one particular labourer who was so efficient that the company always kept him employed. It was great for him because it was the only way he could avoid going to an asylum, where the rest of his family lived.

One night, I left the site office long after everyone else had gone. I quickly noticed that the entrance of the pub had traces of fresh blood on the walls. As I entered, I found more blood on the walls and the floor ... and then a lot more as I entered the main bar. A few crewmembers were sitting at the bar finishing their beers, but the whole place was badly messed up.

The site engineer was one of those sitting at a table, so I asked what the hell had happened. He explained that a local man had entered earlier and demanded a beer, but was refused and asked to leave. Apparently, this man was no ordinary man: he had a military background, but not a normal military background.

The police were called the moment he entered, but when they arrived, they stayed outside, as they knew who was inside. The man demanded to be served again, but again he was denied. He quickly became aggressive and started breaking up the place.

The landlord's son hit the man over the head with a baseball bat, which started the blood flowing, and then the son's mother hit the man with a large beer bottle, which added to his injuries, but still nothing seemed to affect him.

During all the commotion, our industrious site labourer had finished his beer and went to the bar for a refill, totally oblivious to what was going on. The landlady explained to Keith that they couldn't serve any beer until they had got the man out of the pub, which seemed to register something in the labourer's head.

He calmly went over to the crazed man and said, "Get out." The man didn't react at all, so the labourer asked him a second time: "Get out." Again, he didn't get a reaction.

After that, the crazed man tried to return to the bar but the labourer responded by punching him on the side of his jaw, which knocked the man out cold. Apparently he barely moved his arm more than a few inches.

The landlord opened the front door and shouted out to the

police that they could come in. One police officer asked who had apprehended the man, and they pointed to Keith. The officer went over to Keith and thanked him for helping the community. The labourer completely ignored him; he just sat at the table like nothing had ever happened.

The shutdown was completed with time to spare. Luckily for me, before that job had finished I was approached by a new agency with regard to a two-year contract in the Islamic Republic of Iran.

I signed the contract with the Japanese steel company in their London office in September of 1990, but before I could mobilise, Saddam Hussein had popped across the Kuwaiti border, which put my departure on hold. The Japanese are known for maintaining the safety of their employees and contractors alike.

I needed to wait at home in Wales until the Japanese considered it stable enough in Iran for me to fly. After a month, I called the London office to say that I couldn't wait indefinitely as I needed to make money.

The administration manager, a lady from Yorkshire, asked me to check my bank account. Evidently, the Japanese had started paying me from the day I'd signed contracts. This was wonderful news. I enjoyed watching the news about the first Gulf war in my local pub knowing I was on full salary.

It wasn't to last, however. Early one morning, in January of 1991, I received a phone call from London. I was advised that my flight from London, Heathrow was scheduled for later that day.

I had very little time to get my inoculations, but with my mother's help I managed. After that, I headed straight for the Quadrant bus station to catch the coach to Heathrow Airport.

In the meantime, it had begun to snow very heavily. By the time I arrived at Heathrow, the snow was quite deep. By this time, both my arms had seized up due to the injections I'd had earlier in the day; I could hardly move them to manage my suitcase. As luck would have it, the snow caused my flight to be postponed until the next day. I called the London office, and they told me that I'd already been booked into the Edwardian International Hotel near the airport.

Once in the hotel and after looking at some of the prices on the bar and restaurant menus I rang the administration manager again to explain that I didn't have money put aside for such expenses. To my surprise, I was told to enjoy the lobster and sign everything to my room because it was probably the last good meal I'd have for months!

I spent three nights in the hotel waiting for a flight to Tehran. Each day, I would check out and return to the airport to see whether I had a flight. I spent twelve to fourteen hours every day waiting near the check-in counter but finally on the fourth day, I managed to get a flight by way of Frankfurt to avoid flying anywhere near the Middle East.

By the time I got to Frankfurt, I was just in time to miss my connection to Tehran. I had to stay in yet another hotel, but this time with the compliments of the airline.

That night wasn't unlike any other night for an expat in transit. I sat at the hotel bar the whole evening and chatted with a German journalist who was on his way to Baghdad to provide war coverage.

In the airport I noticed on the news channel that numerous Iraqi air-force jets were believed to have defected to Iran. Those jets were supposedly located at the airport I was about to travel to.
The next day, I was on the flight to Tehran. I asked the airline to forward my details to my Tehran office, which they said they would.

There were only twenty-four passengers on the entire flight, so the flight attendant understandably left the drinks trolley next to an Irish engineer sitting next to me. *How civilised*, I thought, as I was going to spend the next four months in a dry country.

Chapter 4
Islamic Republic of Iran

I eventually arrived at Tehran airport at eleven o'clock at night a little worse for wear due to the damn drinks trolley. As we came in to land, I could see hundreds of MiG-29s along the entire length of the runway. In actual fact, the Iraqi fighters had lined the length of the runway two and a half times!

I was soon to discover that nobody had been informed of my new arrival time in Tehran so there wasn't anyone from the Japanese company there to meet me.

Luckily, I had a number to call. After an hour of trying to wake somebody up, I was finally able to announce my arrival. It took over an hour for a Japanese man to get to the airport because the traffic in Tehran was like a permanent rush hour 24/7. As I stood there guarding my suitcase in the freezing cold, Iranian black marketers tried to buy my dollars from me.

The best was yet to come. The next day was a national holiday in Iran, so there were no domestic flights. After catching just four hours of sleep, they woke me up and explained that my taxi was waiting to take me south on a ten hour drive from Tehran to Mobarakeh, near Esfahan.

After a short time in the battered Hillman Hunter taxi, which didn't even have headlights, I heard gunfire all around us. I asked the driver what the hell was happening, and he calmly smiled and said, "It's Revolution Day in Iran. We celebrate this every year." It was quite dangerous outside because everything they were shooting up into the air was coming back down all around us!

I never quite understood why they celebrated 'Revolution Day', as the end result from the revolution was that Iran became a dry country and all bars and clubs had been destroyed. Apparently, the streets of Esfahan were flowing with rivers of beer from the barrels being carried out of hotel bars and broken up in the streets.

It was pitch dark for the last couple of hours, and we were relying on the moonlight to avoid all the potholes in the road. I remember telling the driver to slow down because we were going far too fast. I didn't want an accident in the middle of nowhere. The driver told me that everything was okay because Allah was watching over him. I reminded him that Allah certainly wasn't watching over me, and I told him again to slow down.

Working in Iran was a good experience, and the Iranians were wonderful people. I was always getting invited to somebody's home on my Fridays off. I'd buy a bottle of black market whisky to take along, which was always appreciated. Sadly, I did see a sick sight on one of my trips into Esfahan. As we drove through a small village, the driver stopped the taxi to show me a public execution.

I saw a young man's head placed in a noose, which was tied to the hook of a very small crane we like to call a cherry picker. There was a young girl standing against a wall with her hands tied behind her back. Her head was covered with a black cotton sack. Near the girl were piles of large rocks, and fat old women stood next to them. At that time, only women could throw the rocks at the victim.

The execution was just about to begin, so I ordered my driver to go. He was hesitant because he wanted to watch, but I strongly insisted. Fortunately, he drove away just before they murdered the no doubt innocent young couple.

My heart wasn't into visiting anyone after seeing such a terrible sight, but I continued to visit the family anyway. They understood my feelings on the matter, and they didn't agree with how Iran handled young couples holding hands or caught having a little cuddle in those days.

Alcohol was legal in Iran if you weren't a Muslim, but there was no tolerance if you were caught carrying it into your home. The easiest answer was to make your own, so that was exactly what I did. First, I bought a pressure cooker and a few feet of 8mm copper piping. And then I managed to find a short plastic tube to connect the copper pipe to the safety valve connection on the pressure cooker's lid.

The copper pipe was pulled around an empty bottle to form it into a coil, and that ran from the pressure cooker into the kitchen sink (which was full of cold water). During the distilling process, I left the cold water tap running, allowing the water to run out through the overflow. This helped condense the vapour going through the pipe. I had to be careful not to let the liquid inside the pressure cooker reach over 89 degrees because alcohol evaporates at 89 degrees and methanol evaporates over 90 degrees.

I regularly lit the clear liquid dripping from the end of the copper pipe to ensure that the liquid was producing a very clear blue colour. Any hint of orange, purple, or red would mean that I had to stop the process and pour the remains down the toilet. I had the shiniest, cleanest toilet on the compound.

It took several hours to fill a water bottle full of the uncut alcohol, but that was just the first part of the process. Once I had filled a bottle two-thirds full, I filled the rest of the bottle with raisins.

After that, I would turn the bottle once per day for a month before using it as a rough brandy. It tasted okay mixed with Coke. I never bothered to cut it back with 50% water; instead, I used more Coke and ice.

Apart from my still, I brewed beer from cases of alcohol-free cans. I'd just add dark brown sugar and yeast. This process was much simpler and quicker. For each case of alcohol-free beer, I would dissolve a kilo of dark brown sugar. I'd pour a sachet of dried yeast into a cup of warm water with a little sugar to start the fermentation process, and then I'd add it to my plastic bin with four cases of beer and four kilos of dissolved brown sugar.

After ten days, I'd siphon the beer into empty Coke and lemonade bottles, which were capable of taking the pressure. And then I'd add a tablespoon of white sugar to each bottle and replace the tops as quickly as possible, before the yeast reacted to the additional sugar.

I'd keep the filled bottles in a dark place for another seven days before moving them into my refrigerator. And then I'd wait until they were so cold that the internal pressure was low enough to open them without having them spray all over the place. I continuously poured the liquid into a large jug until the sediment arrived at the bottles neck, which meant it was time to stop.

And then there was the wine. Originally discovered in that region well over four thousand years before Christ, and even earlier in some places, it seemed like a natural choice, plus, it was easy to do. I just bought twelve bottles of grape juice, two-and-a-quarter kilos of white sugar and a sachet of dried yeast. From there, I simply mixed everything together and let it sit for twenty-one days before bottling.

I made an air lock in the shape of an s with a little water and some cotton wool. That way, the carbon dioxide could escape, which stopped the explosions from happening but didn't allow anything to re-enter. The original airlock was just a prototype, but later, I was able to smuggle in purpose-made airlocks bought from winemaking shops in Wales. They were perfect for the job.

Sometimes I needed to acquire whisky at short notice so I made the run into Esfahan myself. I used to go to a jewellery shop, which was more a front for the black marketers peddling the contraband goods. Every trip into Esfahan would pick up a government spy. He was easy to spot, as he'd follow me down every street keeping, he thought, un-noticed and would pretend to be looking into a shop window if I'd turn around in his direction.

The shop knew all about this and made the exchange very fast. I'd enter the shop and discreetly drop my bag on the floor, out of sight of my spy. Then someone would very quickly remove the rags that were used to fill it together with the payment in $$$s and replace with the bottles. The whole exchange was done so fast so I could leave without time to be seen buying anything. I purposely visited a few more shops, normally just looking through the windows to give the illusion I wasn't in any kind of hurry, whilst slowly making my way back to our courtesy bus.

Once safely back on the bus, it was time to run the gauntlet through the periodic roadblocks back to my compound. It was on one of these trips that the bus was held up at a makeshift roadblock and also boarded. Two Iranian police holding Kalashnikov AK-47s searched the bus seat by seat until they came to where I was sitting. I figured this was a good time to pretend to sleep, which is exactly what I did. The officer ordered me in Farsi to open my bag, but I completely ignored his instructions and continued to sleep. He was quite insistent that I open my bag and I began to find the entire situation rather funny. I felt the urge to start laughing, but instead, I bit my tongue to try to control myself.

After a few minutes the police gave up and left me carry on my journey. Once they'd left, I opened my mouth to take a deep breath of relief and blood poured out, all down the front of my polo shirt. I hadn't realised I was biting so hard, but it was a rude awakening of the country I was in.

During the construction phase of the project, we heard that the Iranian president was planning to visit the site. Nobody was told which day he would arrive for security reasons, but I saw numerous people planting evergreen trees all along the entrance roads to the steelworks to prepare for his arrival.

One day, I was walking around one of the five direct reduction iron ore modules where nobody was working. I was checking the status of piping that had been installed, and I lost track of time. A couple of hours must have passed before I realised how quiet the site had got, so I became suspicious and decided to return back to the office to find out what was happening.

As I walked out from under the module, a large group of Iranians ran towards me and pointed their Kalashnikov AK-47s at me. Just before I was totally surrounded I caught sight of Rafsanjani himself. He briefly saw me before I was blocked from view and hastily escorted off the site.

My work rotation was sixteen weeks of work and just ten days' break, back in the United Kingdom. Fortunately, due to the flight timetable, I was able to have twelve days back at home. I always tried to time my home breaks so I would be home at the same time as a friend of mine who was working in the merchant navy as a marine engineer.

In March of 1992 I was presented with my usual home leave flight tickets. My flight home consisted of a domestic flight from Esfahan to Tehran, where I would stay overnight, and then two international flights; one from Tehran to Amsterdam, and a final flight from Amsterdam to Cardiff airport in Wales. On this particular home trip, my scheduled arrival date was a week before my friend would arrive back from the ship he was on, leaving me with just a few days to have his company.

We were quite busy on site at that time with all the piping which I was responsible for, so the Japanese project manager allowed me to postpone my home leave by a week. This was great news, as I'd earn an extra week's salary, plus have my friend's company the whole time I was home.

Unbeknown to me at the time, my original flight wasn't going to make it to Tehran, at least not in one piece. The day I was originally booked to fly to Tehran was a busy one for me. I was on site most of the day supervising the pressure testing of a large process piping system and also air-flushing any remaining debris from inside the piping loops by opening valves wherever there was a pipe branch. It was late in the afternoon when I returned back to my office to update the records I kept of all piping activities and progress records, and a young Iranian documentation engineer came running over to me.

He was very hard-working and had managed to learn very good English in just six months! He asked me if I had heard the news, to which I replied, "How? I've been on site almost the whole day." We entered my office and sat down at my desk where my original flight schedule was still visible amongst the piles of other papers.

The young Iranian immediately put his index finger on my flight schedule and told me that I was one very lucky man. Puzzled, I asked why. He told me that my flight had had a bomb planted onboard and the fully-laden flight blew up just as it neared Tehran. It was later printed in the Tehran Times that the flight was carrying some high-ranking VIPs from the National Iranian Steel Company, which may have been the reason for the bomb on board. There were no survivors. I kept that flight schedule for quite a long time until it eventually was lost.

The Iranians also made new postage stamps to commemorate the project we were working on and each of us in the office were given a full sheet of the first edition stamps. The stamps were of an artist's impression of an aerial view of the steelworks we had built. At that time it was the second biggest in the world; the biggest was in Russia. It didn't feel right that we as foreigners were given such a unique gift, whilst our Iranian contractor received nothing, so I gave mine to the young documentation engineer as they would surely be worth something in years to come.

In December of 1992 I was responsible for pressure testing a natural gas 'header' (pipe manifold) which was one hundred metres long. Due to budget restrictions and lack of chemical consumables, I had to pressure test with water (hydro-test), without any anti-freeze chemicals added to the test water.

The daytime temperature was minus twenty-two degrees centigrade so if I raised the internal test pressure, the entire pipe line would have frozen in seconds, causing it to burst along its entire length, including some very expensive globe, ball, check and gate valves at the same time, with a serious dollar and schedule value. It was a genuine mission impossible for the time of year. At that time, there was something playing on my mind that nothing was impossible. I checked the site's general arrangement drawings, the process and instrumentation diagrams, isometric drawings and any other drawing I could find relating to the area I needed to pressure test.

Eventually, and so conveniently, I discovered that there was a super-heated water supply right at the beginning of the piping I needed to test. The super-heated water supply came from the Italian part of the site, as they were building the steel rolling mill, and their site was segregated from my side of the complex by a chain-linked fence. Unfortunately for the Italians, the fence didn't cover access to the drain valve of their super-heated water supply piping. I had my brilliant Iranian piping gang connect a high pressure hose to the Italians' super-heated water drain valve, so we could run the hot water down the pipe manifold which I needed to pressure test.

The super-heated water was able to keep the internal water temperature to just above freezing and we were able to apply pressure from time to time to search and seal any leaks along the one hundred metre line. We had the vent valve at the far end of our manifold open, with a flexible pipe fitted to it to take away the continuous water flow into our industrial drainage system. We had to maintain a flow of super-heated water continually for twenty-four hours a day to stop ice crystals forming. At pressure, the ice crystals would have taken just seconds to form, and in minutes explode the entire manifold.

Eventually, after my piping team had succeeded in closing all leaks on the manifold, they called me to witness the final pressure test and endorse its success. It was a freezing cold morning with snow and ice everywhere, and my piping team had worked continuously all through the night. I later discovered they'd worked for seventy-two hours with very little sleep out of respect for me, making final preparations for the pressure test. The test had to be completed so that my commissioning group could start earning their salaries.

Failure would have meant dozens of expats hanging around without anything to do until I had successfully completed the pressure and leak test of the manifold.

It was Christmas Day when we finally applied the full test pressure. I nervously walked along the pipe manifold, which ran along a five metre high pipe rack, expecting the worst, but it never came. My Iranian piping team had done an impossible job due to the ambient conditions at that time of year and had successfully achieved the impossible without antifreeze chemicals!

I gave the instruction to totally drain the manifold of all test water, including the opening of valve drain plugs and any other drain location where I could foresee water traps to avoid freezing ruptures. This took the rest of the morning to complete, before using nitrogen to dry the inside of the manifold.

Test completed, I stood at the beginning of the hydro-test, and heard the voice of an Italian process operator as he ran towards the chain link fence.

He spoke perfect English, but didn't have too much hair left since I'd last met him at a party on our compound a few days before. He was distraught and totally beside himself. He explained that all the gauges in his control room had been fluttering around for days and he couldn't find out where all their super-heated water was going.

I was standing on the hose that was still connected to his super-heated water supply and positioned my body so he couldn't follow its connection to my test manifold. I assured him to have faith, and that I was sure, that by the time he had returned back to his control room his gauges would start reading correctly again.

My Japanese senior management were beside themselves once I had returned and announced the gas manifold had been successfully pressure tested, and they immediately arranged a celebratory party in true Japanese style. Needless to say, I supplied the illegal alcohol.

During one of my home leaves I had bought several Welsh flag 'sew-on' badges to give to my Iranian piping gang. My original intention was for them to sew them onto the breast pocket of their coveralls. Instead, they put them on their jeans and proudly walked around the streets of Esfahan and Mobarakeh displaying my countries flag for all to see.

I didn't know at that time that apparently, the dragon on the Welsh flag originated from Persia. The Romans had copied it for one of their flags and the Welsh had taken a liking to it while the Romans were in Wales!

One of my Iranian piping guys lived on a farm. His father grew vegetables and fruit but was also a beekeeper and had over forty beehives. He came to the entrance of my office one morning and asked the security guards if they could call me to the door. Our guards didn't speak any English but I had got very good at sign language and understood I needed to go to the office entrance.

The young Iranian presented me with a full comb of honey extracted from one of his father hives as a gift in return for the little Welsh flag sew-on!

I was quite overwhelmed by his generosity and accepted his gift, not knowing quite what to do with it? It was in a cardboard box and quite heavy. It felt like it was about five kilos in weight and it was held together with a wooden frame. I showed a French Canadian electronics engineer who was working with me and he explained what I needed to do with it. As the daytime temperature got to fifty degrees centigrade in the shade, I was told to hang it outside the back of my bungalow in direct sunlight with a bucket strategically placed underneath it.

This I did the next morning, as there was a clothes line stretching across my back yard. The following afternoon, when I arrived home I went straight out to my back yard to see what condition my honeycomb was in. All the honey had been melted by the intense sunshine and had dripped into the bucket. It had also made an excellent flytrap as the entire surface was covered with sticky flies, which I'm sure were busy doing what flies do in it!

As the heart-warming gentleman which I tried so hard to be, I held back the flies as I poured the full contents into plastic containers and gave it all to my Japanese colleagues. The French Canadian had already reserved the comb itself for his family. The honey was very nice, the one time I dipped my index finger into the clean part of it just to try it.

One Iranian working on the site brought me in a large family-sized coffee jar full of marijuana seeds. Just for fun, I dug the three flower borders in the back yard of my camp bungalow and scattered the entire jar over the soil. I watered them, but I didn't think anything would become of them. In just a couple of days, however, I had a green back yard. After a couple of months, I had a jungle.

A few months later, a Canadian commissioning engineer joined us. We got on very well from the day he arrived. In no time, he said he could do with something to smoke. He mentioned that he'd heard there was good quality hashish in Iran. I told him what I had in my backyard, which he found hard to believe. That evening, he came to my place to see for himself.

Apart from being totally amazed by the size of my jungle, he noticed that my male and female plants were all together. He immediately removed all the male plants and piled them up separately. He explained that removing them would make the female plants produce more resin.

Despite my success, I decided to get rid of the whole lot. After all, it was only meant to be a bit of fun. The Canadian took several bags back to his place because he kept rabbits and rabbits love the leaves (as did his mad, local, feral cat). Later, we pulled the rest up and dumped them into a big pile for drying and eventual burning.

The following weekend, after a few smuggled whiskies, we thought it was a good time to burn the lot. It was so dry that it burnt immediately, and because we couldn't avoid the smoke ... *wow*. Enough said.

In addition to my brewing, distilling, and fermenting activities, I made several black market friends who could supply whisky at fairly reasonable prices. The Japanese expats also bought whisky, but they made the mistake by using the local currency – therefore paying ridiculous prices for the very same stuff.

I knew the black market needed good, old American greenbacks because that was what they used to buy foreign goods. In other words, Iranian Riyals were useless outside the country.

I could buy a bottle of black market whisky for just thirty dollars in those days. That was quite cheap compared to what the Japanese paid which was the equivalent of ninety dollars in local currency.

One night, the Japanese expats were having a party and didn't have enough whisky to go around. One of them suggested that they knock on my door to see whether 'Lang-san' could save their party with a few bottles.

When I let them in, they looked a little shy as they explained that they were looking for some more whisky for their party, which I hadn't been invited to.

I asked them how many bottles they needed, and they answered, "As many as possible." They were probably thinking that I had one or two bottles available.

I took them to the spare bedroom, which I used for storage so they could choose which make of whisky they preferred. They nearly collapsed when they saw 366 bottles neatly placed on the floor according to its manufacturer.

It wasn't possible to order or request a particular brand in Iran; you just had to accept whatever was available at the time.

The Japanese wanted five bottles to start with. I quoted them fifty dollars per bottle, which they found very reasonable. They tried to pay in local currency, but I insisted on dollars. So off they went and returned minutes later with two hundred and fifty bucks.

The twenty dollar per bottle profit helped compensate for all the British scroungers who regularly visited my place. My guests dropped by most nights for a free drink, every time promising that they would see me all right on their next trip, when they had money.

Of course, I never saw any money from any Brit sponging off me, so it was just as well they were drinking my profits. I would have made a healthy profit if it weren't for the British consuming my alcohol almost every night.

The Dutch, Italians, Canadians, and French all paid their way, but not a single time did any of the British pay me anything other than compliments to encourage the free flow of alcohol.

I left Iran in February of 1993, and I met my first wife just a week later. I'd just bought a new soft-top Vauxhall Astra, which was probably what caught her attention. She asked around until someone gave her my number, which she used to call me the very first thing the next day. I was vulnerable after being alone for over two years in Iran, so I was an easy target.

I won't go into the details about her, but I'll say that the valves in her heart would have complied with the engineering requirements for cryogenic service. Her heart would have had no problem passing the toughness tests, either, even at temperatures as low as minus 150 degrees centigrade (engineering talk).

Just a week after meeting her, she joined me on a quick week's holiday to Tunisia. I was quite surprised that she was so readily willing to fly off with such a new acquaintance. Considering the location and local customs, she chose to wear skin-tight cycle pants, which drew a lot of attention from the locals. Wherever we went, the youngsters would grab at her backside and run off.

We visited the usual tourist spots and went on a few excursions including one down south for a camel safari in the Sahara desert. I was given a really ugly animal, which was muzzled to prevent it from biting the other, smaller camels. Considering we went as a couple, the Tunisian safari guides led our camels in different directions so the trip was a somewhat boring one. I'd grown to hate camels since sampling their meat on a number of occasions during my stay in Iran when it was sold as beef.

Other trips included visiting the underground homes, which had been carved out of the sandstone where parts of the Star Wars movie were filmed. The best trips were evening trips, barbeques, belly dancing, horsemanship etc. The week went fast and it was soon time to return back to Swansea and start concentrating on securing another contract.

After no time at all, I was contracted to do another nuclear power station shutdown, this time in Somerset, southwest England. I enjoyed working and staying in Somerset, but it wasn't without its surprises. I chose to stay at a very old hotel, the same hotel as the project manager. This hotel had hundreds of years of history, some of which still possessed the premises.

The first night I thought I was hearing chains being dragged around my bedroom between the door and the window, but chose to ignore it and went back to sleep. The second night was no different from the first, nor the third night. I spoke to the hotel owner and he just smiled back at me and offered to relocate me to another room, which I readily accepted.

I knew noises were a normal part of such an old building, but in my second room the noises had a distinct pattern to them. Every one of the aged floorboards would squeak when I walked over it, each with its own personality. I quickly got accustomed to each floorboard and its location around my bed from the door over to the window. On my third night in my new room I was busy chatting on the phone to my new girlfriend, when I realised that the floorboards were creaking and squeaking in the very same manner and sequence as they did when I paced around the room.

It was clear that something was pacing back and fore from the door to the window continually. I explained what was going on whilst on the phone, which my girlfriend found highly amusing, and she accused me of not sleeping alone. This continued for the following week until I requested for yet another room change. None of this was new for the hotel owner so it was clear he'd heard it many times before from his previous guests who'd had the same experiences.

I explained that I really needed a room which hadn't inherited anything from the past, as I really needed to get some restful sleep. The daytime work was very fast paced and quite exhausting and living in hotels and out of a small suitcase wasn't the nicest lifestyle. Luckily for me, he did have another room which I could use, but it meant sleeping up in the roof of a converted barn. It was the same building in which my project manager was staying, so I agreed as I hadn't heard any complaints about that place.

The building shouldn't really have been converted into two floors and my room was located in the roof. The roof beams were so low in places that I really had to crouch down to save walking into the heavy trusses. The bed had also been squeezed under the roof so I had to enter it crouching down and sitting up in bed was impossible. Fortunately it was still summer so the draft coming through the old slated roof helped to ventilate the little room, even though it was quite fresh in the mornings.

I was to continue the following four months of my contract sleeping in the barn, which went without any more disturbances, and I must say the food in the hotel restaurant was no less than excellent. As a break, we would all go home every two weeks for a long weekend and sometimes I would drive home just for one night and leave very early in the morning for the 8am start back at the power station.

We completed the project with only a few days to spare so I moved in with my girlfriend in Swansea while waiting for my next opportunity, which I hoped would be overseas again. It wasn't long before I was awarded a new contract, but this time to work in Saudi Arabia so the only way my girlfriend could join me there was for us to get married. We rushed around planning everything and got married in September of 1993.

Chapter 5
Kingdom of Saudi Arabia

In October of 1993, I went to Saudi Arabia. I was required, by contract, to work for a three-month probationary period, so my wife had to join me later. Things were fine until then. After a thorough baggage search in Riyadh Airport (where they looked for anything that they might find offensive, such as a Bible), I was allowed to enter.

I was originally based in a hotel on Olaya Street, which ran through the heart of the city. I wasn't to know at the time that I would only be based in Riyadh for the first eighteen months before I'd be transferred to Jeddah for another eighteen months. Staying in the hotel was not so pleasant but at least I didn't need an alarm clock, as a nearby mosque would wake me up every morning at 4.30am, in time to travel at 5am for a 6am start out in the desert.

I remained in the hotel for six weeks until one day my Saudi company arranged for me, together with two other expats, to view a newly renovated compound at the other end of Olaya Street. The compound was quite well positioned, or so I thought at the time, as there was a huge supermarket just a hundred metres away and a few restaurants nearby.

We each picked one of the identical villas, which were all built around a central swimming pool. Two other families were already living there, a British couple and an Indian family, both of whom worked for the same company as I did, but were Riyadh based. The villas were enormous and quite ridiculous for just a couple to live in.

They each had five bedrooms and six bathrooms, a very large living room and lounge on the ground floor and another lounge on the first floor and a kitchen facing the pool. If first impressions were meant to impress, then they'd certainly succeeded in doing just that.

We needed to wait until our company had delivered all bedding, kitchen utensils etc. before moving in, which was to be the following week. We finally moved in a week later and it was quite a lot of work unpacking all the new appliances, bedding etc., which took most of the day, but finally things began to take shape. A week later, we were to go to our head office in Riyadh to collect our keys for the cars that had been allocated to each of us.

We were ushered out to the office car park and shown our not so new cars. It was difficult to tell what colour they were as they'd been sitting in the desert car park for the best part of a year. We all had a Toyota Cressida which was the very same as all the Riyadh taxis. They were noted for their reliability, which was the main importance, as if one happened to break down out in the desert it could quickly become a life-threatening event miles from nowhere.

Once we had used the bottles of mineral water, which we were made to carry to make a clearing on the windscreens to look through, we were allowed to proceed into the Riyadh rush hour traffic. It was the first time I'd driven both a left hand drive car and also on the other side of the road so it was a nerve-racking experience for the first few days.

Riyadh also had an American road system, which was also something new to me that took a lot of getting used to for a Brit. To turn left on the highway, it first meant taking a right hand slip road off the highway before being able to use the overpass to turn left. The secret was to cut across all four lanes of high speed traffic without incident. Any form of accident in Saudi Arabia was automatically your own fault. The logic behind that was the simple fact that if you weren't in the country, nobody would have hit you.

After several days driving around Riyadh looking for the right souk to go shopping in for things to make home more comfortable before my wife arrived, my stress levels were finally beginning to subside and dropped down from a state of outright panic down to high anxiety.

After buying plastic containers and garbage bins, grape juice and alcohol free beer, my wine and beer making was soon underway and going down very nicely with my expatriate colleagues living in the same compound. I'd built up enough of a stock in time for when our wives arrived to join us. Once they had all arrived, I invited all to a barbecue on the first free Friday when we'd all be off work for the day.

Everything seemed to be going okay until the father of the Indian family, living on the same compound, reported me to the head office in Riyadh for making alcohol.

He had never heard nor seen any evidence, but the wife of a fellow British expat from Wick in Scotland had deliberately told his Indian wife who had *naturally* told her Indian husband, who had in turn, *naturally* told my head office. It was all very natural I thought. Not!

Previously, neither my colleagues nor I continued to speak to the Indian husband after he had sold his fifteen year old daughter to a seventy-five year old Saudi for the marriage dowry. He knew the man because they went to the same mosque together.

I was instructed to go to the head office and accept the consequences from our administrative and human resources managers. I had no idea what was happening at the time, and I was actually slightly excited that I was being transferred to Jeddah. The penalty for making alcohol in those days was to be placed in a Saudi jail for twelve months and given sixty lashes with a cat of nine tails spread out during the course of the sentence.

Anyway, those Saudis were rather polite about the whole thing and I was let off with a strict cautionary warning and told to empty any bottles I still had. That was some party. I invited a few of my trusted expats, mainly Swedish and German to help me do just that. What they didn't consume, they took home with them just in case I was inspected.

The Scottish wife who had caused all the betrayal didn't stop at that. She'd have her son climb up the spiral staircase outside my villa and spend sessions on our flat roof spying on our every move and report back. We couldn't even have friends visit without her knowing. With hand-written messages written in the dust on our gate and ugly images of gargoyles it was time to look for a new place to live.

I applied to be moved to an apartment situated at the other end of Olaya Street, which passed all the way through the centre of Riyadh, not far from my original hotel. Many of my Norwegian, Finish and Swedish friends lived there and there were barbeque areas, tennis courts and a swimming pool so it seemed to be an improvement to where we were staying and what we were living amongst.

One Friday morning, shortly before moving to the apartment, I began to feel soreness at the back of my throat. We had been invited to a barbecue that evening across the small pool in one of the other villas, so I was hoping that all I needed to do was gargle with strong salt water to stop it from getting worse.

The salt water did nothing, and I became more ill as the day went on. My wife refused to listen to me complaining about the increasing discomfort in my throat as her only thought was about the barbecue and which bachelors she hoped she would meet there. She was the flirtatious type and always chose to ignore me when in the company of the other European nationalities.

Later in the afternoon, my throat became so bad that I couldn't speak and even my breathing became restricted. Eventually, I collapsed. I tried to get up, but I didn't have the strength to move. The more I tried, the weaker I seemed to get and I was fading fast.

My wife, complaining bitterly, went across the compound to call a British nurse working in the city and she dropped everything she was doing and came rushing over to see what was wrong with me. Within seconds of checking me out, she went running as fast as she could to ask her husband to bring his car around to our outside entrance to rush me into hospital.

I was fading more and more by the minute and I could no longer say anything at all. Her husband came rushing up the stairs to help carry me to his car while my wife just stood there, helpless. While her husband was busy bringing his car around, the nurse had called the hospital to give them advanced notice and instructions to be waiting at the side of the road with a wheelchair and an intravenous drip.

It was a short ten minute drive to the Saudi hospital and sure enough, when we arrived at the side of the road outside the hospital, a Filipino nurse was waiting as instructed. It was quite a struggle trying to get me out of the car and into the wheelchair. I felt totally useless as my friends did everything they possibly could to waste no time in helping me into the wheelchair.

I was in a terrible state by then. The Filipino nurse was desperately trying to get an intravenous needle into the back of my left hand under the bad lighting from the street lights and she kept missing my veins. Soon the nurse took charge and inserted the needle into my arm in seconds. After that, she taped it securely and wheeled me into the casualty's reception.

An Indian doctor soon came in to examine me and using an

instrument, he looked down my throat and wasted no time in prescribing me a strong cocktail of antibiotics and a private room for the next few nights.

Saudi Arabia can proudly boast that they have some of the very best medical facilities in the world, and everything looked immaculate as I was moved to my room. The nurse appeared a short time later to check the settings on my automatic drip.

She made a slight adjustment and told me that the machine was the very latest available. My friends asked my wife whether she'd return later because they needed to go as the car was still at the side of the road, but much to their surprise, she said she'd return with them because the barbecue was about to start.

Early the following morning, the very same doctor came to see how I was doing. He told me that I was a lucky man. He had diagnosed me with ulcerated tonsillitis and explained that the ulcers had become septic and managed to poison my bloodstream and that I had septicaemia. I asked him if all that could possibly happen in less than twelve hours to which he smiled and replied, "It did with you."

My wife visited me that evening after missing the daytime visiting hour due to a shopping trip to see how I was doing. She arrived late, so she could only stay with me for twenty minutes. She didn't seem to think it was necessary to visit me because I had nurses to take care of me. Nevertheless, people kept asking her how I was doing, so she didn't have any choice but to visit.

I was able to speak a little by the time she arrived because the antibiotics had started working. I asked her to leave some money in the drawer next to my bed so I could buy a newspaper to read. She told me I didn't need any money whilst staying in hospital because I had a TV. She coldly left without giving me anything.

I spent five nights in the hospital before being cleared and discharged to return home. Those five glorious nights in the peace and quiet of the hospital enabled me to finally get some restful sleep. Several weeks of living on the compound did not afford such luxuries.

Outside our compound, workers had dug a long trench right along our street. In the daytime, I couldn't get any sleep from working my nightshift because lorries were using the spare ground next to our compound a few metres from my villa as a dumping ground. Every time they dumped a load of earth, the tailgate of the lorries would slam shut, which made any sleep impossible.

At night, an ancient diesel generator with no silencer was started up to power a long string of electric light bulbs along the length of the trench. The noise made our entire villa shake, causing things to fall off the shelves. Several times a night I would sneak over to the generator and pour sugar into its fuel tank and run back inside my villa. After a further ten minutes the generator would shut down affording me an hour or two of sleep before they managed to restart it again.

Driving to and from work was becoming more and more dangerous as I fought to stay awake. One time, I actually fell asleep at the office while standing. It must have only been for a split second and I fell to the floor when I woke up. I really missed the hospital.

There was always something going on and one night, while working out in the desert on nightshift duty, something occurred that would have made it to the newspapers if the project hadn't been classed as top secret. It was one o'clock in the morning and time to drive up from our underground workplace to head to the site canteen. As I neared the area, I found workers everywhere, all looking up into the clear, starlit sky.

I pulled over and asked one of the security officers what was going on. He said that someone had visited the site with three very bright lights that had lit up the ground below it, brighter than daylight could ever have.

I could feel the tension and excitement in the air and once in the canteen, it was clear that everyone was very excited and talking about the same subject. I joined a table full of Filipinos to try to find out more, but everyone had the same story to tell.

After I finished eating, I drove over to my Pakistani security friend to see if he knew anything more. He told me the same as everyone else had and that something had hovered over the site with three super high-powered spotlights. The airspace above the site was a restricted area, so no civilian aircrafts were permitted to fly anywhere near the exclusion zone.

While the object was still hovering silently of the area of interest, the site security had called Riyadh to explain what it was they were looking at. They were told that there wasn't anything showing up in that area according to their Airborne Warning and Control System (AWACS). The Saudi Ministry of Defence always kept their aircraft fitted with AWACS flying around the capital twenty-four hours a day, seven days a week.

The security stressed that everyone had stopped work on the site and all could see the huge object hovering low above them, so they couldn't be wrong. The air defence agreed to send two jets to fly directly over the site coordinates to get a visual of what everyone was claiming to be there. Cameras were prohibited on the site to help maintain its secrecy, so recording the event was impossible.

My friend continued to tell the story with increasing excitement. Evidently, he had returned outside to wait for the jets to fly by with his colleagues, telling them what was about to happen. The object continued to hover silently over the very same area for a few more minutes before it slowly began to move.

Suddenly, it shot off at an incredible speed and disappeared into the night skies just a couple of seconds before two Saudi air force jets flew past at very low altitude, over the exact area the object had been followed by the deafening roar from their engines.

Apparently, the jets hadn't picked up anything on their radars either, but three thousand workers couldn't possibly be wrong.

There was always something happening out in the desert: if not a thunderstorm, a sand storm. One night, accompanied by a colleague, I drove back above ground because we heard there was a thunderstorm from hell going on. As I approached the entrance of the tunnel from one hundred metres below ground, I was met by a most beautiful array of lightning, which fanned out like fire coral.

Excited by our first sight, we drove to the highest point we could, which was on a small hilltop to get a better view. Once I'd parked our jeep we took in the most spectacular free light show we'd ever seen. While we sat there amazed with such a spectacle, we noticed that one particular streak of lightning was repeatedly hitting the ground and heading directly towards us while other streaks continued all over the place. We waited for a few moments until we realised that the lightning really was heading in our direction and decided it wasn't such a good choice of parking spots. We were on the highest part of the site and surrounded by metal!

Without hanging around a moment longer we quickly drove off back down the track we'd just come up. We had only moved a few yards when an intense streak of blinding light drilled the very ground on which we'd been parked. It was a sad fact that cameras weren't allowed anywhere near the site, so it wasn't possible to take any shots of the display, but it was an amazing show to have experienced and one that I'll never forget for the rest of my life.

Whilst working another nightshift, but this time taking my turn above ground, I was walking back towards my little site office when the wind seemed to pick up dramatically. In just a few minutes, it had changed from a pleasurable gentle evening breeze into the strongest wind I've ever experienced.

It was the beginning of a tremendous sand storm of enormous

proportions, which had come from nowhere. As hard as I tried, I could barely make it across the open yard towards my above ground office. The office was a portable cabin and certainly not a good choice to seek refuge, but by that time there wasn't anywhere else closer to seek shelter.

Running wasn't possible as I would have been blown over and I was practically walking horizontally as I made my way across the yard. By the time I reached back to my office, my toes were digging hard into the dust for grip while my hands were just inches off the ground while I was being held up by the storm's force.

Once inside the office, it was clear that the office wasn't the best place to seek refuge as the entire portable cabin was lifting off the ground and at times close to rolling over. The side of the office, which was being lifted by the storm, held all the bookshelves with our construction records. Needless to say, by the time I arrived, all the files were already all over the floor.

Fortunately, the landline was still attached so I called my colleagues based underground for that week and told them to stay where they were as it was almost one o'clock in the morning and time for them to head up to the canteen. I remember looking up into the sky to see an empty fifty-gallon oil drum flying across the yard about a hundred feet above the ground. I would never have believed such storms existed if it hadn't have been for that night.

Driving back to Riyadh the next morning, I noticed that a huge, concealed door, just fifty metres from the road, had been exposed by the sandstorm near our workplace. It was close by, but still a few hundred yards outside the perimeter fence. When I returned to work that night, it had been quickly covered up again. There were many rumours that some of the underground tunnels led off to other underground locations, so I could only assume that what I saw was one of them.

Soon, Ramadan came along, which I was very grateful for. Because my wife never cooked for me, I always arrived at nightshift hungry, waiting for the canteen to open. Fortunately for me, all our site security guards were from Pakistan, and they prepared special food for themselves during Ramadan. I arrived on site at six o'clock in the evening, just in time to be invited to sit with them on the ground and share their food.

They always prepared extra so they could invite friends to join them, however, they were repaid throughout the year. We constantly supplied them with soft drinks that were freely available in the office kitchen, but otherwise inaccessible to them at their posts. Ramadan was their way of saying thank you.

After eighteen months in Riyadh, I heard I was officially being transferred to Jeddah where everyone wanted to go. Being transferred to Jeddah was a good move. It meant I no longer had to see the faces of those who'd revelled in stabbing me in the back time and time again. As I was the only one who voluntarily took on the burden of setting up all the Riyadh site's documentation system and quality records, my company wanted me to do the very same for their site in Jeddah, so all my work had paid off quite nicely.

Jeddah was like a different world compared to the everyday stresses an expat endured living in Riyadh. I knew quite a lot of the contractor's staff as they'd also been transferred from Riyadh. They told me they had their own private beach not far out of the city and that as I was their client, my car pass automatically gave me permission to use it.

My wife and I used it several times and it was like a little piece of Europe. Friday was always the rest day for everyone so we'd always use the opportunity to enjoy the privacy of the beach. They had even built a pier so people didn't need to risk walking over the coral to the drop-off and instead, could simply walk down it and use the steps to enter the Red Sea. Walking over the coral was quite dangerous as it was infested with extremely venomous stonefish, which have spines all down their dorsal fins. If anyone were unlucky enough to step on one of them, their screams would be heard from far away and they'd spend the next six months in hospital having skin grafts until the venom finally wore off.

After just a few weeks enjoying life in Jeddah and still trying to find my way around, my wife insisted on going on holiday on her own instead of waiting just another two months to go with me on my annual leave. As it transpired, she had secretly planned with her mother and aunt to go to Benidorm in Spain and that's exactly what she did rather than stay in the United Kingdom, as she'd told me.

It was in her absence that I found out from a Swedish friend that she had been regularly unfaithful whilst I was working shifts in Riyadh once we had moved to the apartment where all the other Europeans lived. I could only assume that it was the reason for her coldness when I'd arrive home from work so many times.

I called her at her mother's home number to ask how she was, but instead of reaching her mother, however, her brother answered the phone. He didn't realise that I didn't know anything about her going to Benidorm with her mother and aunt and spilt the beans.

Thus began divorce number one after just nineteen months of marital bliss.

Once I had learnt what my wife was getting up to while I was at work, I paid my Saudi site manager a visit. He was a prince, and his family were very powerful in Jeddah and they owned a large amount of the land. He was a very good man and keen fisherman, and we would often talk about our escapades fishing in the Red Sea. I'd go to his office regularly to show him photos of my latest catches, which he always appreciated, and offer him some of my fresh catch to take home.

This time my visit was for a very different reason. I went into his office and as always, he'd pick up his phone and ordered some

Saudi coffee to be brought in. Saudi coffee didn't contain any coffee, but instead cinnamon and cardamom, which he knew I enjoyed very much. He could sense something was wrong by the look on my face and wasted no time in asking me if there was something he could do for me.

I asked him if he could help me with a domestic problem regarding my wife by cancelling her re-entry visa to Saudi. He gave me a warm, somewhat sympathetic smile and picked up his phone. After he had spoken just a few words in Arabic, he put the phone back down and asked if there was anything else he could do for me; it was done.

He was a gentleman and didn't ask any questions with regard to why I didn't want my wife to return to the Kingdom. Maybe he had figured that out for himself, or was just being his usual courteous self.

When my wife arrived back after her sleazy stint in Benidorm, her brother explained that I'd called and discovered where she'd gone. Suddenly worried that I'd found out, she became nervous and wanted to return back to Jeddah as soon as possible. She immediately called me and claimed that she missed me and couldn't wait to return to Saudi to be with me, yeah right.

With the pain I was feeling due to my newly broken heart, it was a real pleasure telling her that her re-entry visa had been cancelled and couldn't be revoked.

She didn't believe me and went to London Heathrow airport to try to return to Jeddah. Only at the Saudi Airways check-in desk, when they did their routine check, did she believe her visa was no longer valid.

She wasted no time getting both my offshore and onshore bank accounts frozen. That was great: she couldn't continue shifting money out of my accounts and into her own as she'd done since I first left for Saudi. It was clear from the beginning that she was probably following her five-times-divorced mother. We had got married on a Saturday, and she had made me give her access to all my accounts that Monday!

Three days after she got access to my money, she claimed she needed to go shopping, but when I offered to drive her, she snapped at me. She said she wanted to go alone. Several hours later, she returned without any shopping bags but instead told me she had met up with a friend and didn't make it to the shops.

I found out two weeks later that she had had a secret abortion. When I quizzed her why she'd done it, she said, "You have to take me all over the world before we can start a family."

My friends in Saudi laughed when I told them she'd frozen my accounts because I was paid in Saudi, and the funds went directly into my Saudi bank account. It didn't affect me at all; rather, the move had protected what I'd already made in Iran and Saudi until its destiny was decided in the divorce court.

I just looked at the experience as a blessing because it had happened so early in my overseas life.

Saudi Arabia became a whole new place to live without my wife around. I was able to enjoy parties again without watching her dancing cheek to cheek with other bachelors' hands all over her.

I was able to take up scuba diving again, and I became a dive master in a few months. I was able to spend money on myself for the first time since meeting her. Life was great again!

I moved from the compound in Jeddah to an apartment that was closer to the site where I worked. I met a Filipino woman at a friend's party called Myatt, and she became my maid and visited my apartment every morning at eight o'clock.

A few of my Riyadh colleagues later joined me in Jeddah, so it wasn't long before all the complaining started all over again. In Riyadh, we used to work twelve hour shifts six days per week, alternating weekly from day shift to night shift. That had been torture because the body couldn't adjust from one week to the next.

In Jeddah, it was set up differently. There were only morning and afternoon shifts with no night shifts. The day shift was from six o'clock in the morning until half past four in the afternoon. The afternoon shift started at four o'clock and went until one o'clock in the morning. I only needed to see the rest of the team for half an hour before having the entire site to myself.

When it came time to choose our work shifts, all my colleagues selected day shifts, thus, I grabbed the chance and volunteered for permanent afternoons. Everyone immediately agreed. After that, I visited my favourite prince in the world's office to explain what had been discussed and agreed upon and asked if it was okay with him, which it was.

I already knew there were no afternoon shifts on Thursdays, so I got paid the same for working a five-day week. This left the others with six days per week waking up at half past four in the morning and leaving at five to start at six.

It took a couple of months for my colleagues to realise their mistake, but it was too late to change things. I used to leave my apartment at three in the afternoon, Saturday through Wednesday, for my one-hour drive out into the desert. I would arrive home just before two o'clock in the morning after a relaxing drive on quiet roads to enjoy a bottle of home brew.

This had so many advantages: the traffic was light in both directions, so much safer, plus I could enjoy the luxury of my home brew every night before going to bed.

Because I was the sole client representative on afternoon shifts, I could organise things exactly how I wanted them to be with the contractor. It was certainly the best move I could have made. Soon, the Swedish friend of mine who was representing the contractor changed to permanent afternoons to join me, and that allowed us to scuba diving together in the mornings whenever we felt the urge.

I was able to build up quite an impressive stock of beer, wine, and rough brandy. I was working when my British colleagues were free, so they couldn't visit me, like they had in Iran. Due to my impressive reserves, I allowed Myatt to invite all her friends to my apartment for a party at the end of every month. Quality of life couldn't possibly have been better now that I was free to enjoy myself again.

Due to my permanent afternoon shifts, I had a lot of spare time to do whatever I wanted. I could visit my favourite fishing equipment shop in the centre of Jeddah or take my scuba tanks to be refilled with air whenever I wanted.

Because I was well settled in Jeddah, I could go scuba diving every day or every night. I preferred night diving, but it wasn't without its dangers, as I discovered one night whilst diving with my instructor. It was a Thursday night at eleven o'clock that we were on the corniche in Jeddah, just a ten minute drive from my compound.

It was surprisingly quiet that night, and I was using a new high-pressure tank, which I'd just bought. It was made in Sweden, like all my diving equipment. The normal scuba tanks were made out of aluminium, and their maximum working pressure was 200 bars, which is equivalent to 3,000 pounds per square inch.

The new tank I had bought was much smaller, but it contained the same volume of air and made of steel. The tank was very heavy on my back, and its working pressure was 300 bars, which is equal to 4,500 pounds per square inch.

As it turned out, this dive was the last night dive I would ever make.

Once fully equipped, we had to climb down the large, hazardous rocks in the dark until we reached the water's edge. Before entering the Red Sea on a night dive, we broke the glass inside our chemical lights and shook them until the fluids mixed together and began to glow brightly. I always took two underwater lamps on my night dives: a primary, rather powerful lamp and a smaller, standby lamp for when my primary lamp had inevitably depleted its batteries.

My primary lamp was a ridiculously powerful dive lamp. It was capable of turning total darkness into bright daylight. It burned up eight D-cell batteries in just forty-five minutes, so the end of each night dive required the use of my spare little lamp, which instantly developed a more claustrophobic atmosphere in the darkness. On this dive, the powerful lamp was probably what saved my life that night.

We began our descent to just ten metres, and we tied a red chemical light to some coral to mark our entry/exit point. We continued our dive, exploring the coral and placed additional green chemical lights every so often as markers to trace our way back to where we started as we proceeded in the northerly direction. We wanted to have our cars close by when we finished the dive so we'd ensure we returned back in time to find the marker before the red light had died.

While underwater, it was a little difficult to stay positioned with all the weight on my back, still everything seemed okay at first. I always wore a wetsuit which was made of Lycra and Polartec, mainly to help protect my body from the razor sharp coral. It wasn't to help me stay warm, as it was 28°C in the Red Sea.

We completed our first thirty minutes of the dive and turned to complete our second thirty minutes in the direction from which we'd come. We were heading back to our starting point exploring a slightly shallower level of coral to ensure that we both had spare air left in case of any unforeseen event and to cover new places.

After about ten minutes, while I was busy stroking a large,

sleeping grouper, I experienced one hell of a surprise. Night diving offers a whole new meaning to the word darkness. The only possible view was in the direction the dive lamp was pointing.

I was focused on the sleeping fish when something caused me to roll over uncontrollably. All I could do whilst struggling to roll back over was swing my dive lamp around.

It is well known that sharks like to eat at night in shallow water. After all, fish also need their sleep. Coral reefs present a perfect lunch venue because most fish like to live in the first ten metres depth and that's exactly where I was.

As I managed to spin around and aim my powerful dive lamp into the dark abyss, I saw what had moved the water in such close proximity to me. It was the tail of a shark of enormous proportions. I had a brief but clear view of the shark's tail, which was tall enough to make it at least sixteen feet long. It was only a few feet away, but in the darkness I only briefly caught sight of it before it disappeared into the night.

I quickly swam over to my dive buddy and indicated a big mouth by spreading my arms. I pointed in the direction the shark had gone, and we both pointed in the up direction at the same time, so we wasted no time in clambering over the coral drop-off where we would be safe and relax again.

Diving at a depth of only ten metres does not require any decompression stops, which was just as well because we weren't in any mood to hang around.

The following weekend, a fellow expatriate stole the show. He had just returned from diving alone, which I never did, in just the same place where we had night dived the week before. His scuba tank had a strong nylon net over it to protect it from getting scratched and to keep it looking like new, but the netting had been ripped to shreds.

There were teeth marks in the tank's hard, enamelled paint that covered most of his tank.

He had been attacked from behind by a large shark that shook him vigorously by his tank and pushed him face first into the sand. He was very lucky that he had been pushed into the only little patch of sand in that area. Had he been forced into the coral, the outcome would have been very different, especially for his complexion!

When he was forced into the sand, his demand valve was ripped from his mouth so he couldn't breathe. Luckily for him, the shark didn't like how the hard aluminium tank felt in its jaws, and it released him. He was able to go on an emergency ascent and clamber over the same coral as I had the week before.

During my stay in Jeddah, I managed to go on over three hundred dives in the Red Sea, and I will always be grateful to Saudi Arabia for granting me a diving license that allowed me to enjoy its west coast reefs.

It is not my intention to deter anyone from diving in the Red Sea; quite the opposite. With over three hundred dives that enabled me to map parts of the seabed of Jeddah for others to enjoy, I can't complain. Therefore, I will only elaborate on two more instances that have remained in my memories.

One instance was when I went on a chartered dive boat fifteen kilometres off the coast of Jeddah. The day and the sea started off too perfect for my liking. The surface of the ocean was like a kind of still calm. The Red Sea is well known to change unexpectedly, but the Saudi coastguard allowed vessels to leave the safety of Jeddah's marina that morning, so off we went.

We did one dive in the morning, which wasn't terribly special because there wasn't very good coral to explore. But the second dive in the afternoon was something quite different. We were diving at a depth of twenty-two metres on a shipwreck. The shipwreck was nicknamed chicken wreck because it had been a cargo vessel carrying thousands of chickens bound for Jeddah when it hit a reef in a storm, broke its back, and sank.

The dive started off fine. The waters were unusually calm. After just twenty minutes, however, the tranquil dive became a different world. I became aware of movement up above me, which caused me to look back up to the surface where our dive boat was hovering.

Due to the Saudi environmental policies in those days, dive boats were not permitted to drop their anchors, which might have damaged the coral.

When I looked up, I could see the ocean's silver surface becoming turbulent and dangerous. As the dive master on that day, I aborted the dive by tapping every diver on the shoulder and indicating that everyone should return to the surface.

At the surface, the real danger became apparent. Everyone's objective was to get back on the dive boat while it bounced more than ten feet off the surface of the water. The main danger was at the transom, where we needed to climb up a ladder. That part of the boat was hammering down on the water, easily capable of smashing one's skull.

Eventually, we could account for each and every diver, and we started our journey back to the safety of Jeddah's marina, which was still a long ride away.

In Jeddah's direction, all we could see was a sky full of sand. The coast was out of sight, which explained the waves we were riding on the way back. We estimated the swell to be around twenty-five to thirty-five feet.

Our dive boat was struggling to ride up the waves, and each time we got to the top of a wave, half the hull would be out of the water, only to come slapping down again on the other side. We had a Filipino skipper who was very experienced and knew what to do. He began to zigzag the waves one at a time.

It was a much slower way to get back, but it was also much safer. We sat on bench seats on either side of the back of the boat. We all gripped the benches with white knuckles: one minute we would be high up in the air looking down towards the guys on the other side of the boat, and the next minute we would be looking up at them.

All the while, we were slowly but surely getting closer to Jeddah and we could see the battering the sandstorm was giving the mainland. It took us several hours to reach the marina, by which time the storm had calmed down a lot. We took advantage of the lull and pulled up against the quayside without being slammed against it, as it was still quite windy.

There was a lot of sand in the air, and all the roads were a mess. We saw sand dunes piled up against buildings and other similar sights. When I got back to my apartment, there were many messages left on my answering machine from concerned friends who knew I was going out on a boat dive that day. I called everyone back to put their minds at rest.

We went on several more boat dives after that event, and they were all well worth the effort. One such dive took us far away from shore to another shipwreck. That ship had been carrying heavy duty electrical cables. Just like the previous wreck dive, the ship had broken up on a coral reef in a storm, which had blown the ship well off its intended course.

The wreck was decently intact. The tonnes of copper cables had been salvaged years before due to their value. As we gradually made our way around it, we found a small oceanic white-tip shark sleeping. There were seven of us, and I was the only diver without a camera. Everyone was busy taking photos of the shark until it suddenly became aware of our presence and darted out quickly, pushing straight through the middle of us.

As it did so, it hit me in my chest with its fin, knocking all the air out of me. It was too deep to make an emergency ascent to the surface, so I had to struggle to get my breath back while the other divers were busy laughing, with clouds of bubbles pouring out of their demand valves.

When I began to start breathing somewhat normally again, I noticed something that could best be described as a small submarine not too far from where we were.

The submarine moved very slowly, but it had noticed our presence. I motioned to the others to look over their shoulders to see what I was looking at. The 'submarine' could have been the small shark's mother, but if so, it was a fully grown mother, approximately sixteen feet long.

This is something new, I thought. We didn't exactly know what to do. The shark slowly swam around us as we huddled against a large coral head until our dive computers starting beeping to alert us of low air. There was no more time to think; we had to go back to the surface regardless of the shark, which was getting closer every time it circled us.

We all began our ascent together and with the dive boat directly above us, it wasn't long before we were all clambering at the transom trying to get the hell out of the water as quickly as possible. The worst part was needing to make a safety stop half way up to decompress with the small amount of air we had left. We stopped at ten metres and again at five metres so I was sucking air by the time I surfaced.

Of course, nobody admitted to being afraid, but there was a strange smell among us … and it wasn't coming from me.

During these months, I'd met a guy from Cornwall who also

worked on the same project, managing the site security. He was ex-British military and his wife worked in a nearby hospital in Jeddah. He had a boat in the marina, so it wasn't long before we teamed up and went fishing every Friday.

They invited me to their compound every Thursday night, which was on a Swedish compound. Someone was always having a party there on a Thursday night, so it was a great place to be. The idea was that I stay the night so we could leave together early in the morning to take the boat out by seven o'clock. We bought squid for bait and sacks of ice on the way to preserve our catch.

We always returned with a cooler box crammed full of fish at around four o'clock in the afternoon. Grouper and red snapper were always popular with the Filipinos I worked with, and I was only too happy to oblige them every Saturday afternoon when returning back to work.

Myatt opened my cooler box every Saturday morning, and the ice was still frozen; and she cleaned all the fish before I got up. When I think about it, Myatt was a diamond.

I told her which fish I wanted to freeze for the monthly party and which fish I wanted to give to the Filipinos on site, and then I gave the rest to her to take home. This went on for several months until, one day, she opened my cooler box and found only two little fish.

I was waiting for her to arrive that morning, but kept out of sight. She didn't know I was listening to her as she made a kind of disappointed moan. Then she saw that I'd taken all the shelves out of the fridge which were leaning alongside it, and she was surely curious as to why.

When she opened the fridge, she couldn't stop herself from letting out a little scream: there was a forty-seven kilo yellow fin tuna wedged diagonally in my fridge. That was the only way I could keep store it as the cooler box was far too small.

I proudly entered the kitchen, trying my best to resemble a character from Ernest Hemingway's famous book, but a younger version, and I found her smiling from ear to ear. She asked me how I wanted it prepared, so I asked her to cut it up into steaks. The steaks were so big that we needed to cut them again into quarters, which would still overhang a dinner plate.

While Myatt was busy fighting with the tuna, I went out to the local supermarket and bought the biggest aluminium saucepan I could find which had two handles and a lid. After that, I went to a garage to pick up a sack of ice.

When I returned, I poured some ice into the saucepan, placed the head of the tuna on top of it, and continued to fill the rest of the saucepan with ice until the tuna's head was fully covered. Finally, I placed the lid on top of the pan.

Myatt asked what I was doing, and I replied, "I'm packing the head for you to take home with you, darling." Later, Myatt explained that she was able to make Filipino fish soup for an entire month!

One of my normal Thursday night visits to my fishing partner's compound presented me with quite a surprise. It came as a little, furry, four-legged kitten. My friends' wife noticed earlier in the day that a black plastic garbage bag was lying on the ground underneath his car. It had been strategically positioned directly again the back wheel of his car but was moving; so she dragged it out to see what was inside.

There were four little kittens inside, which had been strategically placed so they would be driven over. The four little kittens were playing on their living room carpet but one of them seemed to bond with me the minute it saw me, and that was that!

I needed to wait until the next day to take Muffy home with me so I had time to borrow a cat box, buy kitten food, cat litter etc., and also some little toys so she could amuse herself. For a litter tray, I used a large rectangular stainless steel cooking tray, which I had found in a kitchen cupboard.

Muffy was very nervous when she first entered my apartment; she hid under the sofa and couldn't be persuaded to come out until she became hungry. The drive home probably didn't help. It was several hours before Muffy came out and she ate everything placed for her. Muffy's confidence grew quickly and soon she became a wonderful companion to have.

She was certainly a feral cat, always on the wild side. My shoulders were permanently covered in scratches and claw marks because she liked to take rides around my apartment while perched on my shoulders like a parrot.

Her favourite game was helping me when I was rigging more fishing lures. This was quite dangerous once hooks were attached, and we had many a near accident when she came darting out of nowhere to pounce on the lure I was busy rigging. The rigs were composed of a hard plastic head and a soft latex type coloured skirt, totally irresistible to Muffy.

I was coming close to completing my third year in Saudi Arabia, but with all my divorce proceedings wearing me down, I decided not to renew my contract for another year. Meanwhile, my Cornish fishing partner had been busy over the last three months entering us in the annual fishing tournament in Phuket, Thailand, which was held in the first week of November every year.

With my soon-to-have freedom, I left Saudi Arabia in October of 1996 and returned to the United Kingdom for just a couple of weeks to finalise my divorce. Myatt took Muffy to live with her and I replaced the litter tray back in the kitchen cupboard for the apartment's next occupants to use.

While I was back in Swansea, I decided to get my first tattoo to prepare for the Phuket fishing tournament.

I had a T-shirt with an illustration of Ernest Hemingway's book, 'The Old Man and the Sea'. The picture featured a blue marlin caught on an old man's hand line while on his little fishing boat off Havana. Because time was short, I just had the tattoo artist put the fish on my right calf muscle. I figured I could get the rest done the next time I was back in Swansea, whenever that would be. I couldn't have guessed that the tattooist would lose his right forefinger later so it wasn't possible to have it completed.

With my divorce complete, I flew to join my fishing partner, his wife, and their Doberman Sasha in Thailand. They had left Saudi around the same time I had and were already waiting for my arrival in their hotel at the top of Bangla Road in Patong.

Chapter 6
Phuket Fishing Tournament

Previously, while still in Saudi Arabia, we had fishing team T-shirts and baseball caps made in the Philippines by a friend who was visiting his home while on leave from Saudi. We called our fishing team 'The Hot Rods and Hookers' for some strange reason.

My partner had the word Captain on his hat and T-shirts, and he arranged for mine to feature the words 'Master Baiter'. Thankfully, the words were separated by a space. Our team regalia went down very well in Thailand at the bars on Patong Beach!

The tournament kicked off at 6am sharp, so we rented rooms just a five minute walk from the jetty at Chalong Bay to get ready for the early start for the three day event. I met my boat crew at five o'clock in the morning on the first day of the tournament because I needed to know where the hell our boat was out of the thirty-nine other entries.

I hadn't slept the whole night because I was both excited and unsure how well we'd fare with so many other boats. I walked to the area at the entrance of the derelict wooden pier and was amazed to see how busy it was. Even at five o'clock, the Thai TV crew were already busy filming everything that was going on, including my newly completed tattoo of my blue marlin. The whole place was a hive of activity, and I could feel the immense energy in the air growing by the minute.

I recognised my crew, as they were wearing our team T-shirts and baseball caps. They comprised just a captain and deckhand like all the other entries. They led me to the boat, which I hadn't seen before, not even any photos. It was a tradition Thai style wooden vessel around forty feet long with a canopy covering the central area of the deck for shelter from both the sun and rain, which later was well appreciated.

I had already rigged my tournament rod days before, which had been custom built in America by AFTCO with a heavy Penn 80TW reel. I dropped it in one of the rod holders at the port side of the stern because I felt it would be my lucky place for the three day event. Our crew had slept on the boat all night, protecting the live baitfish that they had caught the day before. These little yellow-tailed fish were considered the best live bait for the sailfish that we were aiming for, each of which would earn us five hundred points, and they needed to be protected from any potential thieves from the other boat crews.

The event organiser issued us with a disposable camera and necessary paperwork to prove any claims in the event that we were lucky enough to catch a game fish. At exactly 6am, the horn sounded to start the tournament, and with a plume of black smoke and the load roar from its diesel engines off we went in our old, Thai-style, deep sea fishing boat together with the other thirty-eight contenders.

We didn't think we had enough of the little baitfish, so we wasted the first hour of the day fishing for more of them before trolling out to the most popular fishing area where all the other boats had already gone.

Half way to the favoured fishing grounds our captain suddenly made a sharp turn, causing all of our lines to cross. This was disastrous because we came right alongside four sailfish, but there was nothing we could do except waste more time untangling our lines. An hour passed, and I was finally hooked up with a good-sized sailfish.

Unfortunately the hook hadn't gone deep enough into the fish's mouth, and I only had it on the line for a couple of minutes. I kept the line tight the whole time, but the fish still managed to spit my hook out. This raised my morale, not to mention adrenalin! With no more action on the first day, we sadly turned and headed back to the jetty at Chalong Bay; everyone had to be back before 5pm.

After a rather sleepless night, the second day was more successful. Half way through the day, which was normally a dead time for the sailfish, my reel finally clicked a couple of times. A few moments later, my reel clicked again and then another click: something was certainly interested in my little bait fish swimming around.

My deckhand gently and quietly raised my rod from its stand and positioned himself at the back of the transom. He let out more slack line so the sailfish wouldn't feel any tension and counted to twenty to allow the sailfish to swallow my hook. Suddenly he shouted, "Now," and the captain pushed both throttles fully forward, and with another plume of black exhaust smoke and another roar from its engines, the boat lunged forward while at the same time the deckhand slid forward the clutch on my reel and made a few firm smooth strikes to ensure a safe hook-up.

I was already in the boat's 'fighting' chair wearing my fighting belt for lumbar support and we jumped into action. The deckhand carefully handed me my rod without letting my line go slack and I began to play the fish more carefully than I'd ever played a fish before in my life. I could feel the adrenalin pumping through my veins, giving me all the strength I needed to fight a fish about the same size as I was.

Fortunately, there weren't any other boats obstructing us so it was down to just the fish and me. After just thirty-five minutes of playing the fish, I finally got it to the transom where the deckhand was able to catch hold of its long bill and lift it into the boat for the 'proof of catch' photo to be taken. My heart was still pounding with adrenalin when we released the fish unharmed, and we were now back in the tournament. The sailfish earned us our first five hundred points in the competition and putting us on the scoreboard.

Wow, the game is on, I thought. The tournament followed strict rules, and all 'billfish' had to be released unharmed. We continued trolling for the rest of the afternoon without any more excitement before it was time to return to the pier. We arrived back at the pier at Chalong Bay just before five o'clock that day and handed in our camera and got another to use for the third and final day.

We waited around to listen to the results for the day and see the points from each boat written on the tournament board. Our five hundred points had earned us fifth place so we had a healthy chance of improving it with one day remaining.

After catching my very first sailfish, I was awake all night. My veins were still glowing with adrenalin, which made any sleep impossible.

Our final day was frustrating and didn't raise our score. Our total of five hundred points wasn't enough; so we kept at fifth place out of the thirty-nine boats. We didn't qualify for any prize, but it was great meeting all the other teams of varying nationalities and listening to the stories they had to tell from fishing all over the world that made it all well worth entering.

The end of the tournament was held at the Holiday Inn, situated on Patong Beach. The Holiday Inn had organised an amazing night with food and entertainment, which I'll never forget for the rest of my life.

Each winning team was announced, and the trophies were awarded. I sat patiently waiting for mine. I knew all the prizes stopped at fourth place, but I was told to expect some kind of acknowledgement because it was my first tournament on the island and also my life but sadly, that recognition never came.

Anyway, I was in a very nice and relaxing part of the world so what did it matter? The glory was simply being a part of the tournament and not winning it. In February of 1997, whilst chilling on a Thai beach around the coastline away from all the noise of Patong, the same Japanese company I'd worked for in Iran called me. They asked me if I would be interested in re-joining them in Venezuela to build the very same direct reduction iron ore plant that I had been involved with building in Iran.

Venezuela? I thought. And then I thought: salsa; merengue; tambor; hola, mi amor; ¿qué quieres, chicas? I did not need to think any longer; immediately, I asked, "When do I fly?"

The company were keen that I join their team as soon as possible so I had to end my relaxing little stay in Thailand and get back to more serious times ahead, and fly back to the UK to arrange a work visa in London.

Chapter 7
First Time in Venezuela

Sadly, back in the United Kingdom I wasted no time in taking my passport to the Venezuelan consulate in London for a work visa. The Japanese firm had already sent a letter of invitation, so the process was quick. I submitted my passport on a Monday and collected it again that Friday. My flights were arranged for the following Monday, so I had the whole weekend to prepare for the trip.

Because there were no rotational leaves in my Japanese contract, I needed to ensure that I didn't forget anything. I had no idea at the time when I would be back in the United Kingdom so I needed to pack for all events.

I flew out from Cardiff Airport towards the end of February of 1997, but again, I was delayed due to bad visibility. That time of year always posed problems with the early morning flights, as heavy mist and fog seemed to loom around that area of South Wales so consequently, I missed my connection in Amsterdam. I took a later flight, which eventually arrived in Caracas, where I needed to change to a domestic flight down to Puerto Ordaz. Unfortunately, the Japanese company hadn't been notified of my belated arrival time, which meant there wasn't anyone to meet me at the airport in Puerto Ordaz.

I didn't know I wouldn't be picked up, so I continued waiting at the airport for someone to collect me … all the while turning down local taxi drivers and chancers hoping to get the job. Eventually, there was no one else around. The airport was closing for the night, and it was too late to get a taxi, thus, I began to walk.

I was in a hot country, but I was dressed in winter clothes. The sweat was pouring out of me. I wasn't aware how much danger I was putting myself in by dragging my suitcase behind me.

I must have walked over three miles in the dark before I came to a military installation where I found two guards waiting at their post. Without any Spanish, it was almost impossible to make them understand that I needed a taxi. One of the guards went off and brought back his superior a few minutes later who could speak a little English. I asked him whether he could help me get a taxi to a hotel. He understood my request and helped me out.

Because I was European, I ended up being taken to the Intercontinental Hotel in a beautiful part of Puerto Ordaz. When I got there, I checked in and went straight to bed. The next morning, I called the office to let them know I had arrived in the country, much to their surprise. I was picked up an hour later before being charged for a late checkout.

I was first dropped off at my apartment for a few minutes so I could drop my luggage off before proceeding straight to the site office.

The office was just a twenty-minute drive away, and upon entering, I was amazed at how many beautiful women the Japanese had employed; I wasn't complaining. The piping engineer who had called me in Thailand was the only one I knew from the previous project in Iran, and he had been promoted to construction manager.

I was introduced to all the staff, including the quality manager. If first impressions count, I found him to be a rather inadequate man, someone not to be trusted.

I was later taken to the contractor's office to be introduced to the managers based there, including their quality manager called Hector. Luckily, he spoke perfect English. I was not aware at the time, but I was going to spend a lot of time with Hector because he didn't really have a clue what he was doing as it was the first time he'd worked in such a position.

He seemed desperate for my help, so in order to make my job easier, I gave him all the help and support I could.

Nobody thought to tell me that it was 'Semana Santa' (Easter) in just three days, and everyone had no choice other than to take those days off.

That same day, one of the Venezuelans in the office called Jorge came to me with a distraught look on his face and asked if I had any spare cash. When I asked him why, he explained that his five-year-old daughter needed an emergency operation or she would die. Naturally, I didn't know whether to believe him or not, but I didn't want to hear later that she had died because I didn't give her father any money. Thus, I loaned him the only money I had.

The day before the Easter holidays, I was dropped off at the apartment and told that they'd see me in three days. "Three days?" I asked. "Why?" Only then was I told about the holiday. *Great,* I thought, not knowing where the nearest ATM was, where to shop, or where to eat; I was lost for words.

The next day, I walked around for a couple of hours in the heat and humidity before finding an ATM. I didn't know how dangerous the place was at that time, but kept myself aware of other people's movements the whole time. Fortunately, I didn't have any problems – they would come later – and eventually I found a place to eat. Back in the safety of my apartment and without having any mineral water, I proceeded to boil water for twenty minutes and put it in the fridge.

Once the holidays were over and I was back in the office, I heard Jorge explaining to one of the Filipino workers what a great weekend he'd had in Puerto de la Cruz with his wife and her sister. Jorge didn't have any children!

Because it was my first time in Venezuela, I didn't know that the vast majority of Venezuelans lie, have no respect, and never return money to foreigners or anyone else for that matter.

After not learning a damn thing from my cryogenic wife, I met spouse number two, Carolina, while helping the contractor's quality manager. Unlike cryogenic wife, she was better suited for high-temperature service and I'd met her in my very first week on site. Carolina worked for the contractor on the other side of the site which was a long twenty minute walk in the intense heat and humidity.

I spent quite a lot of time with her in my first few weeks because I was busy preparing all the welding procedures for the contractor. Evidently, they didn't have anyone else capable of writing or qualifying them.

Carolina explained, with the help from another girl from Trinidad, that there was a riot on the site the previous year and the office had been burnt down. Latin Americans are hot-blooded people with fiery tempers; and it didn't take much to start them off. Apparently, the armoured salary van was late one Friday, early in 1996, so the workforce became impatient and started a riot outside her office.

Things quickly got out of control, and the office was set on fire. Everyone managed to escape through the back door, and they could do nothing more but wait outside and watch their office burn down, except for Carolina. When she couldn't be accounted for, the site safety woman told the project manager that one of the men should go and look for her. The project manager refused. He said, "If anyone were still inside, it would be too late to help them in any case."

With that said, and no time to waste, the safety woman jumped into a Toyota Hilux and reversed it straight through the wooden office wall near to where Carolina's desk was situated and found her frozen at her desk. Carolina, stricken with fear, couldn't move, so the safety woman had to physically push her into the truck and drive out, minutes before the entire office was ablaze.

The men watching her heroic action looked quite pathetic when the salary van arrived a few minutes later.

During those early days on the project, I noticed a business card left on a desk in the contractor's office. What caught my attention was that the business card had the Welsh dragon on it. First, I was somewhat angry, thinking a Venezuelan had taken a fancy to my little country's flag. I told the contractor that I wanted the guy who left the business card to see me in my office.

Later the same day, I couldn't believe my eyes when a fellow Welsh man introduced himself. It transpired that Richard Jones didn't just come from Wales, he came from Swansea and the Mumbles where I was from!

Richie had lived in Venezuela for almost twenty years by that time, and he had a lot to tell me, including advice that I shouldn't fall for the beautiful women there. Richie had the contract for the underground firewater piping, so he needed to return to Puerto Ordaz regularly to check on the progress and his workforce.

Each time Richie returned, we met in a local Tasca restaurant for a few beers and a game of pool. There, we'd play pool and have something to eat, inevitably a popular dish called 'mar y tierra' (ocean and ground) in true Venezuelan style.

I continued to spend quite a lot of time with Carolina. Her job was to paste her company's logo on the page headers I was busy writing. While she was busy doing that, I continued preparing the welding procedures. I think she pasted more than the logos, because we got married in her parents' house seven months later.

At the time, my Spanish was practically non-existent, and Carolina didn't speak any English. To me it sounded like a perfect marriage because she couldn't argue or complain about anything.

All wedding plans were arranged in super-fast time, before I could change my mind, and off we went to Ciudad Bolívar, where Carolina's parents lived. We spent the whole day filling up their house with more food and alcohol than there was space for.

Ciudad Bolívar was formally called Angostura, where the famous bitters originated. Ciudad Bolívar is the capital of Venezuela's south-eastern Bolívar State. It was founded as Angostura in 1764 and renamed in 1846 after the death of Simón Bolívar in 1830. Simón Bolívar was the key force behind Latin America's successful struggle for independence from the Spanish Empire. He is still considered one of the most influential politicians in the history of Venezuela.

Later in the afternoon, Carolina went to a salon to have her hair entwined with plastic strings of pearls and plaits and a few other things while I waited for her in a nearby bar.

Something kept telling me to get a taxi back to Puerto Ordaz, but I was quite comfortable where I was in the bar. There was a man they called a vigilante standing at the door with a sawn-off shotgun to protect the customers, so I felt quite safe there.

After three hours of waiting for her to meet me in the bar, I was feeling wonderful. I was losing interest in meeting her family, let alone having a second wedding.

I eventually weakened and agreed to jump into a taxi and return to her parents' house. I'm sure that had I remained sober, I would have returned to Puerto Ordaz, still a single man.

As soon as I arrived, her father and I took his taxi so I could buy even more ice in readiness for the evening. We arrived at the Venezuelan Polar brewery and bought two more blocks of ice.

He managed to borrow an ice pick that would allow him to break it up back at the house. Amazing, really, that they allowed him to borrow the ice pick; I guess they must have trusted or known him very well.

We also found some special music CDs especially for weddings and had arranged for a DJ to play for us. There was enough food to cover the seventy-nine family-only guests, and we purchased enough alcohol to knock out the entire street.

In Venezuela, it is customary for every man attending the wedding to dance with the bride, and for every woman to dance with the groom, but this was not what happened at this wedding.

Yes, every man succeeded in keeping my new wife well occupied while her father kept her away from me the entire wedding night. I, however, spent the whole night being completely ignored. I was left sitting all alone at a table near the road just watching everyone enjoying themselves at my expense.

As I turned around every five minutes to watch wife number two having a wonderful wedding, I could only wonder why on earth I had not taken a taxi back to Puerto Ordaz.

As I watched the family drinking, eating, talking, dancing, and having a wonderful time, my frustration and anger reached an explosive level that was about to escape into the open. I thought those ignorant people were finally going to get a Welsh wake-up call.

I remember asking one lady to dance with me so I could participate in my own wedding, but she flatly refused me, and then another ... and another. The only woman who could actually speak a little English took pity on my frustration and loneliness and explained to me that no lady wanted to dance with a man who didn't know how to dance salsa or merengue very well.

That was it for me. I told all of them to go back to the hell they came from. I was shaking with anger. My new wife's cousin, who was a nurse, went to his car and brought a syringe filled with some kind of tranquilliser, which he had stolen from the clinic where he worked.

The first injection had absolutely no effect on me, so he gave me a second dose. That dose did something, but only enough to stop me from physically throwing each and every Venezuelan guest into the street.

They decided that it would be better for us newly-weds to return to my apartment in Puerto Ordaz that night instead of staying the night in an aggravating environment. We went to take our wedding CDs, but someone had already stolen them.

When Carolina came back from her bedroom where she'd kept her handbag out of sight from her family guests, she was in tears. Someone had stolen all her new make-up, which I'd bought for her the weekend before. I had hidden my wallet in her bag, which someone had also emptied. *My new family,* I thought.

A few days after we got married, her parents presented me with their electricity bill, water bill, telephone bill, and any other bills they could find. I was now family. Carolina had a seven year old daughter who also moved into my apartment in Puerto Ordaz.

Another two weeks passed until I returned home from work one Saturday lunchtime, only to see my apartment's balcony full of Venezuelans drinking!

I was together with an American and German colleague at the time and they agreed to help cover me while the three of us went into the private club in the centre of the complex. We all figured that I wouldn't react too well to my welcome committee, so we went for a few beers with the hope that they'd have gone by the time I got home.

After half an hour, Carolina called me to ask where I was, as I was late getting home. I told her that I'd seen all her relatives and their family friends all along my balcony with beers in their hands and thought it best I didn't arrive while they were still there.

I did all my weekly shopping on Friday nights, and had made several trips back and fore in my truck in all the heat and humidity so I'd be well stocked for the following week, and could just relax after getting home after work. The night before, I'd bought three kilos of fresh prawns, which I was looking forward to cooking that afternoon. With my fridge fully stocked with beers and a few bottles of the finest rum, I wanted to invite both the American and German to share it with me.

After seeing all the Venezuelans along my balcony, I knew there would be absolutely nothing left to return home to.

I told Carolina to call me once they'd all gone home, but she insisted I return as they all wanted to meet me! *How would they expect me to react,* I thought, *seeing them helping themselves to all my stocks?*

It wasn't until five in the afternoon that they finally left. I knew that meant they'd finished everything there was to eat and drink so it wasn't worth them hanging around any longer. Anything that was left over would have been carried out with them as they left in any case. That was their style.

As soon as the last freeloader had left, Carolina wasted no time in coming to the club to meet me. She knew that as there was a large outdoor pool, there was always an abundance of scantily clad ladies who were looking for a foreign man to entertain for free food and drinks. It had been on her mind all the while her visitors prevented her from leaving.

She had a worried look on her face, as she knew how I would react when I saw the mess back in my apartment. I was starving hungry by that time so I agreed to go home so I could start preparing my beloved prawns. She was very quiet as we walked back to the apartment.

When I entered, it was just as I'd expected. There were five cases worth of empty beer cans and empty Black Label whisky bottles all over the place and all the rum had been taken. I opened my fridge, and that too had been emptied of everything, including my prawns.

They'd made paella with all three kilos and I was left with a small amount of cold rice in the bottom of the pan and nothing else!

I went to take some cash from my bedside drawer so I could go out to eat but someone had stolen the lot. There was the equivalent of five hundred dollars, which was about two months' salary for them in those days. I told her I was off to an ATM machine and then a restaurant, as I really need to eat. I told her to stay behind and clean all the mess and I'd return later.

I grabbed my keys and ATM card and off I went to relax and calm down after all I'd just lost.

I banned anyone from visiting my apartment after that, but that didn't always work. The following Saturday her cousin's wife visited and had opened two full cases of beer cans and had just taken a sip out of each before opening another and another so they'd be cold from the fridge. I couldn't begin to understand such mentalities.

This continued throughout the first year – including a new roof for her parents' house, glass in their window frames instead of the bars they had before, a gas cooker, a refrigerator, beds with legs, an air conditioner, and even glasses to replace the jam jars they used to drink from.

I was made to visit them at least every two to three weeks, and I was like a lamb to the slaughterhouse every single time. As soon as I arrived, her father would rush me off to the local off-license to buy three or four cases of Polar beer and a bottle of Black Label whisky.

The entire street was very happy with this arrangement, because they'd pass by and help themselves to the spoils and in many cases they returned home with a couple of six packs without saying a word.

Even Carolina's cousin who lived next door would walk past me without saying anything and take beers back to her house time and time again until everything was gone.

I complained to my new wife that she had to stop her cousin, but she said that we couldn't do anything because her cousin's only job was to perform voodoo on people for a small fee!

Later, voodoo played a big part in my life, causing me to quit my job, sell my Chevrolet Grand Blazer which I'd bought from a German friend, and leave the country to have the voodoo removed back in Swansea.

During that first year, we planned a long weekend on Isla de Margarita with another expat and his girlfriend. The island was quite nice, but the atmosphere changed after we walked to a Tasca restaurant.

We were warned by the owner not to walk back the way we came because the locals were hanging around in doorways waiting to relieve us of all valuables or even worse. When it was time for us to leave, the owner arranged for a taxi to meet us right outside the front door so we'd get away safely.

Working with the Japanese wasn't the same this time around. The quality manager I was introduced to on my first day hated the air I breathed and disagreed with everything I said or proposed. An example was my rejection of sixty tonnes of electron fusion-welded stainless steel piping, which was set to hold natural gas under a reformer – which can be better explained as a giant sixty foot long by forty foot wide cooker.

While testing the welding, we discovered that the actual pipe seams were not fully fused and leaked badly. It was unusual to use such piping for gas service, but this was for Venezuela, so they wanted to go cheaper!

I wrote instructions for the contractor to stop all work on the pipe, but the hateful quality manager told me the pipe was fine and not defective.

This was enough for me. I was sick of him doubting my professional judgement, so I chose to disassociate myself from the project and quit.

Just a week later, I joined a project just up the road called Orinoco Iron. One night, a Japanese friend saw me in my local Tasca restaurant and said, "Andy, you were right about the stainless steel piping."

When I asked what had happened, he told me: "When they introduced the gas into the piping to light the reformer the whole lot almost exploded. There was gas leaking from the pipes, the pipe bends, everywhere you said." The faulty piping put their project back over six months and they fired their quality manager.

One morning, I went to my truck as usual and jumped in and started the ignition. I didn't realise until I'd pulled out of the underground parking lot that someone had sprinkled a type of cigar ash all over my bonnet. The ash was well spread out and covered the whole bonnet. I couldn't imagine what this meant, or who would have gone to all the trouble by doing such a thing.

Carolina didn't see the ash as she was in Ciudad Bolívar visiting her parents for a few days. When the weekend came, I drove to Ciudad Bolívar to collect her. As per usual, I was escorted to the local off-license to buy beers and whisky but stressed I wasn't staying long as I had things to do. Whilst driving back from Carolina's parents' house in my Grand Blazer, a strange smell began emanating from somewhere in the truck.

Soon, the smell got stronger and eventually, my gearbox seized up. We broke down exactly half way between Ciudad Bolívar and Puerto Ordaz, where there wasn't any lighting. We raised the bonnet as a sign we'd broken down and waited for a tow truck to arrive as they constantly patrolled the road.

This was a very worrying time as we were sure we'd meet the wrong people and get into more serious trouble, as we really were in the middle of nowhere.

After waiting there in the heat for over half an hour, we got lucky and a tow truck pulled over to see if we needed a tow back to Puerto Ordaz. The driver and his helper seemed the family type so we began to relax. They wasted no time in attaching the winch on the back of their old truck and lifted the back of my truck up off the ground and we were towed to Puerto Ordaz. They left my truck outside our apartment block next to the security guard, who, for a small fee, promised to keep an eye on it all night.

As my truck couldn't be driven, we arranged for them to meet us early the next morning and again tow us to the Chevrolet dealer, which was fortunately not far down the road in the Southern part of the city. The next morning, the tow truck returned on time, and took my truck to the dealership so they could check it out.

Once they'd examined my truck, they gave me the bad news that my gearbox needed replacing because it had been running dry for some time. The previous German owner had paid a Venezuelan to have the engine oil changed every month, but when the garage checked it, the oil was a thick black colour indicating that it had never been changed.

They needed to order a new gearbox from Caracas, so I rented a small Chevrolet Corsa to get around while repairs were being made.

One night, Carolina wanted me to drive her friend home. I was reluctant because it was already late, but I finally agreed if only to have some peace and quiet. We waited at a red light for quite some time before it eventually changed to green. As I began to cross the junction, there was a terrible *smash*. A drunken Venezuelan running the lights hit the back corner of my car, spinning us around. He had a jeep, so he didn't have any real damage, but my rental car was a mess.

When the police finally turned up, they weren't at all interested in the drunken Venezuelan. Instead, they took interest in me as a foreigner. They took me back to their police station and then to my apartment because they wanted to see my passport. When I returned, they took my passport off me and demanded a hundred dollars for its return. In the meantime, they let the drunk go. Once they had the money from me, they let me go and did absolutely nothing about the accident.

The rental car was collected the next day, and I later discovered that they'd debited my credit card for the full repair even though I'd paid for insurance, which they probably claimed as well.

My truck was ready to collect a couple of days later, and I was issued a four-thousand-dollar bill because they not only changed my gearbox, they also 'fixed' a lot of other things that didn't need fixing nor were they asked to touch. I registered a complaint with Chevrolet in America, but nothing became of it.

The next trip to Ciudad Bolívar was to collect Carolina again. This time, the alternator bearing collapsed, rendering it useless. We made a temporary repair just to get back to Puerto Ordaz, but I had to replace that, too.

A week later, the air conditioning pump failed, next the evaporator. It didn't seem normal for a sixteen-month-old truck to have so many problems.

The same problems began happening inside my rented apartment. I'd have one air conditioner fixed, and then the next would fail. Later, the refrigerator, the washing machine, and again the air conditioners would fail. There was no end to the problems I was having.

While these events were going on, my wife's daughter, who slept in a spare room at the other end of the apartment, used to complain to her mother that something was bothering her when she was trying to sleep. At first my wife ignored her complaints as she was only seven years old, but one day my wife noticed scratches on the little girls back. Scratches, which she couldn't possibly have done herself. The scratches appeared to have been done under her skin.

As I mentioned, I didn't stay there much longer because of voodoo. So many things kept going wrong, it just didn't make any sense to hang around any longer.

I met a friend who recommended I visit his mother in Ciudad Bolívar so she could check me out for voodoo.

I drove to Ciudad Bolívar the following Saturday and met my colleague's mother. She took me into a back bedroom where there were two single beds.

She sat on the edge of one bed whilst I sat opposite her on the other bed. She put an old, battered, aluminium saucepan on the floor between us and unwrapped the first of three fat, hand-rolled, Venezuelan cigars.

She proceeded to smoke the first cigar by continuously puffing on it. Her aim was to produce ash and examine the formation of it.

She repeatedly spat the tar building up on her lips into the saucepan until half of the first cigar was smoked. She looked at the ash and saw that it had divided perfectly into two halves.

She said, "A girl wants to split you up from your wife." She continued until the cigar was too short to continue, and then she gave me the girl's name. It was the secretary from the other project, the girl from Trinidad!

She lit the second cigar and started burning it down in the very same manner and then she asked me if I had been having problems with my truck.

I explained that my Chevrolet Grand Blazer had experienced a lot of problems: the gearbox had seized, the air conditioner pump had died, and the alternator had broken.

As fast as I was replacing parts, other parts were failing. I explained that all these things started to go wrong the day I found a dark grey ash sprinkled over its bonnet. She told me to sell the truck because it would never be the same again. And that's what I did.

The third cigar burnt in a different pattern, and she said that I should leave Venezuela as soon as possible or face death. When we arrived at our rented apartment later that afternoon back in Puerto Ordaz, the very same dark grey ash had been sprinkled outside our front door.

It was impossible to enter our apartment without taking some of the ash in with us on the soles of our shoes. That was an unforgettable night! The first thing I did was open the fridge to have a glass of cold water.

When I tried to drink from the glass, I instantly vomited without any warning. Later, at the dining table, my drink started moving around the table. We watched it happen in front of our very own eyes.

Later, cigarette butts rose up out of the ashtray, floated through the air, down the hall and landed on the middle of the quilt on our bed. And then the next cigarette butt would do the same ... and then the next one. Everything was done in threes.

My colleague's mother had advised me to smoke a hand-rolled cigar in each room of my apartment, which was supposed to reverse the voodoo. I did this, but when I blew smoke at a place which should have normally had a small cupboard and not a wall, a force threw me back. I did it again, and again I felt a force, but stronger. My wife freaked out and asked whether we could leave the apartment and find a hotel to stay in.

I didn't want to leave the apartment as I was made to pay four months' deposit instead of the normal one month as I was from Europe, and I went into our en suite to wash. In the bathroom, I felt a strong presence behind me and turned around. Behind me, I saw the exact same dark grey ash growing out of the white ceramic floor tiles in three piles. It was as though I was hallucinating, but I was perfectly sober.

I called my wife, and she had also felt something pass by her on the way to the bathroom. Again, she asked whether we could leave. We tried to sleep, but we were constantly interrupted.

I could see the indentations of fingers gripping my wife's right arm. I lay there knowing that I had stopped breathing but couldn't seem to be able to do anything about it. When my wife realised what was happening to me she slapped my face to bring me to my senses.

When we turned the lights back on the problems stopped, but each time we switched them off to try to get some sleep, the problems would start again.

That happened two more times, so we decided to leave the

apartment and look for a hotel at three o'clock in the morning. We drove around for what felt like hours until we finally found a hotel, which had a room to spare, and stayed there for at least the next few days. It was only about a week before things started happening again, this time in our hotel room. After we changed hotels, all was fine for about another week … and then it all started happening again. It was as if we were being followed with nowhere to hide.

My only option was to leave Venezuela and get professional help back in Swansea.

Chapter 8
Help from Swansea

Throughout my hardship in Venezuela, I kept my mother up to date with all the unbelievable events that were taking place. Thankfully, she believed me and made some inquiries with friends she knew. A doctor she worked with had heard of such goings-on and mentioned the name of a spiritualist working in Swansea.

An appointment was made before I arrived in Swansea, as I needed the help of an expert and fast. Therefore, the day after I arrived, I went to see what could be done. I kept telling myself that everything that was going on was purely coincidence but at the same time, there was something also telling me that with so many things happening, something was certainly not right.

I went to Swansea's Spiritual Centre. There, a remarkable man called Jonathon welcomed me in. As I walked inside the centre with him, I couldn't stop explaining all that I'd experienced in Venezuela. Jonathon asked me to relax in a very calm voice, and he told me that he already knew everything that had happened to me the moment he laid eyes on me. He had a vivid perception of everything that had occurred back in Venezuela.

He said he could help and told me I needed to sit on a chair in the middle of the large room while he put on some relaxing music of the ocean waves washing up onto a beach. He explained he needed to place his hands over my shoulders, but not in contact with them. He added that it would take around ten minutes. While listening to the music he began his cleansing. Seconds before he began, he explained that I might feel electricity between his hands and my shoulders, and hot or cold sensations.

Wow! The moment he started, I felt a lot of static electricity between his hands and my shoulders. And then I felt a cold feeling that quickly became quite hot. He continued for forty-five minutes before stopping. He explained that someone had done a very professional job on me, and that I'd need to return the next day, which I did. There were no fees involved.

The next day, he performed again and explained that he'd managed, together with some good spirits, to remove some of the voodoo, but I needed to return a third time.

The next day, he repeated the exercise and explained that he'd removed most of the voodoo. Once again, he informed me that I needed to return, but for a final session the next day.

The problem was, I couldn't return the next day because I had a new contract back in Venezuela!

Before I left the Wales, he added my name to a list of people who were sent healing during their Thursday night spiritual meditations. He told me that I would feel something as they helped me, or perhaps a few hours later.

Strangely enough, I did feel something was happening from time to time. I felt a new and very peaceful feeling washing over me and calming me down, even though I was far away.

I should have listened to him when he advised me not to return because my stay in Venezuela ended up being a waste of time. Everything went wrong again, but due to the Venezuelan company and not voodoo. I was working for a Venezuelan engineering contractor and everything agreed and endorsed in the contract was not honoured, which was hardly surprising. I needed to stay in a small Venezuelan village called Puerto Píritu.

Puerto Píritu was actually a beautiful place to be based, which was directly on the Caribbean. My new company had found me a temporary place to stay, which I still needed to rent; it was a small outbuilding of a German-owned villa on the top of a hill. I was to stay there until I could find something better suited for myself. After a month I was able to find an apartment across from the beach, shops and local restaurant.

The Venezuelan house sitters, who the German owners paid to take care of their property, stayed in the main house and were very accommodating. Especially by taking me to the local supermarket so they too could get stocked up for free at my expense. They owned a scooter, which they let me use to get around, which was a great help.

They enjoyed the opportunity of being able to go away for weekends, as I was there to take care of their two boxer dogs. The dogs bonded to me the minute they sniffed me and sensed I was an animal lover. I was alone with the two dogs the night Hugo Chávez was declared the new president of Venezuela.

The minute that it was publically announced, people from nearby houses went outside and started to fire gunshots into the air. It was the second time in my life where bullets were shot into the air! The poor boxers were petrified of the noise and huddled tightly against me while I sat outside listening to the noise, but under a roof.

I bought the two dogs collars and leads and would take them for a run along the beach, as their owners never took them anywhere. We would walk down the hill together and the dogs seemed to sense they were being cared for and never once pulled on their leads, even out of excitement.

In fact, they chose to walk either side of me, so tightly that it was sometimes difficult to walk. The open air restaurant on the beach allowed dogs inside so long as their master was ordering, so I'd take the dogs with me and order three 16oz rare rib-eye steaks, one on the table and two on the floor. I hadn't taught the dogs to sit at the table, but I was sure they were ready to learn.

Even after I had moved into my own apartment, I would still return to the villa to collect the dogs and take them out for the day as if they were family. The dogs' ribs gradually became less noticeable as I fed them as much I as could. Soon it was noticed by their Venezuelan owners that their dogs ate better than they did.

It always amused me in my loneliness that when I, together with the dogs, left the restaurant to return them back to the villa, we never carried a human bag back with us for their owners.

I arranged for the local veterinarian to visit to inoculate the dogs again heartworm, which was prevalent in the area, like most hot countries. It was repeated every month. The poor dogs had only lived off scraps thrown on the ground. With all the flies laying their eggs and other bugs, the poor dogs were ingesting it all out of starvation.

Whenever I took a swim off the beach, the two dogs would sit together guarding my things whilst watching my every stroke. Dodgy locals wouldn't dare to go near my things as the two dogs would turn, stare and growl at them. One day, the dogs sensed something and started barking at me while I enjoyed the warm Caribbean water. Suddenly, I felt a sudden pain as something took a bite, then another and another. The water wasn't too clear so I couldn't see what had taken a liking to me so much so I started power swimming back to the beach.

I felt a couple more nibbles before I realised I was no longer moving as my chest was on the sand in just a few inches of water. The two dogs were already in the water fussing around me, licking me profusely, checking to see if I was okay. As I stood up I found five puncture wounds from whatever had taken a fancy to me. They were only little tiny nibbles, but it was clear that something had sharp teeth.

When I returned to the villa, the house sitters told me that nobody swam in that part of the ocean as it was infested with baby sharks, which would go for anything that moved. *Typical of Venezuelans,* I thought; they only warn you after the event had taken place!

Every Saturday morning, I would meet the night fishermen as they returned to the quaint little harbour at six in the morning to have first choice of their catch. I'd take a new bottle of the finest Venezuelan rum (ron) with me to aid their daytime sleep, which was always a bottle of Pampero Aniversario. It was probably the finest quality rum I've ever had the pleasure of tasting. I'd carry a cooler box full of ice and cans of Coke and some disposable plastic cups.

I normally took the little scooter, but on nights when I couldn't sleep and gave up in the early hours, I'd take the dogs by foot, which took a forty-five minute walk to the harbour. The dogs always got excited seeing the still-alive fish flapping about.

The deal was I'd swap the full contents of my cooler box in return for the pick of their catch as long as it was under two kilos. The Pampero Aniversario was worth a lot more than two kilos of fresh fish, but as I was an avid sea fisherman myself, I enjoyed sitting there chatting to the fisherman, while listening to them telling me all about the big fish that had got away! I know all about fisherman's tales, but due to some of my own experiences, some of them I'd believe as I had my own unbelievable stories to tell which I have deliberately omitted from this book to maintain my professional integrity and reputation!

I had been known to get lucky on some fishing trips, like the day I caught a sixty pound wahoo along with six smaller ones, two barracuda and a small skipjack tuna.

True to style, my Venezuelan company hadn't been totally honest in my contract. They promised me a Toyota Hilux to use as my own, but they hadn't told me it was only for site use and that it had to remain on site when I went home each night. It used to take me at least an hour and a half to get to the site every morning for a seven o'clock start along the coast in Barcelona.

Taxis were not allowed on site so once I had arrived at the site entrance, I still had a thirty minute walk through the dust in the intense heat and humidity to reach my office. The local workers used to look at me wondering why I had to walk as they did. By the time I had reached my office I was in a hell of a state. My clothes were already totally saturated in sweat. I thought this watrs great for a quality manager responsible for all the quality on a one billion dollar project! *Pure Venezuelan style*, I thought.

Back at my newly rented apartment, redecorating was finished and I had bought all the usual essentials to make it more liveable. One day I saw a girl cleaning the road along the beach, so I offered her the job of cleaning my apartment once a week for extra income. She jumped at the opportunity and would also help me when I went shopping and help carry all the bags back with me.

Back in the office I continued to complain about my lack of transportation but nothing changed. I quit, gave all my recent purchases to the cleaner and retuned back to the United Kingdom.

Chapter 9
Pakistan

In March of 1999, I went to Karachi, Pakistan for the last half of a project which had been going for over a year. Karachi was a hot and very humid place. We all stayed in the same hotel in the centre of the city. Sanitation was non-existent in Karachi and all the wastewater went directly into the canals throughout the city. We all went to the job site in a large coach under armed escort. Our office had employed its own local chef who was very good and the kitchen was just inside the entrance of the office.

I would sometimes visit the chef to ask what he was cooking that day. He, together with his helpers would often be found sitting on the concrete floor picking weevils out of the rice, which had been poured onto newspaper. The sacks had become infested with the little six legged brown creatures from the warehouse. Adult weevils can live for two years. The female lays up to six eggs a day into separate grains of rice, which she makes holes in and later closes with a secretion. Those are the ones that ended up eaten. At least the odd ones they'd miss added some protein to the dishes. Everyone suffered stomach problems during their stay and one of the British men working with me caught hepatitis and had to leave the project.

One afternoon, our usual route back to Karachi was blocked, so we had to take a detour through a village. I had never seen so many children in my entire life. They were all so young and completely filled the pavements either side of the narrow street, which our large coach was struggling to drive down. There must have been tens of thousands of them and all well under the age of ten. It was a perfect place to be ambushed, but fortunately nothing happened.

Carolina joined me after three months, but that was another mistake. She had a terrible time while waiting in the hotel all day. She received several phone calls to our room every day from a man who was pimping. He asked whether she wanted to have many boyfriends.

He kept saying that he knew many men who needed a lady, and that he would arrange men to visit her! We had to have the telephone put through the hotel operator to vet each person calling.

If that weren't enough, the minibar stocker visited our room every hour to check the drink status. Of course, that was just an excuse to look at Carolina. We had five hotel employees fired due to this behaviour. There were other incidents, too, such as finding needles in our toilet paper rolls and discovering drawing pins in our room service meals.

While in Karachi, I needed a local man to work for me in the office at site, and take care of the database I'd created. The Japanese firm I was working for set me up with three guys that I could interview. The first two seemed terrified. They only answered yes or no to all I asked them, but the third and final candidate was quite different. His name was Izhar Ali.

Izhar not only answered all my questions, but he also had many of his own to put to me! All Izhar's questions gave me an excellent impression of his professional integrity, and I asked him how soon he could start.

Izhar started the following Monday, and he immediately began dismantling the computer I was having trouble with. With bits all over my desk, he found a loose chip that was causing the problem. He put it all back together again in a few minutes.

That was probably the best first impression anyone has ever left on me. Izhar and I became the best of friends, and we still are today. Fortunately, Pakistan wasn't the last place I had the pleasure to see Izhar.

My wife's problems continued at the hotel. The most shocking one was when we were in the elevator together with a local man who moved behind me, bent down, and tried to sniff my wife's backside! I spun around and cracked him hard on the side of his jaw, knocking him out cold! I was rather proud of myself.

When I told Izhar about the episode the next day, he recommended that I buy Pakistani clothes for Carolina. He said no one would dare look at her the same way again, and they'd leave her alone.

Luckily, there was a clothes bazaar in the hotel the very same week, so Izhar came over to do the negotiations and help us choose two outfits. Carolina looked just like a local lady in her new disguise, plus she already had the skin tone.

Once, she was fed up with staying inside all day, so she tried to lie down by the hotel swimming pool. But that innocent action generated a lot of interest from some locals and they all moved in close to her. She didn't do that again.

Many taxi drivers hovered around the entrance of our hotel. One in particular was a horse drawn carriage. The horse was a big boy called Jack. I'd take an apple back with me every night from the office to give to Jack. Its owner would hold the apple with his hands cupped so Jack could nibble his way around it. Jack would eat the whole apple except its core, which I found very unusual for such a big horse.

I would choose to go with the carriage to look around Karachi on the weekend. It was a hot and dusty way to get around, but still better than inside some of the taxis. I always sprayed a handkerchief with cologne and carried it with me when I went out for use each time we passed over a canal, for natural reasons.

I regularly visited a furniture and ornament factory. All the furniture was made from solid rosewood and sometimes decorated with skilfully inlaid brass. The Pakistani craftsmanship was amazing and I bought many items from the factory shop including onyx carvings. The onyx was a mixture of dark green and brown and of exceptionally high quality, not to mention the brassware. I bought a rosewood captain's trunk, which had my name inlaid in its lid together with the date 1999. It was ideal to store all the other items I'd bought which included a handmade silk carpet.

I continued to visit the place and Carolina also enjoyed going with me as there wasn't anywhere back in Venezuela which sold such beautiful handmade ornaments. Once the captain's trunk was full, the shop arranged for my box to be crated and sent back to the United Kingdom, which arrived in the while I was home on holiday. A friend was with me and was able to help me carry the box into the house from the delivery van. All the items were certainly intact, but the onyx was a different colour to what I had bought. Instead, they had swapped it for the cheapest quality, which I dealt with as soon as I returned back to Karachi two weeks later.

At one of the weekly parties, which the German hotel manager held for expats, Carolina and I were introduced to another Venezuelan man who fully understood and sympathised with Carolina's situation. He gave us the phone number of the wife of one of his Pakistani friends who was also Venezuelan and living in Karachi.

Carolina couldn't wait to make the call the next day. The Venezuelan man called ahead and told the lady to expect another Venezuelan lady to call. The married lady was very excited to hear from Carolina, and she immediately drove to the hotel with her private driver to pick up Carolina.

It turned out that the lady's husband was a very successful company director of a textile company. Carolina had a great day out and came back to the hotel refreshed and excited that she had a new friend to visit. She was also thrilled that she could finally escape the confines of the hotel.

On the weekend, I was invited to the director's house. Because he'd visited Venezuela many times on business trips, we had plenty to talk about. He also owned a farm, which we all visited for a barbecue the following weekend. There weren't any animals or fields of crops, though. He had bought the farm just to have somewhere to relax outside the city, *a place with some much-needed fresh air.*

Because Carolina now had a friend, the shopping trips started. Her friend and her driver took Carolina all around Karachi. She bought more and more clothing for herself and her family back home. Naturally, I went crazy some days. She kept coming back with more clothing, and I was concerned about the baggage restrictions for our flight out.

Amazingly, she had already thought about that: a friend working for KLM had access to the system and made a notation that the excess baggage had already been paid! We were told to say the following when we got to the KLM check-in: "You need to look at the notes. Our baggage has already been paid." It worked!

In September of 1999, we parted company at the airport in Amsterdam. I needed to work in Habshan, Abu Dhabi. Abu Dhabi was a wonderful place, except I was a two-hour drive out in the desert surrounded by sand dunes. My time in Abu Dhabi was short-lived because I received a phone call from an agent in December enquiring whether I'd be interested in working in Venezuela again. At the time of the call I was high up on a pipe rack. As I carefully walked along the top of a large diameter pipe I wasn't afraid of falling as there was scaffold planking underneath the pipe. I wasn't aware until the phone call that the planking had run out long before and as I reached to get my phone out,

I noticed there wasn't anything below me except air, which gave me a little vertigo.

Shortly after getting back to the United Kingdom while I was preparing to return to Venezuela, I turned on the TV to see some horrifying news. Continuous, heavy rains had caused mudslides in La Guaira, on December 17, 1999, where their international airport was situated. The torrential rains, flash floods, and mudslides isolated coastal towns and forced 120,000 Venezuelans from their homes. The storm had claimed many lives.

Security forces patrolled the mud-filled streets of Caracas to halt scattered looting and rescue thousands of people from flooded buildings.

At least 15,000 people lost their homes, authorities claimed, and dozens of towns and villages had been cut off. Venezuela's rainy season normally finished in early November, but not this year. Venezuelan authorities claimed the rains were the heaviest in sixty years.

The disaster shut down Caracas's Simón Bolívar International Airport and closed schools and businesses in the capital. Also, parts of the subway system were closed, which normally transports one million people every day.

Mudslides raged down El Avila Mountain overlooking Caracas, and they carried homes and parked cars with them. Mangled bits of furniture and tree trunks littered many city intersections. The country's National Guard ordered the evacuation of shantytowns clinging to the hillsides and bordering gullies.

I began to wonder whether I should have stayed in Abu Dhabi. I didn't know how long it would take for Venezuela's international airport to reopen, and I was somewhat hesitant to return due to the previous problems I'd encountered there. Still, I decided to go so I could be back with Carolina.

Chapter 10
Second Time in Venezuela

Arriving in Venezuela made me wonder whether my problems were going to return. It started off badly as KLM had mislaid my luggage, which didn't arrive for several days. I even recognised the immigration officer who I'd dealt with in the past, so I let someone else go before me so I'd have a different guy. That immigration officer previously refused me exit unless I gave him one hundred dollars. He figured that I was working without a permit, and he threatened to have me arrested and taken to the main station in Caracas. Considering my options, I paid the bribe and flew out.

I spent the first night in Caracas because the vice president of the company who selected me wanted to meet me in person before I began work. The reason he wanted me was because I had helped his company out so much on my first project in 1997 in Puerto Ordaz, when I first met Carolina. I'd actually visited the site eighteen months before, looking for work, and they had a Romanian quality manager at the time. I was offered the position to support him, but I had declined their offer at the time.

I was booked into the Intercontinental Hotel and scheduled to meet inside the rooftop bar. A very tall, blond-haired man approached me and introduced himself. He was originally from Russia, and he had a very highly-strung personality. He looked like he was heading for a nervous breakdown.

The manager of his head office in Caracas accompanied him. He was a short, weedy-looking man who resembled a ferret.

We moved away from the bar so we could speak more freely and face each other. The Vice President didn't waste any time cutting to the chase, and he started telling me that the project was in real trouble. I put my hand up to stop him from rambling on, and asked if a certain Italian contractor was on the project. The look on his face was that of shock and horror.

He said that they were his main contractor. I replied, "I fully understand why your project is in such trouble." Without allowing him to explain any of the problems, I explained what the contractor had done in Puerto Ordaz. He was all ears, listening to every word I had to say. He knew that I understood the style of his contractor and that they were up to their old tricks again, milking his company for everything they could.

He asked what could be done to put things right. I replied, "You've already made the first move to start putting things right because, when they see me, they will recognise me from before and know what they're in for. They won't be able to screw you anymore."

Previously, I had uncovered many of the scams the contractor had pulled over the Japanese in Puerto Ordaz, and I mentioned what they liked to do. With the aid of our corrupt procurement people in Puerto Ordaz, the Japanese had been charged two or three times the normal prices for materials and services.

His face changed in such a way that I thought he would either laugh or cry. Instead, he bought another round of drinks before retiring for the night as we had an early start the in morning.

The following morning, we all left the hotel together and drove straight to the construction site from hell. We made one stop halfway to the site to have something for breakfast because it was going to be a long day. When we pulled up, the Russian got to hear me switch into Spanish for the first time as I ordered a chicken arepa and a coffee.

Before it was time to pull off the main road, we drove right through the middle of a shoot-out between Venezuelan police officers and someone on the other side of the road. There must have been four or five police cars along our side of the road with officers crouching behind them, firing across the road into the trees. We couldn't see anyone in the trees as we passed, but we were lucky the police paused as we raced by.

The last twenty minutes was spent driving through the Andes Mountains. In the distance, I could see the plant, which was not looking great even from a distance, and as we neared the plant, it was clear that it wasn't a good project to be associated with.

The highly stressed vice president wasted no time showing me around. There wasn't an opportunity to grab a coffee, or any time for formal introductions. I was a stranger to all the onlookers, and I'm sure they were wondering who was getting a personal, escorted tour of the mess they were trying to construct.

The job was an engineering disaster due to the two previous Eastern European quality managers. They had both been fired, and quality records were non-existent to justify their two-year stay.

I could see signs that the contractor's style was well and truly impregnated throughout the construction. One of their tricks was to erect steel beams the wrong way around and later charge for additional work to drill new holes where the original holes should have been. I could see unused holes everywhere.

The project was the worst I'd ever seen; all the structural steel-work was crooked or out of alignment. After a little investigation, I learnt that the former Eastern European quality managers had no control over their Eastern European construction supervisors. Foolishly, the supervisors were being paid a bonus for progress. Consequently, everything was basically thrown up with no regard for accuracy. Faulty bolts had been bought cheap, and they were shearing off when torqued up. They had to replace over fifty thousand such bolts, so additional work claims were totally out of control; they were re-erecting scaffolding everywhere.

The only (but expensive) solution was to bring a team of professional steel erectors to do whatever they could to try to repair what the idiots had built. We had a team of New Zealand steel erectors come over, but I thought it would have been quicker to take it all down and re-erect the entire building properly.

When the new team came in, I met an amazing man from New Zealand's Bay of Islands. Dave was a huge man whose body had been completely tattooed in the old-fashioned way, except for his face. We became good friends, and the Venezuelans nicknamed us *the twins*, just like the movie. When Dave and I walked around the site side by side, I measured up only to his chest.

This giant played the guitar and sang with the softest voice. It was like a Hawaiian lullaby.

We lodged in a small town called La Victoria. It was certainly not a place to walk around in the daytime, let alone at night. The nickel plant we were working on was deep in the Andes Mountains, which had been declared a nature reserve.

The mountains were impossibly steep, but cows managed to live where even goats would have to watch their footing. One slight slip, and that would be the end: there was nothing to stop the fall except the bottom of the mountain, over a thousand feet below.

It was a true engineering accomplishment to dig into the hillside to lay the new road to the site, but the constant risk of landslides was a permanent reminder to drive as fast as possible. Our tires screeched almost the whole way to and from the site.

It wasn't long before Carolina joined me in La Victoria, and she eventually began working in one of the site offices. We were only a one-hour drive from Caracas International Airport, so we took advantage of that fact and went for a five-day trip to a little Caribbean island. That was my first visit to the Caribbean, but unfortunately, it wasn't my last. An Australian and Dave also went at that time, so it was a fun trip. Inevitably, we always ended up at the bar on a beach pier.

After several months of working on site and living in the hotel, life became more boring.

We passed a bottle store every night on the way back to the hotel. One night, when I was driving back alone, I pulled over for a quick beer at a bottle store we hadn't visited. I spent some time talking to the owner, who originally came from mainland Spain and had just had his eighty-eighth birthday.

The next day, I invited my New Zealand colleagues to join me at the same place after work. As it worked out, everyone had a great time. The little bottle store became the new place to go every day after work. The eighty-eight year old owner could not believe his luck.

Word got around until the local bad guys heard about the nightly event, due to all the new targets. One night, I was too tired and needed to walk back to the hotel alone because my colleagues had the truck and didn't look like they were going anywhere for a while. As I was about to start the three minute walk, a local woman called Mary-Eva stopped me. She said that there were two local guys waiting for a straggler at the corner.

Apparently, they had been waiting there every night. In the past, we had always driven back together so they couldn't do anything to us.

That particular night was different. I was getting fed up with the restrictions of living amongst the same dangers from one day to the next, so I walked towards the two Venezuelans, and keeping a safe distance I invited them to join us. In Venezuela, if you offer anyone a drink, you are automatically expected to pay the bill, even for anyone else they bring along.

The two shady looking characters looked at each other and walked towards me. I invited them into the bottle store, much to the owner's surprise and bought them both a beer.

They didn't speak any English, so I explained to my colleagues what I was doing. They understood and played along with my plan. In short, we got the two guys very drunk.

The next morning, the muggers must have woken up with an impressive, free hangover. From there, they probably worked it out that it was better to keep friendly with us for the free hand outs than try to rob us for a few dollars.

Word continued to spread around the small town until every scumbag in the area ended up joining the nightly event. A beer only cost ten cents, so we were not bothered by the added expense. La Victoria became much safer for us all. The funny thing was, the loco locals actually became our bodyguards.

The average attendance rose to as many as thirty locals and as many as fifty or sixty on a Friday or Saturday night. Husbands started bringing their wives, and soon, their wives began preparing food to bring along and share with us. Even my staff began to join us, which further added to the event.

Venezuelans like to spend more on their cars' music systems than the cars themselves. We were guaranteed to have at least one macho man in attendance with a car better suited to being a mobile disco, and that meant plenty of dancing.

The old Spanish man had to order hundreds more cases of beer each month as more and more people joined the congregation. The expats all chipped in some money so the old man could increase his security, and we made it clear to the loco locals that if his business was ever compromised, all the parties would stop immediately. Therefore, nothing happened.

Like most other places in Venezuela, there were often shoot-outs in the streets. One morning, as I left the hotel, I noticed several bullet holes in the walls of the hotel reception. We had all heard shots fired the night before, but we didn't realise the fight had continued into our hotel. Evidently, someone involved in the shoot-out had used it for shelter whilst returning fire.

I became friendly with a local storeowner, and he and his much younger wife invited Carolina and I to visit a beach he liked. I didn't know it would take over an hour and a half to drive there when we left La Victoria. Eventually, after over an hour's drive we arrived at the beach, which wasn't anything special. We hung our bags on the only tree we could find to shade us, and went for a swim. As it happened, we couldn't risk taking our eyes off our things because a man was showing a lot of interest in them and standing nearby, just waiting for his chance to run off with them.

The storekeeper had to go back to guard everything so we could relax and enjoy the warm Caribbean water. Later that afternoon, he drove back a different way, which took us through the winding mountain roads of La Guaira to show us where villages once stood until the December mudslides.

All that remained was what could best be described as dry riverbeds where trees, villages and street lights had once been. Not all the roads had been rebuilt. Instead, many had been roughly cut deeper into the hillsides. The earthen road was so dangerous and narrow in places that we had to get out of the car and walk ahead in case the car slipped over the side. Rocks continued to roll down the steep hillside and some had to be rolled out of the path of the car before we could pass.

There was a very eerie feeling about the place. Knowing that thousands of men, women and children had been washed down these slopes a few months before, buried by millions of tonnes of mud, rock and everything else in the mudslides, the ambience was uncomfortable to say the least. There were no birds singing, no breeze and nothing to absorb our voices in what felt like a lunar landscape.

It became more unnerving when the storekeeper took a gun out of his glove compartment and explained that the area was well known for people dressing up as police officers and holding up cars that they stopped. I'm not the type to unnecessarily put myself in dangerous situations as those happened naturally, and if I'd known about the drive back to La Victoria, I wouldn't have gone in the first place.

After nine long months, we had the work in some kind of shape and it was time to erect a prototype monorail to transport the nickel into the electric blast furnaces. Though I was originally a plater and not a design engineer, I could still see by the design that there was a major weakness. It was an accident waiting to happen.

I reported the design weakness from an obvious and practical point of view, but I was shot down every time I mentioned it. The client directly contracted the crane supplier so I had no say in the matter.

The day came to weight test the monorail, so I instructed my people to keep well off the monorail steelwork, and position themselves safely on independent surrounding steelwork. As per procedure, my contractor followed the usual protocol and made the monorail lift just five tonnes of the seventy-tonne dead weight test, which it managed to do.

And then they added another five tonnes, which it also managed to lift. I remained on the ground standing under some concrete flooring while they loaded another five tonnes. Again, like the other times, it lifted the test weight, but this time they lifted it higher. When it was around thirty feet off the ground, it failed.

Without any warning noises, the monorail broke exactly where I had predicted. It ripped off a German technician's left arm, close to his shoulder. As the test weight hit the ground, many small stones hit me in the face. After that, I turned and ran straight into a concrete column, which didn't help my appearance. Everyone emptied out of the offices to see what the noise was all about, including my two secretaries.

They found me covered in muddy water and blood, which was coming from several little puncture wounds on my face. I was lucky, as were my staff, to be alive. Because we were in Venezuela it was very difficult for the site ambulance to help the badly injured German technician. Apparently, everyone wanted to see the blood dripping down through the open steel mesh flooring.

A few months later, they tried to conduct the test again. Sure enough, the next failure was the steelwork joints themselves, as I'd previously pointed out to the vice president. That time, a man was badly injured on the side of his face.

They didn't need a design engineer to point out the weakest points in the design, but two guys would never forget that project.

On one weekend, when Carolina was home visiting her parents, a friend and I decided to drive to the beach for a change of scenery. The beach we aimed for was famous for a Venezuelan folk dance called the tambor, meaning drum as it was the only instrument used. We drove into a place called Maracay, also known as Ciudad Jardín, meaning Garden City, which is home to the only bullfighting school, Maestranza, in the country.

From Maracay, we ended up following a road that began at the north-western part of the city called El Limón and went to Ocumare de la Costa and the beaches of Cata and Cuyagua. The road is still the most dangerous I've ever driven on. It passed through a rain forest with few remaining barriers left along the edge of its winding route. Due to the frequent landslides, the original barriers had long since been knocked over the edge and down the thousand feet slopes.

Because the landslides had reduced the narrow road over the years to single-line traffic, the road was considered a one-way route with an entry timetable depending on the direction you were travelling from.

We arrived at Cata Beach, where the road first provides access to the coast, and we found a hotel near the beach. It was a quiet place that never hosted tourists due to the dangers in the country. It was lunchtime, so we wasted no time in checking in and ventured down along the beach until we came across a very sorry-looking restaurant. With plastic tables and chairs set out on a rough concrete floor and a rusty, corrugated iron roof full of holes, it didn't look very inviting. Due to the heat and immense humidity, we were both in need of refreshment, so we ventured in just to grab a cold beer before continuing to look for somewhere better suited for our needs.

While standing at the bar, which was made from old wooden pallets, we noticed a large aquarium across the room. I went over to see whether there was anything inside. Much to my amazement, it was crammed full of lobsters of all sizes.

The barefoot waiter joined me, his T-shirt filthy and full of holes, and he asked whether I fancied one. I thought I'd make it easy for him and pointed to the lobster nearest the surface and he dipped his arm in and pulled it out alive and kicking. Even though it was too big for the two of us, we went along with the choice.

He returned back a couple of minutes later and asked how we wanted it cooked. I hesitated as he listed about a dozen different ways. The only choice I partly recognised resembled thermidor, which was always my preferred dish. After selecting that option, we waited well over an hour before he returned with the lobster.

He had placed it on a battered, old, stainless steel tray, and spared the usual presentation, but the food itself looked fine. It wasn't until I tasted it that I realised it was the very finest thermidor I'd ever had in my life. Needless to say, as hard as we tried, we couldn't finish it and asked for the bill. For the beers and the meal, we didn't pay more than ten dollars.

The hotel was set about a hundred yards from the beach, but that didn't stop us from hearing drum beats starting at eight o'clock in the evening. We couldn't hear any other instruments, so we followed the sound until we got to an area of the beach where cars could park alongside.

A few of the local people had already arrived and were drinking Polar beers from their cold boxes; they were still dressed in beachwear. They were already dancing the tambor on the sand, probably still drunk from the daytime. The dance had been invented at

Charoni Beach, which was just a short distance along the coast.

By ten o'clock at night, the area was alive with local people demonstrating their very impressive dancing skills. Because we were probably the only foreigners they had seen for a long time, we were encouraged to join in. Of course, they all found our pathetic attempts very amusing, but they understood it wasn't our natural style. The tambor is a very erotic form of dancing, and couples swapped their partners every couple of minutes, carefully avoiding any physical contact to keep the knives from coming out.

We stopped a taxi and got him to take us to buy some beer and a cheap polystyrene cold box and ice. After that, we returned to the beach so we could pay back the beers we'd been given. We went to the shop two more times before retiring at four in the morning and returned to the hotel for some much needed sleep. From the hotel, we could still hear the drums beating for another four hours.

We checked out in the early afternoon, but we were told that the road back wasn't open until four o'clock. Not knowing what to do, we asked whether there was anywhere of interest to visit nearby. The receptionist recommended we go for a swim in a river, which was on our way, and scribbled a rough map for us. We found the place okay, which was downstream from a derelict hydroelectric power station just above the waterfall. The day was hot and humid as we explored the old works. We were completely engulfed in dense rainforest, and the place had a very uncomfortable feel about it.

We ended up in the river at the base of the thunderous waterfall, but instead of enjoying it, I continued to feel that it was somewhere we were not welcome.

I really didn't like the atmosphere, so we didn't stay long. I felt like I was in a very small humid room with something hanging on my back. We'd spent a short time sitting under the waterfall enjoying the cold water pounding down on our shoulders, however, the next day we felt like we'd been beaten up.

During this contract, Carolina began her old tricks again: demanding a ridiculous amount of money to support her family. I still hadn't fully recovered from how they had abused me back in Puerto Ordaz after we'd got married.

I had practically rebuilt their house on my last stay in Puerto Ordaz. I grew tired of it, and I made Carolina return home. I found a Venezuelan abogado (lawyer) to put an end to it. A friend had recommended him, and he turned up at my office the same week.

He arrived in his full air force uniform, and every Venezuelan on site recognised him but me. He was the major general of the Venezuelan air force, but he was also a lawyer in his spare time. He used his influence to make his legal work easier. He drove me to Maracay, where we registered the first step in my separation.

As we entered a building, everyone who was sitting in the waiting room queuing for their turn noticed who'd walked in and immediately jumped up. *My lawyer is very famous,* I thought. We didn't need to queue. Instead, we walked directly into the local judge's office without even knocking on the door. The client with the local judge got up and left the room immediately when we entered. Just a few minutes later, we were done and on our way back to my office.

I met him a few more times over the following months. He regularly came to visit me at my hotel to discuss my divorce, joined me at restaurants, and even drove me to the military base in Caracas once to show me where he worked.

When we'd finally received a copy of my marriage license from Carolina, the complications started. Apparently, when I signed the marriage paper back in September of 1997, the night I got married, I didn't realise I was also verifying that I was the original father of Carolina's seven year old daughter.

Even though I'd never been to Venezuela before 1997, he explained that it made the whole divorce process more complicated because I now had a daughter to support until she was eighteen years old.

Later that month, he picked me up at my hotel on a Saturday afternoon. He was wearing civilian clothes, and he drove me to Caracas using his wife's car to show me the military base. When we stopped at the checkpoint, the guard on duty casually walked up to his side of the car and asked for his ID. When he produced his ID, the guard jumped to attention faster than a speeding bullet and saluted him.

We drove all around the base before leaving for the centre of Caracas as I wanted to go to a famous bookshop there to pick up a dictionary. Everywhere we walked, people stopped and stared. They probably wondered who the little white guy with the major general of their air force was. We returned back to La Victoria in the evening, and after he'd had a couple of beers, he left for home.

I only met him a couple more times before I returned to the United Kingdom to carry out my first contract there since 1989. My lawyer assured me that everything would be taken care of in my absence and that there was no need to worry. I had no idea that it was the last I would ever see or hear of my lawyer. I later heard that a helicopter, which was flying outside Caracas carrying three top ranking officials, exploded in mid-air. Apparently, a bomb had been placed onboard.

Back in the United Kingdom, I started working at a compressor station in Scotland. I'd heard how beautiful the countryside was in Scotland, but I never imagined it could be so picturesque. While driving through the country lanes each morning to the compressor station, I saw pheasants, rabbits, foxes, and roe deer every day.

The local hospitality was second to none, and many a good night was spent sampling some of the 366 single malts in the lounge bar. A selection, I might add, that put the pub in the Guinness World Records book.

Chapter 11
First Time in Qatar

I travelled to Qatar in October of 2001, which added to my track record of mistakes. I realised after the first day in Doha that I was being paid less than half the amount agreed upon in London. I quit the same day, but the company refused to hand me back my passport, claiming it was already being processed. I asked why it was being processed after I'd quit the day I'd arrived, but I just received a dumb look as a response.

I was staying in one of the few hotels in Doha at that time, and I demanded the return of my passport every day so I could fly home. This went on for almost a month until, one day, we all had received written instructions to find a place to rent.

There was a big seminar that was going to be held in Doha, and every hotel room had been pre-booked. I was about to be homeless, living on the street. A kind Iranian welding engineer working with us offered to help me out. He showed me his rented place, but staying there would mean sleeping on the floor as he did. Out of desperation, I contacted the British consulate for their advice.

They told me that it was illegal for my company to withhold my passport, so they contacted the corrupt project manager and instructed him to immediately return my passport and arrange my flight home.

The day I arrived back in the United Kingdom, an agent called me just five minutes after I entered the house. He asked whether I was interested in a contract back in Venezuela.

Chapter 12
Third Time in Venezuela

On 19 December 2001, I went back to Venezuela to work on two upstream oil facilities in a place called San Tomé. It was another opportunity to see Carolina because San Tomé was only an hour drive away from Ciudad Bolívar. I wanted to know what had happened regarding our divorce. Shortly after arriving, I discovered that I was still a fully married man, as all progress had stopped when I lost my lawyer.

Naturally, it was the Christmas season, and most expats had already flown back home. But not me: I flew out of Cardiff. It was the problem time of year again, and the early morning fog caused a take-off delay. As a result, I missed my connection in Amsterdam. I called my agent, and I was booked on the next flight going roughly in the right direction nineteen hours later.

I went into Amsterdam to waste some time before returning to Schiphol Airport where I'd have to wait to board my flight. My flight took me to a remote Caribbean island where I had another six hour wait. Finally, I boarded an Italian Airways flight to Caracas.

Caracas International Airport can be a very dangerous place for those who don't know the tricks the Venezuelan kidnappers use to get visitors into their fake taxis. They assume a company representative is meeting its contractors in the arrivals hall. Their method is to boldly and confidently approach the unsuspecting traveller and ask for his name and company.

Next, they inform their fellow kidnappers, and they quickly write the traveller's name in big letters on a large card before walking past the traveller with the card held high. The innocent traveller would introduce himself as the person on the card, and the Venezuelan would welcome him with some small talk and proceed to escort the traveller to a car waiting outside, even helping with the baggage along the way.

Once in the car, a gun is produced, and the traveller is taken to the nearest ATM. If he's lucky, he might be dropped off in the middle of nowhere, or he might be retained for future ATM withdrawals, or held for ransom.

The only trustworthy taxis were the official airport taxis. Those taxis required travellers to prepay prior to departure in case something happened to them once they'd left.

For those familiar with working in Venezuela, the oil-rich areas are all high risk for expats moving around. Every week, I heard a gunfight somewhere outside as the rival mafia groups tried to gain more territory. I was sure to keep clear of the windows during such events in case of stray bullets.

One night, there came a powerful reminder of the dangers when I heard a knock on my apartment door in the early hours of Sunday morning. It was our piping engineer, Paul, and he was standing at the door in quite a bad shape.

He had been shopping just down the road at the local supermarket called Cada 2000. After shopping, he had opened his car door to dump his shopping bags and had a gun pushed against his head and another into his ribs. The muggers forced him into the passenger well and drove him off to a very remote road about three kilometres away, which led to Puerto Ordaz. There were no lights on that part of the road, just rough bush land that didn't have any paths where people might have been walking.

It was shortly after six o'clock in the evening, and the sun was beginning to set. Being close to the equator, it only took the sun fifteen minutes to set. They pulled over to the side of the road and made Paul get out. He was forced to remove his work boots and walk towards a small ravine about fifty yards from the road. The muggers had obviously known about the place as it was perfect to dump a body and Paul knew what was coming. As they neared the edge of the ravine, Paul distracted the guy with the gun, punched him as hard as he could, and started running for his life.

The other two accomplices saw him running in the bad light, so they reversed Paul's company car back down the road, shooting at him the whole time. Paul, running as fast as he could, ducked and weaved until he was out of sight, just like he'd seen in the movies. With so much adrenalin flowing through his veins, he didn't feel the pain of all the thorns, glass, or even the barbed wire fence that he ran into in the dark adding to his injuries.

After two hours of walking in the darkness with just the moon to light his way, he finally got to the nearby town of El Tigre, where he found one of the few Venezuelan police officers in the area. None of the Venezuelan policemen spoke any English and Paul didn't speak any Spanish, but luckily for Paul, the policeman could see he was in a bad state and agreed to help him by driving him back to our compound. Paul removed his torn coveralls inside my apartment and we could see that his hands, stomach, and feet were all badly cut, torn, and bleeding.

With the help of Carolina and our part-time live-in maid, we spent a couple of hours removing pieces of wood, thorns, and glass from Paul the best we could. We poured surgical alcohol over his wounds to help prevent any infection setting in and wrapped them the best we could. Fortunately, we had a spare bedroom for Paul to stay in because he didn't have his keys anymore to get into his own apartment in the next block.

Later in the afternoon, we went to the local police station and helped Paul obtain a police report and gave him enough money to go to Caracas for a new passport from the British Consulate, because the criminals had taken everything. Carolina cooked for Paul all week while he was around and cut his steak into bite-sized pieces, as he couldn't hold a knife and fork due to his badly cut hands. Our maid did his laundry on a daily basis so he didn't have to worry about that either.

Paul visited us two weeks later. It was a Saturday afternoon and he wanted to invite us out to the local Chinese restaurant as a token of his appreciation for putting him up, feeding him, and taking care of his laundry.

As always, I had a fridge full of beer, so we sat there chatting and drinking for a couple of hours before Paul said that we should go to the restaurant before it closed.

Carolina didn't feel like going with us; she just wanted a take away, so the two of us went out alone. When we arrived at the Chinese restaurant, it had already closed. We thought it was very strange because we had never seen the restaurant closed before, especially in the evening.

We discovered the next day, once back in the office, that the restaurant had been raided by probably the very same muggers who had taken Paul just two weeks earlier. Everyone in the restaurant had lost any valuables they had on them; the alternative would be getting shot.

Fortunately we'd missed that. If it weren't for the beer in my apartment, the same guys could have mugged Paul twice in a fortnight, or shot him, considering the fact that he knew their faces! I thought, *this just proves that beer really is good for you.*

That was the final blow for Paul and he left the project and went back to live with his wife in Trinidad. After that, Carolina went to the supermarket with our maid to do all the shopping without me. It was too dangerous for her to be associated with me, because she would become a target to be kidnapped for ransom.

During the project, life became more difficult because Venezuela underwent a national strike. The biggest problem, apart from the rise in crime, was fuel. The government had limited fuel distributions, so eventually, even the public transport was stopped. I was working an eight week by two week rotation on the project and was well overdue for a break. I was nearing my sixteenth week and becoming really tired working seven days a week.

Unfortunately, because I was reorganising the mechanical completions for the project by utilising my own copyrighted system, I couldn't take my first rotation, as I was too involved at the time. We were working seven days per week, which involved an hour's drive both to and from the site. Towards my second opportunity to take a break, the national strike became a real worry.

By that time, the oil refineries had also joined the strike. With limited fuel supplies and no public transportation or domestic flights, I was really getting concerned as to whether I'd ever be able to leave the country. The domestic flights to Caracas International airport had been cancelled because all aviation fuel had been reserved for international flights to continue.

My main concern was getting to Caracas by any means possible to fly out. For something to look forward to, I went ahead and booked my domestic flight to Caracas, along with my international flight back to the little Caribbean island of Aruba.

Due to the odd flight times, I needed one night in a hotel near the airport in La Guaira, Caracas. My British colleagues took full advantage of my stress and revelled in reminding me that there was no chance I'd be able to take my much needed break. After working twelve hours a day, seven days a week for sixteen weeks straight I was getting desperate. I'm happy to say that they were all wrong.

The very day I was due to fly out of San Tomé, the strike was lifted. The entire country was about to run out of fuel to run the power stations, so if the strike had continued for just two more weeks, the whole country would have been without electricity. With no electricity to power the freezers in supermarkets, communications, and domestic supplies, the country would have died.

Carolina wasn't going with me this time because I wanted a relaxing break, not a family shopping trip. I travelled light; very light. My luggage only consisted of a camera, a toothbrush, and a razor, so I set off for the airport in San Tomé all the same. There were only daytime flights at the single-strip airport because the runway didn't have any lights.

My flight to Caracas was on time, so off I went with a smile. When I arrived, I was surprised that nothing had gone wrong yet. I began to get suspicious – something always went wrong, normally due to the local people abusing their authority.

I passed through arrivals without any problems, and I found the official taxi office right away without anyone waiting. I was in a taxi a few minutes later and thought this is great, as we pulled out of the airport to take the twenty minute drive to the hotel in La Guaira.

The peace wasn't to last, however. After five minutes driving towards my hotel, all hell was let loose. We were on a dual carriageway, and there weren't any exits we could use to get off. We drove around a bend and came face to face with thousands of Hugo Chávez supporters.

They had filled all lanes in each direction, and they were rioting and smashing everything in their path. They were excited and angry, very angry. They were wearing red berets, and all of them had used lipstick to draw two red stripes on each of their cheeks. They were all very macho.

They were wielding machetes, iron bars, and anything else they could use to cause havoc, death, and destruction. My new problem was that they were heading straight towards me and there wasn't anything I could do to avoid them. It was too late to try to turn around or reverse; all we could do was slowly drive right through the middle of them.

My pale complexion due to sixteen weeks of all work and no play was not working in my favour, and I risked being torn apart. The driver was well aware of that danger, and he motioned to me to crouch down on the floor in the back of his taxi so it would appear empty. Fortunately, he had a newspaper that he was able to spread apart to better cover me.

Seizing the irresistible opportunity for some great holiday snaps, I managed to unzip my bag and get my camera out while continuing to hide under the newspapers. The driver noticed my hand coming up with my camera, and he quickly slapped it back down.

I noticed, through a gap in the newspaper that I was trying to read, that my taxi driver had opened his window. He was slowly waving his left hand out of the window with a closed fist, which indicated his support for the riot. The noise was deafening. It brought back memories of Cape Town years before.

After a very long fifteen-minute crawl through the enraged group of Rambos, the crowd began to thin out. Finally, we passed through the stragglers at the tail end. When it was safe to look around, I came up from my hiding place to see cars on fire, shop windows smashed, and a trail of debris from where the mob had been.

Once outside my hotel, I tipped my driver twenty dollars. In those days, he could exchange that bill on the black market for ten times its value in local bolívars. He was happy, but he still needed to return to the airport. I wished him the best of luck, shook his hand, and made my way into the reception.

I could see stains up the hotel walls from the mudslides in December 1999. They must have been over six feet high. All the walls outside were the same. The receptionist explained that the whole floor had been filled with mud. They had to close the hotel for several months to dig it all out and make repairs. She added that all the streets in that area of La Guaira were the same. On a gruesome note, when the big cleaning operation began, many bodies were uncovered.

People in Venezuela had avoided eating shellfish for over three months due to all the bodies that had been washed into the ocean and never seen again. A local fisherman in the marina had the sense to tie together all the boats moored there and take the flotilla out to sea for safety. This turned out to be a smart decision when boulders the size of houses came crashing down the hillsides. I couldn't see the full extent of the damage, however, until I had got to my room later on the fifth floor and looked out from my balcony.

Because I only had my shoulder bag, I didn't bother going straight to my room as I usually liked to do to drop off my things. Instead, I went to the bar for a couple of cold beers to chill out after what I'd just been through. I was the only customer at the bar, so I chatted with the barman. He said I was very lucky to have got through in one piece because his countrymen were all loco! That wasn't exactly news to me, so I told him to tell me something I didn't already know.

The next morning, I checked out and had an uneventful trip to the island of Aruba. I checked in to the same hotel I had used before with Carolina. The trip was more pleasurable the second time around because I could actually walk past the shops in the lobby and go straight to my room.

I had slept well the night before and worked up an appetite, so I wasted no time going to the beach shops for some holiday clothes. I took one last trip back to my room to change into my new tourist guise and headed back to the bar on the pier where they served very nice seafood platters.

Because I was alone, I had a great time sitting at the bar and talking with an American. He was staying in his timeshare, just a five minute walk from the pier. He ended up joining me for the rest of the afternoon and evening. In fact, I met him and later his wife on the pier almost every night. They, in turn, introduced me to their friends, who also had timeshares along the beach.

He was the perfect guy to have around on holidays. He liked to party in true American style, making him very popular on the beach pier. Due to his timeshare, he had visited the island three or four times per year for many years. It wasn't surprising that I met him again the next time I returned in April of 2009, which was when I made the biggest mistake of my entire life.

Totally refreshed from my singles holiday, I was greeted in San Tomé by a disappointed wife who couldn't believe I hadn't returned with arms full of presents for her family.

The reality of work hit me when I got back to the site office to find that my team of ladies hadn't really done anything during my absence. The work that they had bothered to do was all messed up, which had drove the commissioning team crazy in my absence.

The reason was clear: they had all brought their earphones to work with them so they could listen to salsa all day instead of concentrating on the job at hand. Previously, I had removed the speakers from their desktop computers for the very same reason. It was like having a classroom full of disobedient children. Back at the office, I was received with a cold welcome because my presence meant the return to work as usual.

The peace after the national strike didn't last long before we encountered yet another problem on the project. The new dilemma directly involved the contractor's workforce. They could see that the work was nearing completion, so they tried to slow things down to make it last as long as possible. This was a usual trend on Venezuelan projects. The workforce used any excuse to strike, which was more annoying than dangerous. In short, the streets of El Tigre were crowded with construction men who didn't want to work.

This continued on and off for a number of weeks until it began to heat up. The main contractor, together with his subcontractors, started to direct their anger in our direction. A false rumour was sent around that the reason they had not been paid was because we weren't paying their companies.

This certainly created a volatile situation, and we were told to stay home a few times because there were threats that the workers would storm the site offices. With three thousand angry Latin workers, the concern was legitimate; plus the majority of them held gun permits and carried their guns all the time as a part of their macho image.

The situation continued on and off for several weeks. With very little construction going on, I had plenty of time to bring all the documentation up to date. With my staff using every possible opportunity to avoid showing up for work, I carried on doing everything myself; that was the silver lining.

My staff even arranged to go to Puerto De la Cruz for a weekend, even though there was work as normal. They switched off their mobile phones so they couldn't be contacted until after their holiday weekend. They were all presented with disciplinary letters when they finally came back to work, which made me more unpopular.

Shortly afterwards, there was a genuine fear that the workforce would riot, so everyone was told to stay home. Only a few members of senior management risked going to the site, including my immediate boss Chris and myself, but we didn't stay long.

That day, to avoid any problems on the road to the site, I left my apartment at four o'clock in the morning. I had already made the coffee before Chris arrived shortly afterwards and the site construction manager arrived half an hour later. When he saw the lights on in my office, he came over and asked what the hell I was doing there. I explained that, after so many false alarms, I decided to take the risk and come in anyway. He wasn't comfortable and said that he'd keep Chris and me informed if he heard any further developments from security and also our community spies.

As it turned out, there were further developments, but by the time we found out, it was too late to evacuate down the only main road from the site. It was ten o'clock in the morning, and Chris asked me whether I knew of another way out of the area. As luck would have it, I did know of one way back to El Tigre, but it still meant using part of the main site road. We just had to hope the mob hadn't already reached it. The road I had in mind was almost impossible to navigate in anything other than a four wheel drive vehicle, but it was the only chance we had.

I was okay because I had a Toyota Hilux, but Chris was in a Corolla, which I found very funny at the time. We couldn't waste a minute, so we each took a site radio in case we got split up, locked the office, and hastily headed to the car park. There wasn't time to scrape off the ridiculously large yellow windscreen sticker making me a perfect target, which was for car park entry, so we left it and drove off. I figured it wasn't the time to stick to the 30km speed limit either, set by our wonderful HSE guys, and I floored the gas pedal.

Chris hadn't driven home using the track I was heading for, so he was close behind me as we raced down the site road to beat the mob to the junction.

I could soon see my left turn in the distance, but I could also make out the mob approaching it from the other direction. They had completely filled the road. Four wheel drive vehicles aren't designed to swerve around potholes at high speed, so I flew over them instead, which wasn't so good for the Corolla, though. Chris was following close behind, and I could only laugh each time I saw him angrily flash his headlights in my rear view mirror when his wheel hubs were almost ripped off with the potholes he couldn't avoid.

We made it to the junction with only seconds to spare. The angry mob was almost on top of us, but they couldn't make it to us quickly enough to block our escape as they were all on foot.

The track I turned into was badly broken up, and some of its potholes were over two feet deep and too wide to jump at speed. We were already out of the main danger, but we still didn't know whether the workers' unions had had the brains to organise another group to use the same track we were on. Out of sight and in the middle of nowhere wouldn't have been a good place for Chris and me to be caught.

We continued swerving around the potholes for another half hour before the road began to improve, but it was still slow going.

There weren't any signposts at the junctions out in the middle of nowhere, and I had only been along that route from the opposite direction once in the past. Luckily, I navigated correctly in the right direction, which was a first for me, so we didn't get lost and eventually ended up back at the little village of El Tigrito without incident. This day there weren't any workers hanging around as before; they were all outside our site entrance, picketing without an audience.

I was receiving death threats from anonymous emails because my mechanical completions system was reducing the project schedule. The project was seven months behind when I had first arrived back in December, but using my system I had succeeded in bringing it forward by around three or four months. This enabled the oil company to make an unplanned $437 million in early oil exports.

As a change from the usual boring road to the site, I began using that old track more often. I continued working for a few more months before leaving in September of 2002 and returning to the United Kingdom. In August, one of the girls working for me began working to rule, and would threaten the other girls not to assist or cooperate with me as she was in charge.

She also relayed the same to the contractors' workers who were also involved with completions. She'd go to the Colombian project manager behind my back with stories that she could do my job and that he should make me hand over the administration password of my database so she could make improvements to it. One day I was requested to go to the project manager's office, and as I entered, I found all my staff already sitting there.

The project manager explained that I needed to give my admin password to the girls so they could make changes to my database, at which I just laughed. I asked if the company would like to first purchase my copyright protected system, as I was the sole owner. This changed everything and I was permitted to leave without giving my password, which I wasn't about to give freely after the years it had taken to create in any case. I took my truck keys off the girl and made her travel in the company bus to better assert my authority over her.

During those last few months, Carolina had started demanding yet again, and insisted that I helped her married sister, her sister's husband, her two brothers and the rest of her family, which continued until I was about to fly home. Eventually, I weakened and left her with sufficient funds, including extra for a lawyer to get us divorced for the second time.

I was given a business class ticket back to Wales and a thank you handshake from the project manager without any bonus at all. All the staff employees had received mega bonuses for bringing in the project months earlier than forecasted. It amused me to think that their project was already seven months behind due to their genius, and it was my unpaid-for system that was responsible for putting it back on track!

Chapter 13
Libya to Nigeria

July of 2003 was my first introduction to Melliteh, Libya. It was mainly an LNG tank farm and jetty. I was based on a desert camp near the ocean with very poor facilities. We needed to queue in the hot daytime sun to use one of several computers to check our emails, which didn't help matters very much. My stay was shortened, however, because I wore shorts in the camp canteen one evening, which offended the locals also living on the men-only camp.

Basically, they could see the tattoo of the blue marlin on my right calf muscle, which I'd had for the international game fishing tournament in Thailand, and they tried reprimanding me for having it. What angered them most of all was that I'd desecrated a body created by Allah.

Needless to say, I was instructed to visit the project manager's office the next morning where I was told never to wear shorts again in front of the locals, so I voiced my opinion and quit the project at the very same time. My thinking was: If I have to accept their religion, then they should equally accept mine. I always made a point to respect the local laws and customs in the countries I visited, but often wondered why they didn't return the same respect when they visited the United Kingdom. It all felt like a single direction attitude, one I didn't agree with.

I managed to get a seat on the afternoon flight from Tripoli so off I went. In the meantime, Chris, who I'd met in Venezuela, was doing his best to fix me up with a contract working with him again; but this time in Nigeria, so I knew it wouldn't be too long before I was earning again. As it worked out, I was only out of work for three weeks.

In September of 2003, I arrived in Lagos, Nigeria en-route to Port Harcourt, which was in the Rivers State, which Chris had secured for me. I was travelling on a Dutch airline which didn't go to Port Harcourt, so I needed to spend one night in a Lagos guesthouse before taking a domestic flight the following morning for a short, one hour flight southeast.

It was a slight culture shock, but not too different from what I'd already experienced in Pakistan and Venezuela. Being in a third world country naturally made one cautious of the surroundings and the thought of being so far from home was always on my mind. A representative of my agent was loyally awaiting me amongst the disorganised chaos in the arrivals area. There were some barriers with people hanging over them, so I was lucky to have seen the representative holding such a small card with my name written on it.

He walked me to where his car was parked and tried his best to ward off some dodgy-looking followers all wanting to exchange their local Nigerian naira for US dollars. The drive to the guesthouse took over an hour and some of the sights I saw on the way are better not explained.

The guesthouse was situated in a quiet, urban part of Lagos, with a high wall surrounding it like most houses in Nigeria. The tops of all the walls were covered with broken bottle bases cemented in place and supported with coils of razor wire. Armed guards protected the entrance equipped with the usual AK-47s. The guesthouse supervisor was there to welcome me and explained he'd also be the one to make me breakfast in the morning and take care of any requests I had to make me comfortable. All the rooms were large with en-suite bathrooms and the television had European channels.

I noticed that there were many mosquitos in the room, so the supervisor wasted no time in spraying it for my own protection. Almost all the Nigerians suffered from malaria, which was a much bigger concern for me than the dangers of being a victim of kidnapping.

After an early start we left for Lagos airport the following morning where I was again swamped with local men all trying to see what they could make from me. They were actually rather amusing and I'd get to see them every time I was on rotational leave.

My flight to Port Harcourt wasn't the most comfortable. I was quietly sitting in a window seat with an empty seat next to me, with the aisle seat already occupied. I was looking forward, towards the other passengers boarding, when I noticed a man of mammoth proportions struggling to make his way down the narrow aisle. I was wondering how a man of such proportions could possibly fit into the narrow seats onboard the aircraft when he stopped at my line. The passenger in the aisle seat got up to allow the man access to the empty seat next to me.

This huge man was a gentleman as well as a gentle giant and apologised to me that the empty seat was his. He seemed to use his body weight to force his way down into the narrow seat, but with his immense width, I was squashed up against the window for the entire flight, as there really wasn't anything he could do about it but sympathise with me.

After my short domestic flight, I'd figured out how they got sardines into the little cans and arrived in Port Harcourt so I could expand my lungs for the first time in over an hour. It was a very basic airport with a single runway. The runway was made from concrete and even had cables running across towards the end of it which aircraft taxied over. There was the body of an old crippled aircraft at the side of the runway, which had been completely overgrown by the dense undergrowth.

There wasn't the usual tunnel to connect to the aircraft, but instead, steps to exit onto a hard standing outside the terminal. Port Harcourt felt more humid than Lagos and there were many flies and mosquitos in the air, together with some other flying insects which I'd never seen before, and passengers were made to wait outside while queuing at immigration. Eventually I collected my case and exited the airport and immediately saw a rather skinny man holding up a sign with my name on it. This new skinny man was called Kenneth and he was to be my personal driver for the next twelve months.

Kenneth was a cheerful character who always had plenty to say and would keep me up to date with local news and political movements. It took well over an hour to drive to Port Harcourt from the airport and by the time I arrived at my hotel, I felt like I'd known Kenneth for years.

I stayed just a ten minute drive from the office, in the Genesis Hotel on Old Wogi Road. I enjoyed my stay at the hotel, and I thought it was much safer to spend my spare time there instead of venturing out to the local bush bars like many other expats liked to do.

Due to my contract, I was required to stay for a full three months before having my first rotational leave. The project involved attending a kick-off meeting in Yokohama, Japan, and I was grateful to have my time in Port Harcourt broken up.

I explained to my colleagues before we left Nigeria all about the important Japanese customs, which had to be respected if we were to get contracts successfully signed. I guess all my advice was ignored as we were the client for the project.

The trip to Japan was a long one. I took a domestic flight from

Port Harcourt to Lagos and after a six hour wait, took a midnight flight to London for another six hour wait. From London I flew at midday directly to Tokyo by flying over the North Pole. This was quite a strange experience. It was a sunny day in London as I took off, but after just a couple of hours I looked outside my window to see the sun setting in the distance so day became night even though my watch still told me it was the afternoon.

We all left our Japanese hotel at the same time the day after we'd arrived to visit our proposed contractor in Yokohama. In just the first few minutes of formal introductions, I knew we could forget any contract being signed.

The Japanese respectfully handed each of us their business cards using both hands to hold their cards, their thumbs over the top of them, in their main meeting room before we were seated. My colleagues took their cards using just one hand instead of taking them in the same manner with which they were given and simply glanced at them before putting them into their back pockets! They may as well have slapped our hosts in the face. I knew then that we shouldn't waste any more time and fly back to Port Harcourt.

Due to all the years working for the Japanese in the past I was able to return their respect and do the ceremony correctly, plus exchange some pleasant dialogue in Japanese to add to the respect of being a guest in their country. After five long days spent in discussions all day in our host's office, we were invited out on the final day to a very reputable local restaurant, which is also a part of the Japanese professional business ethics.

We were courteously escorted into a private room in a restaurant, which could sit all of us around a large round table. Much to the dismay of my Nigerian Project Manager, I was seated in between the Vice President and proposed Project Director of our Japanese hosts, opposite him.

It is customary in Japan, as well as South Korea, to pour the drinks for your guests or hosts yourself, and for them to pour your drinks. A very warm custom which I have maintained since. My problem was that as I had the Vice President on my right hand side and their proposed Project Director on my left hand side, I was basically kept busy the whole evening topping up wine and sake glasses.

While pouring drinks, you had to touch your pouring arm's elbow as if to support it with your other arm's hand, to show your intention was with full respect. I was swapping my arms all evening while turning to the left or back to the right. Needless to say, I had two sets of glasses. One set on the right of my plate and another set to the left of my plate. This was so I could drink with each of my Japanese hosts individually. I have loved Japanese customs ever since.

It was no surprise that contracts were never signed by that contractor, or should I say corporation, and I'm sure it was due to the total lack of respect that my fellow colleagues showed during the introductions on the first day's opening meeting.

It was Christmas time when I left Japan and I flew directly to London, before taking a coach back to Swansea. My three month trip was well timed so I could have Christmas with the family. After a brief two week break it was back to Nigeria for me.

In Nigeria, my stay was not without its surprises. Often, I encountered roadblocks, which stopped me from returning to the hotel unless I paid off the police several times per week.

One night, while enjoying a few beers in the hotel bar, I was invited to join the hotel owner and two of his local friends. I liked to smoke cigars in those days, and the owner's two friends also fancied a smoke. I went back to my room and brought some more to share; as I was going on my rotational leave the next day, I didn't need them and gave them the box. That gesture was received very well and proved to be a good move.

One of the two introduced himself as the chief of police for Port Harcourt, and the other was the High Court judge. We had a good time, and the chief of police asked whether I was being harassed in 'his town'. I mentioned that it was rather humiliating being forced to stop at police roadblocks and having a gun pointed at me. I explained that I was never allowed to go on my way without giving away some Nigerian naira.

I also mentioned the risky drive to the airport when I was leaving on rotation. He fully understood what I was saying and gave me his card. He told me to call him and hand his officer my phone the next time I was stopped. *That will be the last I'll ever see of my phone,* I thought.

He also added that he would lend me one of his officers who would sit in the front seat of my car whenever I needed to go to the airport with his AK-47 in full view. I was thrilled because there were often community roadblocks along the airport road, and the people at those roadblocks always demanded payments for passage as a kind of unofficial toll. Basically, nobody went anywhere in those days without money to 'dash' out in such times of need to avoid more serious problems arising.

The Chief of Police also said that he would have a letter prepared that would give me the freedom of Port Harcourt!

In Nigeria, people couldn't be caught driving down the street when it was the first Saturday of the month. That day was called sanitation day. There wasn't any real infrastructure in Nigeria, despite its enormous wealth from its oil and gas reserves, and that included no garbage collection. Therefore, sanitation day was invented to try to reduce the garbage in the streets and possible diseases it may cause. Everyone was required to clear and burn everything outside their homes or businesses on these days.

On sanitation days, the air was thick with the acrid smell of smoke from all the plastic materials, old car and lorry tyres, and even dead animals, so it was better to remain indoors until it was over. If I needed to go to the office, I'd leave very early in the morning and remained in the office until late afternoon when it was possible to drive again.

My stay in Nigeria did wonders for my waistline, much like Pakistan had in 1999. I contracted dysentery from either the food of water while I was there, which lasted a few months. Once the initial painful cramps were over, it was more of an inconvenience than anything else and I managed to lose two inches off my waistline before taking the correct antibiotics to cure me.

I made some good Nigerian friends whilst staying in Port Harcourt, and have maintained email contact with them ever since. It's no secret that Nigeria has a bad reputation, however, there are so many wonderful characters in the country who would happily be the first to come to your aid, whatever it may be. A few years later, the true warmth of Nigerian hospital and helpful support came to light when I really needed it the most.

Chapter 14
France

In October of 2004, I found myself working in Paris for a subsea company. It was an interesting change to write documents for subsea installations for Angolan and Nigerian oil projects, rather than represent the client and only ask to see what someone else had written.

The local French in Nanterre adopted me the very first week I arrived. The French in Nanterre were totally different from the other Parisians. They used to pick me up on the weekends to show me around including Paris at night. I enjoyed it so much that I even agreed to work through Christmas and the New Year to take advantage of a quiet office!

I'd be collected every Sunday morning by a local man on his scooter, taken to a few micro bars to introduce me to his friends, and then to a wine shop where he would buy a couple of bottles to accompany lunch. In the meantime, his wife would be busy preparing lunch in true French style, together with their two young daughters. It was a really welcome break from the hotel, which didn't serve any food on the weekends. After lunch, we'd go to a nearby forest where he could exercise his dogs for a couple of hours, before returning back to his house again.

December was a great time to be in Paris and I was just a half hour walk across a park to La Défense where there was a well-organised street market specially for the month, just outside a large shopping complex.

I will never forget the New Year's Eve, which I had with my new friends whilst enjoying Paris. The event started by meeting at noon at the local restaurant which was next to my hotel. We had lunch, which turned into dinner, and then we ended up in somebody's apartment deep in the heart of Paris. We finally battled through the traffic and arrived at the Millionaire's Club on the Champs Élysées hoping to enter the club just before midnight.

Paris isn't the easiest place to park and we couldn't find anywhere to leave the car, so we pulled up onto the pavement just before midnight. My friend, who was driving, opened the boot of his car and produced a bottle of champagne and some flutes. A police officer came over to us and told my friend that he'd have to move his car because it was illegally parked. After giving the officer a flute of champagne, he allowed us to leave the car where it was. He said he'd keep an eye on it, so off we went to try to get into the club.

I wasn't prepared for such a place and was wearing white training shoes, blue jeans, and a red Welsh rugby shirt so I was stopped at the door and asked whether I had anything more appropriate to wear. I said, "No," and the girl at the door went inside to ask her manager whether I could enter. She returned a minute later and said, "No problem ... as long as you buy a litre of Blue Label Vodka at 380 euros per bottle." After agreeing to the crazy price, we were escorted to a table next to the dance floor, which was just perfect.

Wow, what a place! I thought. There were Russian women everywhere and just a few Frenchmen, all in evening dress. They couldn't believe their eyes when they saw me dressed so casually. After an hour, the Russian women couldn't hold back any longer and wanted to know who I was to be able to enter dressed in such a way. First, one lady approached me and asked if I wanted a dance, which I readily agreed to. In no time at all, I had over a dozen women dancing with me in the centre of the dance floor.

There were very keen to know who I was and kept asking me question after question which I avoided answering to just play along. After a while I asked them whether they'd seen me on TV before, to which they all replied that they hadn't.

I continued having fun with them until I had almost all of them dancing with me at the same time. By the time we left the club, it was already daylight and time to find somewhere for breakfast. In the daylight, I could see countless telephone numbers written all over my arms using eyeliner, lipstick and pens.

It's amazing what reaction you get when you tell Russian ladies that you own a Paris nightclub!

Chapter 15
Tunisia

In March of 2005, I found myself working on a gas plant in Tunisia. This was a big difference to working in Europe and also a welcome change of scenery. Up until that time, the journey was the most fragmented one I'd needed to make. From flying out of Cardiff in South Wales, I needed to change flights in Schiphol, Amsterdam and again in Charles de Gaul airport, Paris, to arrive in Tunis. From Tunis I'd need to wait for a further three hours before taking a four hour train ride east to Sfax, where I'd meet a company driver to take me to the desert camp, another forty minute drive away.

The camp was very well organised and ideal for a desert base. There were tennis courts, a squash court, swimming pool and clubhouse. The camp shop had all the usual items one needed for the six week trips so it wasn't any kind of hardship, being based there. I enjoyed cooking in those days so I'd make a regular early morning trip to Sfax every Saturday to buy fresh seafood as the fishing boats unloaded their catch. My cooking was soon discovered by my colleagues; especially my curries, chillies and prawn dishes. One night I cooked for everyone, which took me three days to prepare for, and it went down very well.

The gas plant had been built twelve years previously, so all I had to do was set up a documented quality management system that the company would hold contractors against during planned maintenance and shut down operations. The contractors didn't have their own procedures at that time, so they would need to follow the ones I'd prepared.

Because the company received its gas from its own offshore platform out in the Mediterranean Sea, just a twenty-five minute helicopter trip away, I needed to obtain my offshore survival certificate to visit it legally. The closest place that offered the course was Malta, so I arranged to make good use of my time and go to Malta on my next rotational leave.

It was July, a very hot and humid time of year to be in Malta. The Maltese were very hospitable, and my weeklong visit went too fast for my liking. The survival course was conducted on a large training facility near an old Second World War air base. It was ideal for training purposes and very well organised. Its own minibus collected me from my hotel early every morning, which made things even easier.

Because it was an international training facility, there were several nationalities taking the course. Among us were three West Africans who made everyone's day particularly interesting. They were attending so they could work offshore somewhere off West Africa, but none of them understood a single word of English.

The course syllabus had to fully comply with international requirements for offshore survival training, and it included as much theory as practice. Part of the classroom practice entailed basic life saving techniques, including cardio pulmonary resuscitation for accident victims. Each of us needed to demonstrate competency by using a dummy called 'little Annie'. The doll was developed by a businessman who lost his young daughter in a yachting accident, as he couldn't save her from drowning.

To maintain the coursework schedule, all the English-speaking attendees went first as more time was required for the non-English speakers. After two of the West Africans completed the test, the last prepared to demonstrate his competency at administering artificial respiration. He remembered the sequence, but he didn't know when to stop.

The instructor motioned to him several times that he could stop and return to his desk, but he continued for some reason. Again, the instructor asked him to stop, but still he continued, as he wanted to save the dummy's life. After the instructor repeated himself several times, he left him alone to continue, which he did for yet another hour.

After lunch, we received practical fire-fighting training, and we were taken to the changing rooms to dress in coveralls and rubber boots. Once dressed, we noticed that the same African was missing. The centre was alerted and searched, but to no avail.

He couldn't be found anywhere. As a last resort, the centre took their minibus out and found him walking down the main road about a mile from the training centre. He was looking for a new life and new career out of Africa.

Back in Tunisia, and for a weekly break from the desert life, I took the chartered helicopter to the offshore platform early every Monday morning to check out the ongoing quality and maintenance activities.

Hydrogen sulphide is the main danger working in the hydrocarbon industry both on and offshore, and one had to carry an emergency breathing kit everywhere outside the accommodation module. For safety reasons, the accommodation module was a separate platform adjacent from the main platform, connected by a bridge.

Should the main platform catch on fire, staff would be evacuated from the accommodation module instead, where the helicopter deck was situated. These emergency breathing kits were heavy and cumbersome units in those days, and certainly not comfortable whilst carrying them over one's shoulder. They simply comprised a steel compressed air tank and facemask. In an emergency, one would first fit their own mask before assisting anyone else with theirs, and proceed as quickly as possible to the muster point on the accommodation module to be accounted for and evacuated.

Up until that time I'd never really been one for routine work on ready-built installations, so I began to explore younger projects with more activities to control.

In December of 2005 I joined a new project, which was based in Seoul, South Korea, which was still in its front-end engineering design phase for a new challenge to design, procure and build a new refinery in Ras Laffan, Qatar.

Chapter 16
South Korea, China, Japan, Singapore, Indonesia, Dubai, Qatar

After working closely with Koreans in Pakistan, guys who were always happy to share their kim chi with me, I saw the move to South Korea as the perfect opportunity to see the country where that dish originated and eat myself healthy.

Kim chi is made by soaking Napa cabbage in salt water for a few hours to dehydrate it, and then after washing it, it is mixed with a large amount of finely grated ginger, garlic, and chopped onions. Then it is all mixed thoroughly together with ground Korean chilli flakes and left at room temperature for a day, before refrigerating it for three more days.

The smell of kim chi doesn't appeal to all foreigners, but with its strong anti-oxidants and ability to remove toxins from the body, it is ranked as one of the top five healthiest foods in the world. There are hundreds of variations of kim chi and I enjoyed trying different the types whenever I had the opportunity. While living in South Korea, there were plenty of opportunities everywhere and I ate it all the time. I actually lost eight kilos in just three months due to a diet of kim chi and plain boiled rice.

As the kim chi was removing all the toxins I'd built up in my body over the years, I began to feel fitter and more awake than ever before.

The project in South Korea was still in the engineering and procurement phase. Consequently, I had to fly all over the world to visit vendors to conduct pre-contract award audits, kick-off and pre-inspection meetings, and factory acceptance tests. I clocked up over 500,000 air miles with one airline and another 90,000 with an Asian airline at the expense of three forty-eight-page passports in the first nine months. Every month, I went back to Japan, sometimes revisiting a manufacturer, and other times going somewhere new.

On one visit to Japan, I took the opportunity to visit an ancient Japanese castle that once had an army of three thousand women.

In the year of 2006 I visited China nine times. I also used to visit other places like Thailand, Singapore, Dubai and Indonesia, every month. Other places included Italy and Qatar.

My first visit to China entailed conducting a pre-contract award audit to assess the company's ability to fabricate structural steelwork. As I was originally a plater and had served a full apprenticeship in a similar fabrication facility, I was looking forward to the visit.

I flew from Incheon airport, an hour drive outside Seoul, for the short fifty minute flight across the Bohai Sea on the northeastern coast of mainland China to a city called Yantai, in the Shandong province, on a very cold February morning. The original name of Yantai came from lookout towers constructed on Mount Qi in 1398, during the reign of the Hongwu Emperor who was the founder emperor of the Ming Dynasty. 'Yan' means smoke in Chinese and 'tai' means tower. The smoke towers were built to serve as lookout towers to warn against Japanese pirates.

Everything was fine until we were about to touch down on the Chinese runway. I remember looking at the runway from my window seat expecting to feel the wheels touch its tarmac at any second, when suddenly the pilot put the engines into full thrust and pulled the aircraft up as steeply as it could go. What an adrenalin buzz that gave; we were going ballistic. I had a faint suspicion as to what was going on, but didn't want to think about it while I was still in the air.

The pilot continued flying deeper into China for another fifteen minutes before making a turn to return back to where we'd almost landed. The second attempt went fine and as we pulled up outside the terminal, I could see a Chinese lady dressed in uniform bow to the aircraft as it came to a stop.

Once inside the terminal building, I took a minute to ask an airport representative if they knew anything with regard to why my flight had aborted its first landing attempt. The lady explained in very good English that we were head to head with another flight as it was taking off and we'd flown right over the top of it, just missing its tail, before it left the ground! It reminded me of the flight I decided not to take back in Iran that had a bomb on board. I felt like a cat with several fewer lives.

I was accompanied with one of my main contractor representatives and after completing two different arrival forms and clearing the Chinese immigration we found our driver patiently waiting for us in the arrivals area.

Our first venue was to check in at the pre-booked hotel. As I entered the hotel I was speechless! It was an incredible place and probably the most finely furnished and decorated hotel I've ever had the pleasure of staying in. With its highly polished marble floors and huge columns all highly decorated with carvings, I could have spent hours walking around to absorb its full grandeur. The contractor had booked me a corner suite, which again added to the luxury. I had views over the sea and also down along the coast.

When I asked my contractor representative why his company had booked a suite in such a lavish hotel, he explained that I'd need somewhere very comfortable to rest after the Chinese hospitality, which would follow later in the day!

After we'd finished checking into the hotel, we left to visit the fabrication company an hour drive away.

That part of China sported the most beautiful scenery. As we drove along a very straight and perfectly flat highway I observed the flowers, which were fully cared for all along the verges on either side. As I arrived at the contractor's facility I had a very pleasant surprise as I pulled up outside their office. The entire management team were all standing outside the main entrance of the building in a line saluting me with their right hands held to their heads underneath a huge cotton banner with the words 'Welcome Mr Andy Lang' printed in very large red letters. I only wish I could include the photo, but my laptop was later stolen in Ghana, West Africa, when I lost almost all my photographic evidence!

My driver had stopped so that my door was lined up with a red carpet for me to walk on, which continued all the way to the main entrance.

The audit began after all the usual introductions in their main meeting room and took only three hours to complete, before moving outside to review their fabrication capabilities. In fact, all seemed to be going very well until they took me for the walk-about to view their fabrication shop and the general layout of their facilities.

I was taken to their 'laydown yard' where steel profiles were grouped and stored until required. The set-up was more than impressive as the facility was directly alongside the sea and they had their own quayside for ships to deliver steel anywhere around the world.

I was freezing cold, even though I had prepared for the sub-zero temperature, but not enough. The wind was slicing my throat as we walked around outside their facility until they showed me where they stocked all their materials. There, I saw two Chinese girls standing to attention wearing only very thin, summer style cotton pants and jackets. *Was this their winter working uniform?* I wondered.

Immediately, I questioned how long the two girls had been

standing outside and why they were there, in the middle of nowhere in the freezing cold. I was told that they had been instructed to stand there from the minute I had arrived, three hours before, so I could see that their company had stock controllers in their laydown area. The company didn't have a contract at the time so there wasn't any material to control.

I felt totally sickened that the two ladies were subjected to such extreme temperatures on my behalf, and ordered the company director to send the girls back inside to a warm room for the rest of the day, and added that I would later check that they were cared for to ensure their comfort. I explained that my company had very strict health and safety policies, which included any contractor, subcontractor, vendor or supplier, and any violation would result in no purchase order being placed.

I added that it was all part of the pre-contract award audit which I was conducting. The company director said something very fast and strong in Chinese and one of his guys ran over to the two ladies and together with them, ran back inside their main building. The way the two ladies moved indicated that they were both frozen stiff.

I added that if I had the purchase order awarded, I would visit without any warning from time to time to ensure that conditions had been met. Later, I did visit and all the Chinese employees were sporting well insulated and padded winter clothing.

After all the formalities had taken place, the Chinese hospitality went overboard: they invited me out to their favourite restaurant later the same day. I'm not sure whether the food was meant to impress me or frighten me.

The local restaurant was beautiful, and had a private room with a table large enough to accommodate all fourteen of us. As their honorary guest, each new dish that was brought to the table was spun around until it was directly in front of me, to take the first portion. I like sushi and sashimi, but even I have limits.

The Koreans had hardened my appetite by bringing live jellyfish, octopus, and starfish to the table, but the Chinese really stole the show.

One of the dishes consisted of freshly gutted sea cucumber. They gutted it with water still dripping off its hairy skin, and while it was still moving it was a very difficult mouthful, not to mention the white, milky soup with a baby octopus swimming around in it. The method was to slurp back the soup using both hands around the little white bowl until you were able to catch the little octopus in your mouth and crack its head between your teeth. It was not a pleasant experience as its little skinny legs were over my bottom lip while I needed to murder the poor little thing. But what really stole the show was a plate of grilled, black snakeheads. They were crunchy; I almost broke a tooth!

All the while we ate, I tried my best to be polite and maintain some sort of smile on my face. Frequently, they would shout 'gam bei', meaning dry glass, and we all had to knock back a small glass of 24% Chinese wine. Each time I put my empty glass back on the table, a waitress standing behind me would fill it back up.

There is a Chinese proverb that goes as follows: "If you leave a social meal sober, you did not truly enjoy yourself." As far as Chinese proverbs go, I had a great time. It was difficult to maintain anything like sobriety with the waitress standing behind my chair!

Traditionally, Chinese people believe that it is impolite to talk too much while eating. A good meal was regarded as too special to be spoiled by conversation. Keeping reasonably quiet during the meal was easy for me because I didn't understand anything they were saying, plus some of the dishes left me speechless in any case. Their interpreter made things even worse, while I quietly worried about what dish I would be presented with next.

The Chinese had employed the services of the interpreter, but her version of English was new to me. I could understand some Scottish, but almost everything I said was lost in translation. Some normal things I wanted to say got wrongly translated into phrases the Chinese thought were hilarious. After that, they shouted 'gam bei' even more. I decided it was best not to say anything that could possibly be misinterpreted, but that didn't always work.

Once we'd finished the food, for want of a better word, I was driven back to the hotel. We pulled up a little short of the hotel, outside another building which appeared to look like another hotel. It was a Chinese massage place, which was four stories high. I was escorted to a changing room where I had to remove my shoes and use their flip-flops to enter the main building. After that, we went downstairs to change into clothes closely resembling pyjamas.

I was given their largest size, but they still pinched a bit in all the wrong places, which made them not so comfortable after all. We were each given a private massage room and the cutest little Barbie to do the work. Mine kept trying to talk to me, but my Chinese was as non-existent as her English. Still, she never stopped trying to chat while beating the hell out of me with incredible speed. She continued doing that for a solid hour without even breaking into a sweat. Amazing, but so very true; I should have married her!

Once my massage was over, my little Barbie took me to a huge room with large, reclining leather chairs in rows from one wall to the other. I arrived a little late due to my intense conversations with Barbie and the other guys were already seated, waiting for me. I was given an ice cold Chinese beer whilst I watched a Russian show that entailed girls in bikinis simply walking around and doing nothing else. It was as boring as it gets. Moments later, a new Barbie proceeded to give me a foot massage, and then another Barbie gave me a head and neck massage.

I thought to myself, *this is all part of my job. I shouldn't fight it; I should just accept it like a man until it is three o'clock in the morning and time to leave.*

The next day, I needed to visit another company that would galvanise much of the steelwork being fabricated by the first company. Again, they took me to a restaurant after I had concluded my appraisal of their premises. This time it was to a different restaurant, but every bit the same style as the one the night before.

Just like the previous night, everything I said was lost in translation, and some of the dishes were very difficult to swallow whilst trying to maintain an appreciative smile on my face. Fortunately, I was taken directly back to the hotel this time, so I could catch up on some much-needed sleep.

After my first experience of Chinese hospitality, I took the early morning flight back to Seoul in time to collect my tickets for Singapore the following day.

Arriving in Singapore late in the afternoon, I wasted no time in checking into my usual hotel on Orchard Street. I always chose the same hotel as they had a good choice of restaurants on the ground floor. The famous Orchard Towers nightspot was just across the road, but I was normally too tired to spend long there.

The Orchard Towers was basically a building consisting of four floors of bars. Some bars had DJs and others had live groups, but all had the same in common: ladies, a lot of ladies. In fact, there were so many ladies, it made getting to the bar quite difficult, as the competition was fierce. There were Thai ladies, Chinese ladies, Vietnamese ladies, Indian ladies, Singaporean ladies and other nationalities; a perfect paradise for bachelors, or travelling men!

Waking up in the morning after visiting the Orchard Towers was a painful experience requiring paracetamol and coffee, before removing any evidence from the night before.

After my hard night in transit, I would take the 10am ferry

out from Singapore's Harbour Front for the one hour ride over to Batam Island, which is a part of Indonesia, to have a meeting with a Japanese company. I would buy a $10 US dollar visa upon arrival, which was good for a five day visit, before meeting the driver assigned to taking me to the office.

My business was always completed the day I arrived, but I'd always plan the visit for a Friday so I'd also stay the Saturday night to try to get some much-needed rest before making my journey back to Singapore on the Sunday and then on to South Korea the same day.

The driver would take me straight to their fabrication facilities, which was just half an hour from the ferry terminal, but the roads on Batam Island left a lot to be desired. They didn't have curbstones along their edges, so it didn't take long for the surface to break away, especially during the rainy season.

At the office, the Japanese president always welcomed me in person. They had been contracted for the manufacture of large shell plates for oil and gas storage tanks to be erected in Qatar. My monthly visits were to conduct a document review for the release of a shipment of tank plates for the refinery, which included a physical inspection in the storage yard prior to shipping. The intense humidity in the summer months was very uncomfortable, but as a form of compensation, the president would always invite me to join him for lunch at a nearby Japanese-built golf course. He did this every time I visited him.

Several big Japanese companies owned the private golf course, and the restaurant had been built in true Japanese style: both the president and I had our own personal waitress quietly waiting behind us in true Japanese style.

To make it more comfortable for foreign guests, they had built a floor well under the table, like many of the South Korean restaurants had done, so patrons didn't have to sit cross-legged.

After we'd eaten, the president had his driver take him back to his office, before instructing him to drive me anywhere I fancied on the island for the rest of the afternoon.

My first stop was my hotel so I could check in, leave my small case in my room and freshen up before going for a foot massage. I did this on every visit before driving around several beautiful island beaches like a tourist. The driver knew from previous visits that I was fond of fresh seafood and took me to an outdoor seafood restaurant so I could try their famous chilli crab.

The restaurant was built half on land and half over the ocean. The driver planned to wait in the car until I was ready to leave, but I insisted that he join me. Inside, there were concrete tanks with everything imaginable to choose from. An Indonesian man who explained what was on offer escorted us around. I chose a mud crab, and encouraged the driver to choose what he liked to drop off for his family on the way back while it was still hot.

The restaurant had washbasins dotted all over the place. The general idea was to eat with your hands and make as much of a mess as you wanted. Once we had finished, the driver dropped me off at my hotel so I could catch up on some much-needed rest, due to the Chinese hospitality a couple of days before.

To help me with my permanent jetlag, I called the hotel spa and asked if Diana was available to visit my room. Shortly afterwards, little Diana entered my room to give a very professional massage. Half way through her massage she needed to wake me up to roll over and later wake me up again to tell me she'd finished! I guess I didn't need the massage after all.

On this occasion, my return trip to Seoul was interrupted by an unplanned visit to Dubai to meet one of the suppliers we had there. Once I got off the ferry in Singapore's Harbour Front, I had a six hour wait before my flight to Dubai on Singapore Airlines. To pass the time, I decided to pay the Raffles hotel a visit and have a Singapore Sling in their famous long bar.

The hotel is a beautiful place to walk around, and the long bar was up a couple of flights of stairs close to an elevator. Entering the bar, I could see monkey nut shells all over the floor where customers had been, as was the custom. I ordered my Singapore Sling but it was simply poured from a pre-mixed jug. I complained and asked why as I wanted to see the usual cocktail performance. I was told that they only did that for television cameras.

I arrived in Dubai the next day, and took a taxi to my pre-booked hotel. I always chose to stay in the same hotel for its comforts, convenience and large choice of restaurants. At the reception desk, a message was waiting for me from my office in Seoul, which detailed a flight to Qatar on the Wednesday. My wonderful project control manager thought it would be a good idea for me to visit the construction site in Ras Laffan because I was so close in Dubai.

With the Tuesday meeting complete, I made my way to the Mall of the Emirates, where I liked the huge restaurant on the ground floor at the base of the ski slope.

Against All Odds

The menu covered most types of cuisine from around the world, so there was something to please everyone. Then came the spice and gold souks to occupy the rest of the afternoon. Due to so much travel I had learnt to fly very light and just travelled with a carry-on case. As soon as I arrived in a new hotel room, I would call laundry service and sign for the executive service so my clothing would be returned to me in just two hours. That way, I flew around from country to country with just a change of three sets of clothes, plus my toiletries in a zip-locked bag for the airport security checks.

I spent three nights in dusty Doha before returning back to Dubai on the Saturday. From Dubai, I headed back to Seoul via Singapore due to my flights. After just two days back in the Seoul office, I took a fourteen hour flight to Amsterdam to spend another six hours in transit before flying back to Italy for a meeting. With just a one night stop-over in Milan, I headed back to Seoul with another six hour wait in Schiphol airport.

During all my business trips in 2006, I needed to make several trips to Thailand to meet another contractor involved with the project. In February of 2007, a new wife entered my life. I met Wi in a salon in Bangkok on Sukhumvit Road, just a five minute walk from the well-known Nana Plaza. I got to know her well during my business trips to Thailand, as she was always the one who cut my hair when I visited the salon she worked in.

Wi was the one I always chose to cut what was left of my hair each time I returned to Bangkok. Most probably due to her smile and personality, not the fact that she was the best stylist in the salon. With my crew cut, there wasn't anything to style anyway.

Every five or six weeks, I'd meet her when I returned to Bangkok and stayed in the same hotel. The purpose of each trip to Bangkok was to visit a large fabrication facility that was very experienced with fabricating equipment for the oil and gas industry, which was situated near the Cambodian border.

Again, I travelled with a representative from our main Korean contractor, and I always endeavoured to make time to visit Wi; I was due for another haircut by that time anyway. I always remembered to bring Wi little presents from the airport duty-free shops, and we became very good friends.

Whenever possible, I'd steer away from the usual restaurants my contractor invited me to so I could take Wi out after she'd finished work, often with one of her salon friends. That wasn't always so easy with the hospitality of my contractor as there were millions of dollars at stake, depending on their performance.

I had to cater to Wi's work schedule, though. One week she'd work from nine to nine, and the next week she'd work from eleven to eleven. To the Thai people, holidays seemed to be something that only tourists had.

Wi took me to traditional Thai restaurants outside the usual tourist venues, and as far away as possible from the smutty places in Bangkok. Being the daughter of a rice farmer, Wi hated bars with a vengeance. She wouldn't allow me to pay the usual prices tourists became victims of either. She scrutinised every bill before I got to see it, and she didn't hesitate to question any entry she didn't understand.

I learned not to take a Bangkok taxi to a well-known restaurant, because the driver could order takeaway food from behind the scenes and have his meal added to the final bill.

This was especially the case with the tuk tuk drivers who persuaded unknowing tourists to go to particular restaurants. Later, they'd return for their commission of whatever the tourist spent. Many shops offered tuk tuk and taxi drivers a commission just for bringing prospective customers, even if they didn't buy anything.

For those who travel to Bangkok to take advantage of the sex industry, travelling from one venue to another by tuk tuk would result in a bill that's at least twice as high as it should be. I have a love/hate relationship with Bangkok, mainly due to its darker side, which it is so popular and famous for.

Nothing disgusts me more than seeing a hugely obese man proudly walking down the street with a tiny, skinny little Barbie doll that he had recently rented holding his hand. I am very well known in Bangkok to interrupt such romances and pay the girl to go home. That's better than imagining what she'd have to endure later in the evening. The customer would often take personal offense and sometimes become aggressive, but the Thai doormen in the street all knew me very well and what I liked to do, and would have jumped in to protect me should the need arise.

In February, I decided to leave the project I'd been flying around so much for because I had only contracted for the detailed design and procurement phase and returned back to Bangkok.

Chapter 17
Thailand

In February of 2007 I returned back to Thailand so Wi and I could get married in her family's house in Sakon Nakhon, near Laos. It took a forty-five minute flight to reach the area. It was a very green area, like everywhere in Thailand. There were miles and miles of rice fields.

I was still officially married to Carolina in Venezuela, however, so we couldn't formally get married. Instead, we married Buddhist style by having the all-day ceremony without signing anything. Wi knew all about Carolina, and she longed for the day I would finally be free so we could get married officially.

We were well received at the airport by Wi's brother and one of her sisters. We drove for almost two hours before we got to Sakon Nakhon where her mother and father were eagerly waiting to meet me for the first time.

Wi's father had already started cutting very fine sticks, very much like tooth picks, which were needed to form part of the flower arrangement that would later become the centrepiece of the ceremony. Other ladies in the village joined in to help with the plaiting of banana leaves, which would also become part of the flower arrangement.

Wi, one of her sisters and I went out into the rice fields to a place where a certain type of white flower grew. We collected all we could find to add to the arrangement. Hidden inside the final flower arrangement was a small bottle of Thai whisky and a small bowl of sticky rice: offerings to Buddha. To drive around the rice fields, Wi's father had handed me the keys to his brand new Toyota Hilux, purchased with his life's savings.

As I reversed out from beneath his house everyone was watching me. This freaked me out a lot and as I reversed very slowly, I backed into a concrete lamp post, which caused a little dent in her father's back bumper. I could see the lamp post, but just as I touched the brake and changed into the first gear there was a little bump.

I felt terrible as everyone rushed over to see the damage; it was so embarrassing. A few minutes later, Wi and one of her sisters jumped into the Hilux so I could drive them to where the flowers should be. As I was still in shock and total embarrassment for denting Wi's father's pride and joy, I drove over a little puppy, which was sleeping in the middle of the road. I love dogs so much that it ruined the rest of my day. I felt two little bumps and a squeak and that was it, poor little puppy.

It must have taken a full six hours to complete the flower arrangement. Strands of white wool completed it, and it was my job to carry it up the stairs of their house, which was built on tall wooden legs as part of the tradition. I nervously picked it up and was surprised to discover how heavy it was. I couldn't see the steps in front of me as I slowly made my way to the first floor. Luckily, I made it without any incident. I believe the flower arrangement weighed around fifteen kilos by the time it was finished.

The last job was for Wi. She had to arrange the three hundred thousand Thai baht wedding dowry in a pattern on the floor in front of the flower arrangement. She rearranged the money three times before she was satisfied. After that, she added the finishing touch: a necklace and bracelet made of pure Thai gold. The jewellery also became part of the ceremony, along with the rings.

Everyone in the little village was welcome to visit the house to see the dowry arranged on the well-polished wooden floor, which I thought rather patronising for the poor rice workers. Sandals and flip-flops filled the entrance outside their house as guests went in to see my offering to join the family.

With all preparations complete, it was time to change into traditional clothes, which was highly amusing. I had to wear a sarong, which was something new for me. It caused a lot of laughs when the garment ended up around my ankles in front of Wi's mother and sisters.

Making and hand-printing sarongs had been Wi's mother's profession, and her sarongs were well known in that part of the country. She still had many left from when she used to make them, and the patterns and colours were beautiful. To wear it, I had to pull the loop, which was all they were, tight against my waist and fold the spare material back against myself and then fold the whole sarong down over itself. Because my first attempt failed miserably, they decided to cheat and allow me to wear a belt underneath the fold of the sarong so it couldn't be seen. I didn't like its colour, but didn't mention the fact so as not to disappoint them.

I also needed to borrow a white, long-sleeved shirt. I could have bought one back in Bangkok, but I wasn't told in time. They went all around the village collecting white shirts until I finally tried one that almost fitted, but it had to do. The finishing touch was a silk sash that rested on my right shoulder and draped down to my left hip.

We were ready to start the ceremony. I was taken away from Wi and made to walk to the entrance of the village. There, quite a congregation of family, relatives, and friends who were waiting outside joined me. Once we got to the entrance of the village, we turned to prepare for the slow walk back the way we had come. I was made to hold three pampas leaves and three tiny candles, like the type you'd find on a birthday cake.

The music started, and the slow walk back to the house began. I was shaded from the sun by an umbrella held above my head while others played instruments: harmonica, guitar, panpipes, and bongo drums. I felt like all eyes were focused on me, which they were. I tried to walk a little faster to get it over and done with, but each time I tried to speed up, I was made to slow down. The walk back to Wi's parents house felt like hours instead of around twenty minutes.

Finally I made it back to the house. There, I found one of Wi's sisters waiting at the entrance to the house. As part of the ceremony, she had to traditionally hand wash the dust from my feet before I stepped onto a banana leaf to enter the house. I had no idea how much trouble Wi's family had gone to to make all the professional arrangements. I've often thought how good they'd fare on oil and gas projects!

As I made it back to my starting block, I was surprised to see so many people already sitting around on the wooden floor. I was ushered through the crowd and made to kneel down alongside Wi. She looked more beautiful than I could ever have imagined. She was in full national costume, including a slim-fitting handmade silk dress with a pink and white Thai orchid in her hair.

It is very bad manners to show the soles of your feet in Thailand, and I found it almost impossible to kneel down normally because there were people behind me, sitting against the wall. I had to try to sit to the side, but because it was such an awkward position, my ankles hurt against the wooden floor. Whatever position I tried, I felt pain, so I decided to cross my legs. Unfortunately, I couldn't maintain that comfortable position for the following four hours with my anklebones on the hard floor.

Wi's uncle began reading from a thick, handwritten book while everyone kept quiet.

I don't think I've ever kept quiet for four hours in my entire life, but I was afraid to breathe at times. Towards the end of the ceremony, I found out the purpose of the white wool that had been draped on the flower arrangement.

Everyone in the room began to place money in our hands and securely tie a strand of wool around our right wrists. I felt guilty about accepting the twenty baht ($0.65c) donations from all the poor rice farmers, but it was all part of the ceremony, a bid of good luck for our future together. With our rings exchanged, it was all over; thank you Buddha!

After the four long hours on the hard wooden floor, I managed to pass through the pain barrier several times until I lost most of the feeling in my lower legs and feet. When it was time to stand up, I couldn't. The Thai people understood and found the situation highly amusing.

They all helped me to my feet and kept me steady until the blood rushed back into my muscles. The pins and needles feeling didn't take long to disappear and I was able to go back outside where we spent the rest of the evening. I kept myself active slapping mosquitos and swatting the flies, as there were many chickens amongst us, not to mention Wi's father's four cows next to the house.

Wi's father had only the four cows remaining from his herd but I was to add to them later.

Wi was the only one who could speak English, so she regularly joined me to ask if I was alright. Everyone else was speaking Thai to me, to which I could only nod my head, smile, or laugh.

The next day involved the final part of the wedding ceremony. We went to the local village temple to give the three monks an offering. I couldn't believe my eyes when I saw the size of the village temple. It was big enough to house the entire population of the village and still have plenty of room to spare. It was quite a sight with its huge wooden roof, which would no doubt last for generations.

Again, it was time to kneel down and cover the soles of my feet for yet another hour. Fortunately, the time passed quickly, and I welcomed the time to go to the three monks and make my offering. The congregation of onlookers joined us, which was very comforting. They were all there for me.

On the walk back to the house, I called Carolina back in Venezuela to tell her what I'd been up to. Carolina was more surprised than upset, and she seemed understanding. She knew there was no real point in waiting for me; she had to continue her life. I explained that my Thai marriage did not include the signing of any documents, so no laws had been broken. I later learnt that my Venezuelan wife has posted photos of her new-born daughter on Facebook from her live-in boyfriend!

She said she'd pursue the divorce that the second lawyer had initiated in Venezuela. Two days later, she called me to let me know that the second lawyer, as expected, had done nothing. Thus, the second three thousand dollars had been another wasted investment.

Wi's place in Sakon Nakhon was the main area of Thailand where they ate dogs, but thankfully, the King had made that illegal. I was busy looking for another contract in Southeast Asia in order to stay close to Wi, and was lucky to secure a staff position in Kuala Lumpur to work on a 138-kilometre subsea pipeline.

With contracts signed, off I went to Kuala Lumpur for the first time.

Chapter 18
Malaysia

After arriving in Malaysia in February of 2007, I found myself back in Italy after just ten days and back in Japan two weeks later. I could only stay in the company-provided hotel for a week so I needed to find an apartment quickly. It didn't give me enough time to get to know Kuala Lumpur so I chose the first apartment, which was high enough away from the mosquitos. Mosquitos don't normally fly higher than the fifth or sixth floor and the apartment I chose was on the twenty-fourth floor in a place called Mont Kiara.

Mont Kiara wasn't the ideal location as the apartment block was at the top of a long steep road and over half an hour walk from the nearest shops. In the heat and humidity, it wasn't a pleasurable trip to get the beginning of the most urgent essentials.

Once I had bought all the usual accessories, which were rarely found in a rental apartment, Wi quit her job in Bangkok and joined me. Wi didn't need to use the air conditioners in the daytime while I was busy working, so she kept them off all day to save on expensive electrical bills! Even though we lived on the twenty-fourth floor, it was still too hot and humid for me, even with the windows opened to have a through draft. Wi would close all windows and switch on the air conditioners half an hour before my return every day.

After a few more weeks, I was able to buy a new car from a local dealer situated in the heart of Kuala Lumpur, near the twin towers. All was fine until I tried to drive it back to Mont Kiara. Malaysia's roads were very unforgiving and if you missed your exit, you were in immediate trouble, as there didn't seem to be any means to make a U-turn and try again.

The day I took my new car back to the apartment took me almost three hours instead of a brief thirty minute drive. I was stuck on a highway heading in an easterly direction towards the coast without any way to turn around. Eventually, I was able to flag down a taxi, which led me home.

Wi was an amazing cook. A friend of mine, Terry, who lived lower down the same road, would often join us when we went down the road to a local bar and Wi loved to cook for him. Terry was already in his middle sixties and Wi called him uncle Terry. One time, Terry's son docked in Malaysia off a nuclear submarine and Wi invited both her uncle Terry and his son for lunch one Saturday afternoon.

I, together with Terry and his son, sat watching an action movie while Wi remained in the kitchen all afternoon producing course after course of Thai cuisine. Wi brought us many little dishes during the afternoon, each one different from the last. We'd gone through at least twelve courses until we couldn't manage any more and had to ask her to stop cooking.

Wi was not just the best choice of companion; Wi was also my closest possible friend. She never stopped fussing around our rented apartment, which was just up the road from a place called Sri Hartamas, just twenty-five minutes from the centre of Kuala Lumpur.

Wi was forever putting things away in drawers so I couldn't find anything. I'd arrive home from work and look for my telephone charger so I could simply plug my mobile in before doing anything. My charger was never in the wall socket where I'd left it. I needed to ask Wi every day where my charger was, and Wi would reply, "Drawer darling, in drawer. Charger must live in drawer, not floor."

Laundry was another issue. My clothes from the day before were always washed, dried, ironed to perfection and aired every day, even though I could have waiting a week.

During our time together in Malaysia, I discovered that Wi wasn't actually her real name. I knew Thai people liked to be called by their chosen nicknames, such as Nok, Lek, or Hoy, because their original names were often too long.

When I originally asked Wi to write down her name and phone number back in the salon she worked on Sukhumvit Road, she wrote Wi because W and I were the only letters she knew in English. Her real first name was Vipaporn, which she has since changed to Narawadee because her favourite monk told her it was a luckier name. The monk was no ordinary monk, as I later discovered; he was the personal monk for the royal family.

Through Wi, the monk would send warnings to me of events that wouldn't be good for me and advised me to avoid them, whenever possible. For some strange reason he knew all about the voodoo in my life before, back in Venezuela. He warned that voodoo would repeat itself in my life with life-threatening consequences. He warned me to be careful and warned me about a large black woman who I'd later meet. He also warned me of the need to have a major operation in the future, but that I would survive it.

He had explained to Wi my past, which I could never have done due to the language barrier that existed at that time before Wi later took up English lessons to increase her vocabulary.

Even though I was pleased that Wi had accompanied me in Kuala Lumpur, Kuala Lumpur was not a very good move for Wi. Wi couldn't walk down the road to the local gym without cars pulling up alongside her trying to proposition her, and Malaysian, Indian and Indonesian construction workers used to follow her along the road until it got so bad that she remained in the apartment like a prisoner the whole day.

As Wi didn't have a residential visa, she needed to fly back to Bangkok every thirty days, and then return for another thirty. This was a welcome break for her and sometimes she'd stay a few days, visit her friends, family etc., before returning back to Kuala Lumpur.

As a product of all the flying I had done, I had found that I had vein thrombosis in a most personal place. Whenever the vein filled with blood, the vein would become like a hard piece of plastic, raised and terribly uncomfortable. I went to the local clinic and a lady doctor was on duty. After her brief examination she referred me to a surgeon just three days later. The local clinic was actually a part of my apartment's complex and conveniently located on the ground floor.

I met the surgeon and he prescribed a course of blood thinning drugs just to see if they would clear the suspected blockage in my vein. A week later I returned in just the same condition, so he informed me that I needed to have surgery.

The surgery was booked for a week later and I took a taxi to the hospital, which was positioned in a very beautiful part of Kuala Lumpur where the surgeon practised. Unfortunately, it was a Saturday and Wi had only flown to Bangkok the night before, so I was alone. At the hospital, they were all very professional and prepared me for the surgery under just a local anaesthetic. I couldn't believe my best friend was going to be cut while I was still conscious! I was prepared for surgery and left to wait in a very cold area, which felt like hours. The air conditioners must have been on full, and I was shivering the whole time.

Thankfully, eventually a very nice old nurse wheeled me to the operating theatre where I would next meet the surgeon. He had previously informed me that he had qualified in America so I felt I was in safe hands. With the job in hand, I was worried about friendly fire, blue on blue and have a nice day! The surgeon fitted an intravenous needle into my left arm and injected something before he injected something else, which he told me I would enjoy.

He had a pleasant smile on his face and to cut a long story short, I never stopped talking the whole time he performed the necessary surgery, much to the amusement of the two nurses swabbing blood. I wasn't encouraged to lean up to see what was going on, nor did I want to, but I was presented with the end result in a test tube full of some kind of clear liquid. The vein, which was removed, was the whitest possible white I had ever seen. It was like chewing gum, but so brilliantly white.

I left the hospital still enjoying whatever the hell they had injected me with and took a taxi to a shopping mall in the centre of Kuala Lumpur. I wanted to buy another suitcase, or so I thought at the time, still under the influence of the drugs I was given. While I walked to the shop I noticed everyone looking at me. I didn't know at the time, until I arrived home, that my blood had managed to soak through my dressing and also my jeans leaving a large wet, red patch for all to see going down my leg.

I was instructed to return after fourteen days to the clinic, to have my stitches removed, but due to the itching, I couldn't wait that long. Instead I bought a razorblade, a tweezers and some surgical spirit and decided to become a surgeon. It was the second time I'd carried out such a procedure, the first time was when I was circumcised at the age of five years old, and I'd performed a similar procedure in a well salted bath my mother had dropped me in.

Everything went perfectly as I cut the knots and plucked out the rather coarse stitches. Perfect until I cut the final stitch and pulled it with the tweezers in the wrong direction. I left it until last as it was caked in hard dry blood so I soaked it with surgical spirit to soften the blood, thinking I was being sensible – not.

Once I had cut the last stitch, I pulled the stitch in the wrong direction due to the blood, which caused its knot to pass through the first side on my skin, but ended up stuck inside my wound.

I was bleeding quite a lot, but relieved that the operation was over I guessed things would only get better. I continued to pull the problem stitch but it ended up in disaster. My wound opened up more and I needed to quickly stand up so my blood wouldn't make a mess on my soft leather sofa. It wasn't a nice night as I spent the rest of it with my friend in a mug of strong salt water, just like the baths I'd had when I was five years old.

The following evening I needed to collect Wi from the airport as she was returning from her visa run. All was fine until we started to drive back to Mont Kiara. As we were driving on the highway and about half way home, I checked my rear view mirror and noticed the front window of a five series BMW. The car was practically touching my back bumper as I couldn't see its lights. I pulled over and it went past my car and then swerved across my lane forcing me to brake heavily, until I was only going thirty kilometres an hour.

It had blacked out windows so I knew it was a government car, which were licensed to shoot! Guns were permitted in Malaysia if you were security, but Malaysian law did not permit everyday people to hold a loaded weapon. Security guards outside supermarkets etc., held guns but their shells were not permitted to be loaded unless they encountered a problem. Fortunately the government car pulled away, but both Wi and I were quite shaken by the threat for the rest of the night.

After we had lived in our apartment for three months, new people moved into the apartment directly above ours. The new tenants seemed to keep themselves busy dragging furniture all day and most of the night, making our lives quite a misery. With the twenty-four hour construction of new tower blocks being built all around us, and the terrible driving in Kuala Lumpur, we decided to pull out of Malaysia whilst we were still both in one piece.

The company I was working for still owed me over four thousand dollars in expenses from several months of business trips, and despite many complaints, there was no sign of it being paid. It no longer felt as though anything was going well for us, so we left Malaysia and returned back to Bangkok.

I left my four–month-old Volkswagen Golf I had bought with a British friend living in Kuala Lumpur to sell on my behalf. Unfortunately, he fell for the oldest trick in the book and handed over my signed logbook to a Chinese garage owner who sold my car and kept all the money, so I lost everything. The garage owner had done that to numerous other clients before bankrupting the company, which meant nobody got their money. That was a loss of another thirty thousand dollars.

Wi went back to working in the same salon on Sukhumvit Road in Bangkok, but her personality began to change because she was worried that I was not working. Tensions continued to rise until I was able to start a new contract in Qatar as the consortium quality manager of three companies. As I left Thailand, I had no idea when I would next see Wi again so we decided to go our separate ways.

As it happened, this wasn't the last I'd see of Wi, as I discovered five years later in December 2012.

Chapter 19
Second Time in Qatar

In January of 2008 I mobilised to Qatar. The Qatar contract came at a perfect time; plus, I got the opportunity to see Izhar again. I was looking forward to seeing him again so I was able to contract him for his unique computer database skills, working directly under me.

The company I was working for were struggling to create a mechanical completions database that they had committed themselves to in their contract, so the only chance they had of completing it was Izhar. They had turned my offer down to rent my own Q-Pack database, which was already a well proven system.

The first few weeks were spent sleeping in our assigned apartments in Doha, before our rooms were ready on the site camp in Ras Laffan. We needed to leave very early in the morning to start work at the site office, which was an hour's drive out into the desert. It was a boring drive as there was nothing of interest to see along the only road, at that time, to and from the site.

The social life in Doha was fine with its Rugby Club, European Club, and very nice hotel bars and restaurants; there wasn't anything to do out in the desert. Senior management had made all the usual assurances, much like politicians, but nothing ever materialised once you were out there. With no television channels, no Internet and no other facilities, time went very slowly.

The canteen didn't cater for Europeans either, so it was curry three times a day, or starve.

Soon the summer came along so all the mosquitos left due to the daytime temperatures, but the flies chose to stay, so you were never really alone. We were all required to wear orange coveralls all the while we were inside the site's perimeter fence, including the office. As we returned back to the camp all dressed in the same colour to the rows of white containers, we realised it was an exact replica of the detention camp at Guantanamo Bay, Cuba. Razor wire was also included on the top of all the chain-linked fences, which prevented anyone getting in, or us getting out!

Soon, the day came when Izhar walked into the office reception, just as I was passing by. All the office staff started laughing because it was obvious Izhar and I were the very best of friends.

Again, Izhar made me proud. In return, I got him the maximum salary the budget would allow. I lost my temper with the project director negotiating for Izhar, because I am a firm believer that salaries should be based on capability, and not where you came from. I don't agree with exploitation.

During our time living out in the desert camp, someone had mentioned that an Indian restaurant had been seen somewhere outside the site's perimeter fence. One lunchtime, together with Kenny, the construction manager, I ventured out of the back security entrance of the Ras Laffan industrial complex and went to see for myself. Sure enough, in the middle of nowhere, someone had opened a restaurant.

It wasn't much to look at from the outside, and even less from the inside. The food was prepared to order, as they had no idea when they would ever have a customer, so the wait was quite a long one. The outside temperature was around fifty degrees centigrade in the shade and the restaurant didn't have any air conditioning. We had checked inside the kitchen before ordering and found the temperature was intolerable with the added heat from the gas cookers.

We were sure that much of the salty flavour was from the chef's own sweat! The curry, however, was very good despite our surroundings. We arranged for the restaurant staff to have site entrance passes and deliver to our office every Thursday, so everyone could enjoy their food under the comfort of our office air conditioning.

I organised a desk for Izhar in my office because we had a lot of catching up to do; it had been quite a few years since Karachi. As part of my demands to my company, Izhar got his own private unit on our desert camp, like every manager had.

Managers were also assigned an apartment in Doha so they could escape the desert and enjoy city life whenever they wanted. Needless to say, there was a spare room for Izhar in mine. Izhar joined me in Doha a few times and made me proud to have him with me every time. Beer was not cheap in the hotel bars in Doha, but Izhar always insisted on paying his way even though I wanted to cover his turn.

I took a break after four months of living in the desert camp six nights a week and went to Thailand to meet up with two British friends in the same business.

They both lived in Pattaya, which was an hour and a half's drive east of Bangkok. I'd always avoided going there up until then as it was a bit too much, with its thousands of bars. I preferred the quieter and more cultural areas of Thailand.

I met Neil on my first night at a bar we'd arranged. The last time I'd seen Neil was when we worked together in Tunisia on a gas plant. Neil entered the bar with one of his friends to whom he promptly introduced me. His name was Mark, and he was an electrical engineer in the oil and gas business and also lived in Pattaya.

Together, we were later known as the three Alans. This is how that happened, as per Neil's personal request for my story to be more complete!

One night we met up together and proceeded to go down Pattaya's 'walking street', for a change of scenery. We had walked half way down the notorious street before deciding to take on some fluids. There wasn't anywhere quiet down walking street so we walked into the first bar that looked okay.

The moment we entered the bar, the lady managing the establishment came hurriedly over to us and spoke to me first. In true Thai bar fashion she said, "Hello, what your name, where you come flom (from), please sit down, what you want to drink?" to which I replied, "My name is Alan, I come from England and I'll have a beer please." Next she turned to Mark and asked the same question. Mark replied, "My name is Alan, I come from England and I'll have a beer please."

The lady looked at us and said, "Two Alan's … from England?" The best was yet to come. She turned to Neil and again, asked the same question. Neil replied, "My name is Alan, I come from England and I'll have a beer please." The poor lady looked somewhat distraught at our responses; hence, this night was the beginning of 'the three Alans' and we consequently rode into the sunrise.

Returning back to the bar I was staying above in Soi 13, I walked past a tattoo studio, which was still open at that time in the morning, whatever time it was. The same day, but in the afternoon, when I woke up, I faintly remembered something about promising the Thai tattooist that I'd return later to have the Chinese dragon and tiger tattooed on my back.

Not to disappoint the man, I returned to ask if I had seen him in the early hours that same day. As I entered into his studio he quickly showed me the artwork he had spent hours preparing for my tattoo!

If I was thinking more clearly I would have paid him for his time and trouble preparing the artwork and left, but instead, I wasn't thinking at all. I blame the two other Alans for that!

Instead, I removed my T-shirt and lay face down on his tattoo bed. He started by shaving the hairs off my back and applied a thin film of gel before placing a tracing of his artwork on top of it. He then pressed it down firmly to transfer the ink from his tracing onto my skin as a guide to the pattern he had developed.

I was already thinking that it wasn't too late to pull out, but instead, I fell asleep! Again, I blame the two other Alans, and still do to this day!

I woke up suddenly with the most gut-wrenching pain, similar to someone cutting through my side with a blunt chainsaw. *Alans*, I thought, *wait until tonight!* As it worked out, I didn't leave the studio for ten hours, which took me past midnight so I went straight to my room with my back feeling like I'd slept on a BBQ. After two days the tattooist had finally finished the outline, so the next step was to colour it all in.

When I tried to return the next day, I couldn't get out of bed as my blood had glued my back to the sheets. Together with the soreness I couldn't move. Luckily, the room maid entered to clean my room and helped to painfully peel the colourful blood stained sheet from my very sore skin. After I'd enjoyed my traditional Thai breakfast consisting of rice and chillies with some vegetables thrown in, I half-heartedly returned back to the studio for some more voluntary agony. *Alans!* I thought again.

After another nine hours of unadulterated torture, I stopped the tattooist, as I really couldn't take any more pain for that day. The following three days were much the same until his not-so-handy work was finally over. I thought my friends were joking when they informed me that the tiger's eye on my back was poking out of its head until someone took a photo to show me! Nobody could locate the end of the dragon's tail either. Maybe that explained the tiger's eye?

I often thought, if Wi had been with me, she would have prevented the entire escapade from taking place.

Back in Qatar, I wasn't too happy with how the project was going because we were getting badly let down by our procurement department back in Paris, but taking the blame for them on site. One afternoon, an agent called to ask whether I'd be interested in a lead quality manager position back in West Africa.

My curriculum vitae was submitted and accepted, and I said goodbye to Qatar. I felt a little guilty for taking Izhar from his family to work for me and then leaving him alone, but I had a hidden agenda which I couldn't explain to him at the time, as I didn't want him to endure another disappointment if my plan didn't work out.

Chapter 20
Ghana, Togo, Benin and Nigeria

In August of 2008, I moved to West Africa to take care of the quality assurance and quality control in Ghana, Togo, Benin, and Nigeria on a project that had been running for a few years.

Apart from the usual security problems in Nigeria, Ghana, Togo, and Benin were all fine as far as work locations go, whilst taking the usual precautions for that part of the world. The people were friendly, and it was reasonably safe to walk around, especially Ghana, where nobody really bothered me. English speaking Ghana was really rather safe to walk around, French speaking Togo needed some precautions, French speaking Benin additional precautions but it all stopped at the Nigerian border where my heavily armed escort would be waiting for me.

On the 14th September 2008, I started the long drive from Ghana to Nigeria to meet with our main contractor's quality manager. Driving down through Ghana was a real pleasure as most of it was either bush or farmland. Spaced out along the road would be makeshift market stalls selling fresh fruit and vegetables etc., including barbeques selling bush meat.

When buying bush meat, it was not a good idea to enquire what the meat was. Rats were a popular dish, but the barbeques also hosted road kill, which might have been from the day before.

Sometimes, both my driver and I would use these barbeques, but we didn't seem to suffer from them.

Crossing into Togo, all English stopped as it was French speaking; the same in Benin. It would have been difficult to get lost, as there was only one main road from the Ghana / Togo border to the Benin / Nigeria border. The driving in that part of Africa left a lot to be desired. It seemed as though anyone could drive, and drive anything that had wheels. There was not any lane discipline and accidents were a daily event, sometimes terrible. On one occasion, a motorbike carrying gasoline from Nigeria was run over by a car.

The bike ended up underneath the car with the motorbike's rider trapped in the wreckage, and the whole lot had caught on fire. The remains were still on fire as I drove past, which upset me for the rest of the day. I don't recall a single trip driving through either Togo or Benin without seeing an awful road accident. It was as if a traffic jam wasn't a reason to stop and motorbikes would continue to try to squeeze through impossible gaps between large lorries, only to end up crushed between them as they slowly continued to pass each other.

The borders were always a hive of activity and no less than chaos every time. To make them more congested, salespeople would line the narrow tracks trying to make a living, selling all they could carry. It was always the best time to change currency as one could negotiate the best rates, much better than the hotels.

In Togo, I would stay in a hotel in its capital, Lomé. I would only stay there for one night, as I would continue on my journey towards Nigeria the following day. It was a short drive before crossing the Benin border to spend another night in a hotel in its capital Cotonou.

All was fine until I reached the Nigerian border. I had passed through the Benin border without any issues, but as always, stress levels raised when it was time to pass through the Nigerian border officials. As usual, I remained in the safety of the car while my driver carried my passport to be stamped into the country. He returned after a few minutes, saying that they wanted to see my face to ensure the passport was really mine.

This I did, but they weren't interested in seeing my face at all, but instead the colour of my money. They refused to stamp my passport until each of the five representatives had been 'dashed' in any currency I had on me. I tried to avoid making the payments, but after two long hours in the sun I gave up the fight; but I insisted they stamped my passport for a twenty-eight day visit. This they agreed so I was able to meet my armed escort and continue with my journey.

My armed escort was late arriving on that occasion, so due to my delay, they arrived just in time to safely escort me through the seventeen roadblocks to Lagos Bay. Once on the road, I always checked my rear view mirror to see if they were close behind me as they were instructed to be.

In Lagos Bay, the contractor's quality manager who I'd travelled so far to meet was delayed by a few days, which forced me to stay three weeks instead of the two I'd planned for. The hotel complex was a great place to stay for anyone who liked sand, malaria and dengue fever carrying mosquitos and watching out for black mamba snakes, which were killed on a daily basis. There were also green tree snakes, so we avoided standing under the trees in case a snake mistook us for a chicken and dropped on us.

After I'd concluded my visit, three weeks had passed by the time I needed to return back the way I'd come. I also needed to visit our Benin and Togo sites en route to Ghana. My driver and armed escort arrived late as usual, but we eventually got on our way.

Once on the road to Benin, every car that came near my Land Cruiser was considered a direct threat. My escort would sound their siren to keep them away from me, as one of our guys was shot in the head and chest on 17th March 2008 on the same road. He was ambushed and sprayed with bullets just ten minutes from the Nigerian / Benin border.

With that in mind, I always became tense as I approached the very same border. This day, it all seemed too easy. All seventeen road blocks opened up when they saw my truck approaching at high speed and heard the escort's sirens. The flashing blue and red lights were also a visual deterrent that I had an armed escort.

Once past the last checkpoint, we were home free, or so I thought. We had just a few easy kilometres to go before arriving at the Benin border.

I didn't hear the shot fired, but my driver suddenly grasped his right arm with his left hand and almost rolled the Land Cruiser when he realised he'd been hit. I grabbed the steering wheel, but it was too late: we ploughed into the skinny trees at the side of the road, but at least my driver managed to stamp on the brakes.

My escorts were too far behind us to provide any protection, but they could see what was happening ahead. They were actually quite brilliant, even if they were late. They pulled over, positioning their Toyota Hilux to block any direct fire in my direction, and proceeded to return fire.

My driver only had a flesh wound and the shootout lasted for just ten minutes, but it felt a lot longer at the time. Once my escort had succeeded in controlling the situation, I felt more deafened by the sudden sound of silence than their AK-47s. There weren't any additional casualties on my side, but I can't say the same for the three ambushers.

Just another ten minutes took us to the Benin border, which was as far as my escort could take me, as they couldn't cross the borderline. Their instructions were to wait there until I had cleared both the Nigerian and Benin border police desks before returning to their camp, back at Lagos Bay.

My Land Cruiser pulled up just before the borderline so my escort could still stand alongside my door for added protection. With a shot-out windshield and several other bullet holes, we looked like easy pickings for the mob around us. Several locals came rushing over to my truck shouting and demanding money. The situation didn't look very good as more and more people came over to where I was.

Another of my guards, who had been patiently waiting in the

Hilux, approached the guard standing alongside my door and handed him two more magazines for his gun, which he promptly slipped into a large pockets on his left trouser leg.

To encourage my protection, I gave the last of my Nigerian money to my escort and remained safely inside the Land Cruiser. My driver took my passport to the immigration officers as he usually did whilst I remained out of sight, as I must have been the only white man for miles around.

Five minutes later, my driver returned with a worried look on his face. He told me that the immigration officer wanted to see my yellow fever vaccination card. Surrounded by locals, I went over to the immigration officer and explained that my yellow fever card was still in Ghana. I told him that I didn't know I was required to show it when exiting the country?

Then the big act started.

The Nigerian officer shouted at me and told me he could not stamp me out of the country without the card. I tried arguing that I was leaving the country, not entering it, so a yellow fever card shouldn't matter anyway.

Arguing with him was fruitless. He told me I had to 'dash' him something or I would not be permitted to exit his country. This added to the stress I was already suffering, as I wouldn't be allowed to leave Nigeria, nor re-enter it!

All I had on me after giving the last of my naira to my armed escort were British twenty-pound notes. I walked away so I could discreetly take a note from my wallet, which I never normally carried at the border crossings, and folded it up into my right hand and returned to his little wooden desk.

Still totally surrounded by locals who were all looking for a hand out, I approached his desk trying to maintain a false smile for him to see. He ordered all the people waiting to move out of the way so I could go directly to his desk. I said to him, "You are a lucky man as you're going to get a thank you handshake to stamp me out of your country!" I shook his hand, transferred the bribe, and that was that, or so I thought.

I wasted no time in returning back to the safety of my truck and after another five minutes had passed my driver came back with a worried look on his face. He nervously informed me that now the chief immigration officer wanted to see me. I got back out of the car and, surrounded yet again by angry beggars, went back to the same immigration desk.

A new man wanted to speak with me this time. He wasn't dressed in uniform, but instead national dress comprising of a bright blue outfit with a matching hat, so I insisted on seeing his identity card. He immediately produced his ID for me to examine and took me behind the scenes where I was held at gunpoint while he explained that I had over-stayed in Nigeria for seven days.

That time they were right! When I'd entered Nigeria three weeks before, the immigration officer had stamped my passport for just a fourteen day stay, even though I'd asked for twenty-eight to be on the safe side and had dashed him accordingly. Like an idiot, I hadn't checked the stamp he'd given me.

The immigration chief had one of his police officers hold an AK-47 to my head while he shouted at me. He said I was an illegal alien in his country and that he'd have to have me arrested. He continued to shout at me, and he informed me that the penalty for being illegal in his country was a twelve month prison sentence. He said that my embassy couldn't help me because I was guilty.

By that time my stress level switched to overload and I couldn't contain it any longer. While the gun was held to my head with its safety off I started laughing. I could see the remains of the red paint on the left hand side of the AK-47, which indicated the safety had been disabled and the gun was ready to fire.

I'd got to the point where I didn't give a damn anymore and wanted to put up a final protest. I had a feeling that they wouldn't squeeze the trigger so with my left hand I grabbed the barrel of the gun, and held it firmly downwards. This infuriated the immigration chief and he demanded to know what I found so funny and instructed me to release the weapon.

I was tired and way passed caring by this time so I said, "In the entire history of your country, I must be the first white man to have over-stayed seven minutes, let alone seven days!"

His expression changed as he realised that I had already been pushed too far and I noticed a slight grin on his face in respect of my defiance and will to fight back.

Even though he was technically correct, I knew all he wanted was to be dashed some money, so I cut to the chase while still holding the AK towards the floor and asked to speak to him without an audience. He took me to a tiny little office while he continued to shout at me, asking me what he should do with me.

I admitted that I hadn't checked the date written in my passport and that I was glad he was there to help me. I said that whilst taking a British twenty pound note out of my wallet. His expression changed to a friendlier, more relaxed grin, and he said, "Dash me two more, and I will make sure you are fast-tracked and your passport stamped immediately."

I did as he asked, and my stress levels began to drop as I again, tried to walk back towards the Land Cruiser. Suddenly, I heard shouting and turned, only to see the immigration chief running towards me. He claimed that I was now his brother, and he asked for my phone number. I asked him why he wanted my phone number, and he explained that when I needed to pass into Nigeria in the future, he would meet me and get me fast tracked every time!

Fine, I thought, *it will cost me, but at least I'll have easier cross-*

ings in the future. I gave him my number and he also gave me his before I got back into my Land Cruiser to wait for my driver to return with my finally stamped passport. Minutes later, my driver returned with my passport together with an immigration form to fill out to enter back into Benin.

I thanked my escort so they could leave, completed the form, and we drove just a few metres and parked again at the Benin border post. It was quieter this time without the mob being allowed to cross the border, and off my driver went to the Benin immigration counter. Like the Nigerian border, my driver took my passport and completed form to the desk while I waited in the car as per our security protocol.

A couple of minutes later, he returned and said that the immigration officer wanted to see me. *Oh, not again!* I thought. I asked what the hell the problem was this time, and angrily got out of the truck and went over to see the Benin official. It was like a repeat performance. The immigration officer wanted to see my yellow fever card, which I knew was not required for Benin.

I wasn't in the frame of mind to argue anymore and simply dashed him. He immediately stamped my passport and I stormed off back to my truck without saying anything.

On the way back to my car, a very angry-acting idiot who tried to convince me he was the chief immigration officer accompanied me. He demanded to see my yellow fever card in order to let me enter Benin. As I already had a Benin stamp and was already on Benin dust, so I told him to procreate off.

The rest of the drive was relatively normal, or at least for that part of the world. With just a few accidents and a couple of dead bodies in the road, which I considered quite normal for that area, I was soon nearing my hotel. It was always a relief to get across the two borders, probably the worst twenty metres I've ever travelled in my entire life, but the downside was that I had to go through that very same process every four weeks.

The only compensation was getting to the hotel bar in Cotonou just in time for happy hour.

There, I would meet a colleague by the name of Tim. He was our company site representative in Benin, who found my border experiences highly amusing. Tim never needed to travel into Nigeria or endure the same problems I did. I hate Tim!

The next day was Sunday, and Tim had planned for us to leave the office a little earlier to show me 'The Point of No Return'. It was the very first place where slaves had been taken from Africa hundreds of years before, and it was appropriately named because the Africans would never see their homeland again.

We drove for about half an hour down a very long, sandy road with weird looking voodoo statues alongside the road every twenty metres. There wasn't another road leading in the same direction, just rough bush land. I could only imagine the thousands of slaves who had walked down the very same track wearing ankle shackles and chains so many years before.

When we got to the beach, I saw the large arch built in memory of all the Africans who had left from that very same place. I couldn't help thinking that the slaves had walked all the way along the same sandy track wearing shackles that would have been cutting deep into their ankles.

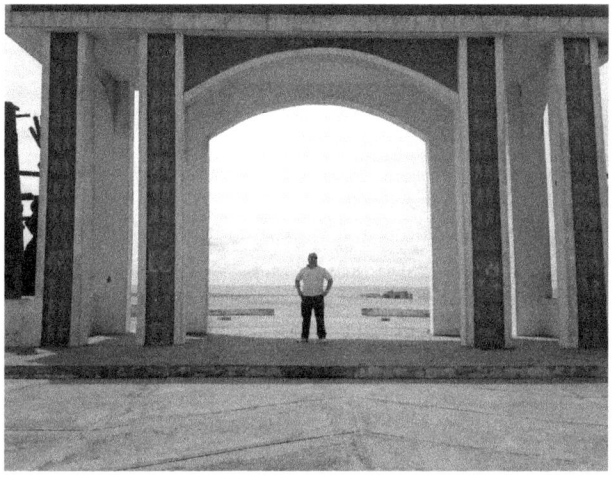

Voodoo statues protected each side of the arch, and they were decorated with images of snakes and lizards and other creatures. The place was completely silent and had an ambiance which didn't feel too comfortable.

There were still the remains of the buildings where the slaves were documented before boarding the ships, which would take them away permanently. All the other buildings along the shoreline were made of palm leaves, but these were western-built, and built of bricks. The sand had been swallowing up the buildings over the years, but their remains still poked up on the sandy beach.

Further down the road, we saw a voodoo temple, which I didn't want to get too close to after my past experiences in Venezuela.

Voodoo may be hard to believe for some, but in Benin, it is still their main religion and practised daily. January holds the world international voodoo festival every year.

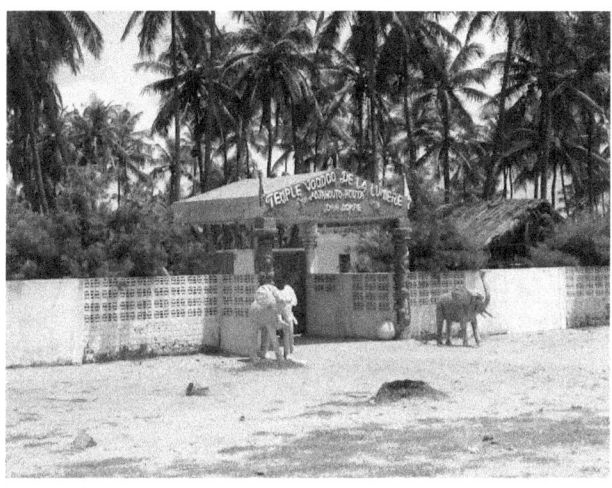

As we continued driving along the sandy beach road, we passed many people going about their daily routines until we passed by their tribal village that lived off the ocean.

Because there were no stones, bricks, mud or straw for miles, all their little houses were built entirely of woven palm leaves.

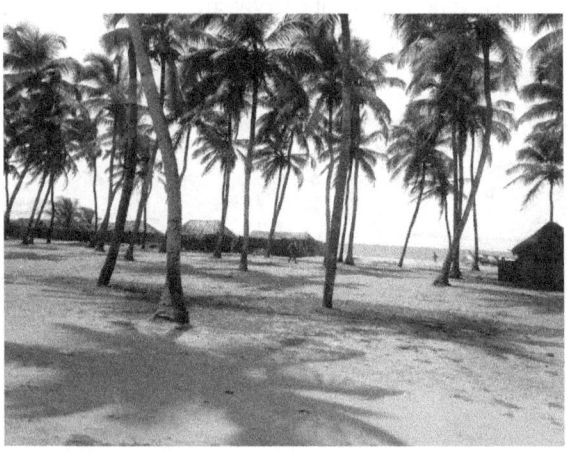

The tribes used to take out huge fishing nets using a flotilla of small wooden boats, leave the nets overnight, and work together to pull the nets back to the beach by hand the next morning. There could be a group of up to fifty to sixty men and women pulling one end of the net and another group pulling the other end. They sang all the while to a rhythm so they'd all pull at the same time. Sometimes there would be excitement when they'd find a large shark trapped in their nets.

Further along the sandy road, we turned left into a really narrow, track in the middle of nowhere. I asked Tim where we were going, but all he said was, "You're not going to believe this."

After just a few minutes, we came to a rough sort of car park in the sand where a few other 4x4s had parked. I still couldn't see anything though. Tim took me down yet another little path by foot until we came across a jetty at the beginning of a mangrove swamp. We were constantly on the lookout for snakes, which was why I chose to walk behind Tim!

A small wooden boat appeared through an archway in the mangroves, pulled up to the rickety wooden pier, and allowed us to jump in. It took about ten minutes to go through the mangroves, and we often needed to duck down when the branches were too low. Eventually, it opened out into a huge, inland lake, which no roads led to.

We went across the lake and found a very secluded bar and restaurant. With good food, cold beer, and a choice of French wines, we decided to call it a day.

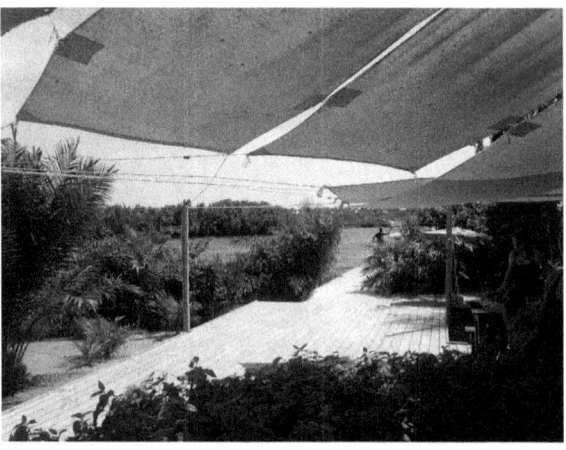

The next day I continued to drive on towards the Togo border and saw a terrible accident in the road. A lorry had driven over a small motorcycle with two people riding it. There wasn't much left of them in the tangled wreckage and many people had gathered around, causing a blockage for all the traffic.

We eventually passed by, but after seeing such events so many times in that part of Africa, it made you build up a slight emotional resistance. I arrived in the hotel in Togo and went directly to my room. I had no idea at that time that there was a cholera epidemic going on and that seventy-six people had already died that week.

My body had built up quite a high resistance to the usual hygiene problems in that part of the world so I had become complacent and didn't take the usual precautions like use bottled water to brush my teeth. I was soon to regret that simple little precaution. The next morning I continued to drive for the last few hundred miles to Accra in Ghana. During my journey I began to feel sick. I had stomach cramps and just put it down to the food I'd eaten the night before.

Later, my lower abdomen began to ache and then my muscles. By the time I arrived back in Accra my whole body was affected. I met the contractor's new quality manager that I'd travelled hundreds of miles to be introduced to, and went back to my room.

I was too exhausted and chose not to eat anything when I arrived at my accommodation, but instead went straight to my room with a few bottles of mineral water. I needed to leave early the following morning to return back to Togo and Benin the day after to carry out an internal audit.

Actually, it was ridiculous being called back to Accra just to shake a new contractor's hand and then travel hundreds of miles back to where I had just left. It just showed the mentality of my so-called British colleagues who were both too lazy and too afraid to do such journeys themselves.

Against All Odds

My condition deteriorated rapidly during the evening and each time I drank water, I had to rush to the bathroom where it would come back up. I became more and more dehydrated and drank more and more water, each time resulting in the same way. Eventually, every single muscle in my body ached. It became almost intolerable, but I knew I needed to travel again the next morning. After a sleepless night, I packed fresh clothes and started my way back to the Togo border.

Once I'd left Accra I asked my driver to look out for a pharmacy, as I desperately needed medication. He asked me if I was sick, to which I replied yes. He became concerned and explained to me that there was a cholera epidemic in Togo which we had only left the day before. Actually, with every single muscle in my body screaming at me in pain, it didn't take much to self-diagnose what I had contracted brushing my teeth with tap water!

I was feeling terrible and deteriorating by the minute as we drove down the road through the busy traffic. As we left the city limits, we were on the main road to Togo with nothing at either side of it. To my amazement, after twenty minutes my driver pulled over to a small wooden shack in the middle of nowhere which was set back from the main road, and stopped outside it in the dust.

He lifted his right arm and pointed to the tiny little shack and said, "That's a pharmacy." The shack didn't even have a sign outside it, but I was getting desperate and hurriedly got out of the Land Cruiser and quickly made my way to it.

Working in remote countries you learnt the basics of self-preservation so I asked if the pharmacy had an antibiotic called 'Flagyl', as I was previously prescribed it for something I had picked up in Iran.

'Metronidazole' is used to treat a variety of problems. It belongs to a group of antibiotics known as nitroimidazoles, which works by killing the growth of bacteria and protozoa.

The pharmacist could see that I was in a bad condition and much to my surprise, she reached below her counter before handing me a bottle of Flagyl! I asked her for a second bottle together with all the rehydration power sachets she stocked and a few more bottles of mineral water.

I was in a really bad shape by this time so I swallowed three Flagyl tablets in one go, together with drinking mineral water with four rehydration sachets mixed into a bottle. I continued to drink the mineral water heavily mixed with rehydration powder and took another Flagyl tablet every three hours while we continued to make our way to the Togo border. After a few hours, I began to feel a little more stable and slightly better.

I eventually passed through the border into Togo and arrived at the hotel an hour later, still very weak, and went directly to bed. I continued taking the Flagyl all through the night, but still felt awful the next morning. It took five full days before I returned back to normal and wondered what would have happened to me if it weren't for the little wooden shack of a pharmacy. I have since regretted not having the opportunity to return to the little pharmacy and explain to the pharmacist how grateful I was for meeting her.

I conducted my audit the following day in Benin, stayed the night and again returned back to Accra with a one-night stopover back in Togo in the usual hotel in Lomé. The hotel in Lomé had a nightclub in its basement down a huge marble spiral staircase and the doorman became a good friend of mine.

His name was Alain and he spoke perfect English and would accompany me to the bar he worked to keep the local ladies away so I could simply relax and chat with him. He arranged for video CDs to be made by the DJ and presented them to me as a gift. They were music videos of the local tribal music, which I really liked until they were stolen among other possessions later in the Caribbean. I still maintain email contact with Alain to this day.

I needed to make another trip back to Nigeria on 26th October of 2008. By this time I was growing tired of the border crossings, so I decided to fly into Lagos from Ghana. On arrival in Lagos airport in front of the immigration desk, I saw a Nigerian official who was pre-checking visas before allowing travellers to proceed to the immigration desks.

He was a very big man, and he towered over me as he asked to see my passport. I handed it to him, and he began flicking through its pages, looking for a valid visa. He finally came to my visa, which had been issued in Ghana which had been good for a number of entries by land. Strangely, it was unconditionally rejected. *Here we go again,* I thought.

He told me that my visa had to be issued from my country of origin, not from Ghana. Actually, he was perfectly correct, as I later discovered.

I asked why the Nigerian embassy in Accra had issued the visa if it wasn't any good. I also explained that it worked on several previous visits, which he could clearly see by the stamps but my words fell on deaf ears. I knew exactly what he wanted, but I was not in the right frame of mind to dash him as his mannerism was too aggressive for my liking.

After being made to wait there for one and a half hours, I was escorted back through the departure immigration area to be deported. I was then held in police custody in their office for another four hours before being deported back to Ghana.

There wasn't any air conditioning in the police office, and after a short time, I was completely drenched due to the high humidity. When I asked for a drink of water, I was refused and told it was not a café.

By this time I was seriously dehydrated, and in quite a bad state until a different immigration officer escorted me to the departure gate of Virgin Nigeria. All the seats across from the window were occupied, so I had to sit against the glass windows with the sun beating down on my back through the glass for around another hour.

Eventually, I was able to board the flight. The flight attendant noticed the state I was in and gave me four bottles of mineral water, which I downed in record time. I'd also asked her for a lot of salt and sugar which I poured into the bottles to help with my rehydration.

My company contacts were tracking my progress from the moment that I was denied entry, and they were quite relieved to hear I'd landed back in Ghana. They booked me into the African Regent Hotel so I'd have a little luxury to recover from my ordeal.

The following day, I returned to our head office and told everyone what had happened. I mentioned that I needed another visa, and that it had to be issued from London as the United Kingdom was my point of origin.

Preparations were made, together with my agent back in Liverpool, and my passport was sent off via courier. After a few weeks had passed, my new, London-issued visa was safely in my hands for any future visits to Nigeria.

During months of assessing the project, I could see the need for a more formal control over the contractor's activities. I made a presentation of my own copyrighted system and succeeded in renting my Q-Pack mechanical completions database, which I had pioneered back in 1992. The only requirement I built into the rental contract was that Izhar would administer my system.

My database rental contract was approved, so I called Izhar. My first words as he answered his mobile phone in Qatar were,

"Hey, brother, it's Andy in Africa. Quit your job and come over here. I have a contract for you." After I had explained everything, Izhar handed in his resignation and joined me a few weeks later.

Izhar went directly to Nigeria to start his assignment, so I needed to drive from Ghana to meet up with him, which took me the usual three days.

Feeling quite confident on 15th February 2009, I drove up to the Nigerian border immigration zone from the Benin border, armed with my new visa.

As a further precaution, I carried my yellow fever vaccination card to reduce the reasons they might name for not allowing me into the country. I thought, *what can they possibly do to me now?*

All was fine when I reached the Nigerian border. I waited in the safety of my car as usual, out of sight of the Nigerian immigration officers whilst my driver took my passport to the Nigerian immigration desks for processing.

After a few minutes, he returned and said the immigration officers wanted to see my 'yellow card', as they called it. Feeling rather pleased that I had remembered to bring it, I handed the card to my driver. I figured that would be the end of my troubles – wrong!

My driver returned to the car after just a couple of minutes telling me that they wanted to see me. I knew the fun was about to start all over again.

I approached the desk, shook the immigration officer's hand, and asked whether there was a problem. He explained that there was a big problem, and that he couldn't process my passport because my yellow card didn't say yellow fever. I found where the words were written, and I showed them to him. I explained that my card was issued in the United Kingdom by a competent tropical clinic.

Not to be outdone by solid facts, the immigration officer asked me for my meningitis card. I told him that no such card existed, and that such information was simply recorded on a normal vaccination card with other inoculations.

He wanted to see the card on which my meningitis data was recorded, but that was back in the United Kingdom with my other records, such as hepatitis A and B, cholera, typhoid, tetanus, and polio. I called the immigration chief who had given me his number before to ask where he was. He told me he was home in his village four hours away and therefore couldn't get to me.

Here we go again, I thought. It was dash time all over again.

Carrying all those cards would have been a total waste of time in any case because it would just prolong the agony and force me to listen to excuse after excuse before I resorted to having to dash them in any case.

The only amusing part of the whole fiasco was winding them up to see just how far their excuses and imagination could stretch. Those guys had the patience and the power … and all day to abuse it.

My new brother of an immigration chief was useless, he didn't want to deny his fellow brothers from making a score in his absence.

After I'd finished dashing them all, I returned to the safety of my truck before saying something that I might later regret. The truck was locked, so I had to wait outside in the direct sunshine until my driver returned. Bogus salesmen, currency dealers and other types of profiteers surrounded me whilst I continually guarded my pockets. They all wanted to sell me fake watches and used clothing, or just beg me for money and cigarettes.

After five minutes, I was called back to fill in immigration forms, which the driver normally did. Later, I was again called back so the officer who was sitting in a wooden kiosk could compare my face to the one on my passport.

Eventually, my driver returned with my passport, so we buckled up and started rolling towards the borderline. *I'm free to go now,* I thought. Wrong again!

Another Nigerian police officer stood right in front of my car and held an AK-47 directly towards my head to stop us. An official asked my driver to get out of the vehicle so he could show him my passport, which he promptly did. As soon as the official looked at my passport, he approached my window and signalled for me to roll it down. He introduced himself as a Nigerian Drug Enforcement Agency officer.

I'd just about had enough yet again, so I asked to see some ID. He produced his DEA card, which looked official enough, so I asked what he wanted. He ordered us to put the car in reverse, park up and bring my entire luggage to his shabby wooden desk so he could search through everything.

Everything he saw he liked, and he asked whether it was his present. I replied no, so he continued going through everything until there was nothing left to search. Surrounded by local onlookers, I had to cover my back pocket where my wallet was, plus keep an eye on everything in my small case.

He particularly fancied my shiny new mobile phone, which I had just replaced after the previous one was stolen two weeks before, along with my laptop, wallet, and a lot of hard cash, from the guesthouse I stayed in Accra.

I was also carrying a couple of dozen large Cuban cigars, which he was sure were a present for him. Luckily, I managed to hold on to those, too.

After repacking my belongings, I was permitted to carry on,

so we proceeded towards the borderline, when another Nigerian dressed in a police uniform appeared. She was a rather arrogant police officer who demanded to see all the papers for the car before we went another yard.

Fortunately, all the papers were in order, so we were finally permitted to cross the border. My armed escort had been patiently waiting for over two hours to escort me, but they were used to the tricks their fellow countrymen played.

The problems I encountered were everyday occurrences for westerners trying to cross the notorious Benin / Nigerian border. My British colleagues in the head office in Ghana refused to do the journey because it was becoming far too dangerous.

They had formed quite a corrupt little clique and as I was the new to the team, I had to go to all the places where they were too afraid to visit. They preferred to sit in the head office waiting for their 'brown envelopes' from contractors which I wouldn't and didn't fit into!

I do think, however, that I may have brought the wrath of the DEA upon myself by wearing a particular T-shirt. I bought it in Amsterdam a few days before on a business trip, and it had a large marijuana leaf on the front. The text of the T-shirt read: 'Don't Panic, I'm Organic'. I told the DEA officer, "Honestly, I only bought it because the colours went well with my jeans."

Against All Odds

I left the project in West Africa in March of 2009, and decided to return to a certain Caribbean island in the Dutch Antilles, just off the coast of Venezuela, to visit some friends I'd met there years ago when I worked in Venezuela.

Chapter 21
Caribbean

My intention was to visit the island in the Caribbean for three weeks and then fly to the island of Cebu in the Philippines and look for an apartment to buy there.

Because I was on a sort of holiday, I had a great time and went deep sea fishing twice a week. On my first fishing trip, I caught a ten foot blue shark. It was quite a fight, which lasted over three hours. During the fight, a huge container ship was heading directly towards us as we were reversing our boat to regain some line that the shark had practically stripped from my reel. It was my first sunshine for a long time so I kept myself covered up while fighting the shark.

The ship was contacted by radio and asked to divert its course because we had a big fish on the line. To my amazement, the ship did exactly that. It was also the first time I'd gone deep sea fishing for a few years, so by the time I got the shark to the boat, every one of my fingers had a large blister ready to burst. The shark was spinning like a crocodile on the side of the boat while the deckhand grabbed a gaff to drag it onboard. The boat was far too small to accommodate the shark, however, so I instructed the deckhand to cut the line to let it go.

Seeing the island through the eyes of a tourist, I enjoyed the place and moved my return flight back another month. British tourists were only permitted to stay on the island for a maximum of thirty days, so I had to do a visa run every month. For my first visa run, I decided to stay on a nearby island called Curaçao for the weekend, and my hotel receptionist joined me for a break.

Because I was having a nice time and making new friends, or so I thought at the time, I changed my mind about buying an apartment in Cebu and started to look at condos on the island I was on.

My original plan was to buy a condo with some security guards, so I could just lock the door and fly off overseas to work. I was deterred when I found out I had to pay a maintenance fee of over five hundred dollars every month, which I thought to be quite ridiculous.

In the meantime, another thirty days was about to expire so I needed to make another visa run. I chose Havana, Cuba, or Habana as it is spelt in Spanish. There were no direct flights to Cuba from the island so I needed to change flights in Panama. Panama airport was quite impressive but I only had two hours there before boarding my Cuban flight.

At that time, bird flu was an international concern so waiting at the airport in Havana was a line of doctors waiting to question everyone entering the country prior to being allowed to proceed to the immigration desks. After passing through immigration were the drug sniffing dogs and then the wait at the carousel for my little case. Drug sniffing dogs were also paraded all around the hall and even over the baggage as it went along the carousel; all very impressive. I was only planning to stay in Havana for four nights, but regretted not booking the hotel for a full week.

Upon arrival at my prepaid hotel, I was made to pay the full amount again. The hotel manager was called and presented with the receipt, which included a paid in full stamp. That didn't make any difference as the hotel manager claimed they hadn't received anything so I went to the ATM and withdrew the cash and paid a second time. This wasn't a good start, but I figured I'd reclaim my booking costs when I returned back to the island I was on.

I loved it in Havana and went everywhere as a regular tourist. Of course, my first places to visit were the cigar factories of Cohiba, Partagas and Monte Cristo, my favourite three brands. They were all just walking distance from each other and I hired a Cuban guide to show me around for the four day stay.

My guide was a young lady in her twenties who I'd met at a salsa club on my very first night. She spoke perfect English and took me to places a normal tourist would never find. Due to the communist rules existing in Cuba, she really wasn't allowed to be with me. So many times, she had to avoid being noticed by the police as we went from venue to venue. It wasn't possible to mention Fidel Castro's name anywhere on the island. I once made that mistake at the hotel pool's bar and the manager immediately closed it for the rest of the day!

One of the places I desperately wanted to visit was a bar called 'La Bodeguita del Medio'. It had been Ernest Hemingway's local bar while he stayed in Cuba. When I entered, I could see a wall full of his 'scribbles', which had been preserved behind glass picture frames. La Bodeguita del Medio was also the bar which was famous for inventing the mojito cocktail, or so it was believed. The mojito was a particularly refreshing drink in the heat of the Caribbean and consisted of sugar, lime, mint leaves, rum and soda.

The mojito's exact history is still arguable to this day. It did originate in Cuba and is one of the most popular cocktails, like the Cuba libre, 'libre' meaning free. Some historians believe the mojito was invented in the fifteenth century when Sir Francis Drake landed on the island, to get everyone drunk to steal the city's gold. An associate of Sir Francis Drake, named Richard Drake, had tried to make a version of the mojito called 'El Draque' out of an early form of rum, which didn't really make it into popularity.

Some people believe African slaves working in the sugar cane plantations invented it. Mojito is believed to come from the African word 'mojo' that means to place a spell on someone. Wherever it came from, it's delicious in any case.

One day I went for lunch with my guide and listened to a live group playing and singing in the background. They were so talented I sent them a round of drinks in appreciation. In return they all came over to my table and presented me a gift of their music CD, which they normally sold. They had even taken the trouble to sign its cover, which made it an extra special gift, but was sadly stolen from my island house later. I loved Havana and the people living there, but my four nights went like a flash and before I knew it, I was travelling back to the island.

Rather than continue to look for an apartment, I was advised to buy a house, which I eventually did, which turned out to be an even bigger mistake. On the island, there were two types of property: lease hold and property land. With property land, you fully owned the land, and there was no planning permission as such required for building, altering, or extending your property, which seemed like the best option.

A Colombian girl, Lisa, who I'd met in a bar where she worked, offered to help me find a house, as I didn't know any of the areas on the island. Lisa was great company and also the lead dancer for the island dance group.

The real estate company was owned and run by a Dutchman and his Colombian wife. His wife drove Lisa and me around a few properties until I saw a house that interested me. With just a three minute walk to the ocean, I thought it would be a good choice.

I chose to live away from the main tourist area because prices were too high in that region. I also wanted to get away from all the noise and bar culture. After viewing several more properties, I decided to buy the three bedroom house on property land, which was about a thirty-five minute drive from the tourist area, down the southern end of the island towards Venezuela.

Once a deal had been agreed upon, I negotiated with the owners to include the entire house contents as it stood to make the place liveable until I was able to buy things that better suited my taste.

The Colombian woman from the real estate company was supposed to return later the same day to take photos of the contents of each room so that all the main items would be left there as agreed.
She didn't return to take the photos for five days, so it gave the owners plenty of time to remove most of the furnishings before any photos could be taken. The owners were going through a divorce as the husband was in jail for being a paedophile.

As my luck would have it, I needed to return to the United Kingdom for a month, so I had a Dutch waitress who was recommended to me to housesit while I was away. She was also going to continue living in my house when I returned to work overseas, and assured me she'd take care of things whilst I was away.

After transferring funds to the local notary, I was told it would take around five or six weeks to complete all formalities and receive the keys.

The first thing I noticed when I eventually received the photos of inside the house was that there weren't any photos of the bedrooms. When I asked why, I was told that the rooms had all been emptied, so there was nothing to take photos of.

I didn't make too much of a fuss because even though I'd paid for the beds and other contents, I would have replaced the beds at the earliest opportunity in any case. I later discovered that the washing machine had also been taken, along with the stereo system and all the contents of the kitchen.

The owner's excuse was that those items didn't belong to them, but they failed to mention that when I bought everything. I was later to learn that it was typical of the people on the island.

I gave the house sitter money to buy new beds and a few other things so I would at least have a bed to sleep on when I returned.

The Colombian real estate company informed me that their surveyor had been to the house and found everything to be fine. They told me that the house had even been rewired. I later found out that it had not been rewired and still had the original, eighty-year-old wiring throughout.

The purchase took ten weeks to complete, so I waited in the United Kingdom to avoid the expense of staying in a hotel room for the final few weeks. When I returned to the island as the new owner, the horror story really began.

In addition to the money I had left with the waitress to buy beds, I supplied extra money for her to continue buying bedding, kitchen utensils, and other necessary items. I also provided the funds to pay for the electricity, water, gas, and cable TV.

After just the first two days of living in my house, the waitress started to make me feel terribly unwelcome, which created a really bad atmosphere. She shouted her objections to my plans to build a fourth bedroom with en suite at the back of my house. She also rejected my idea to add an additional air conditioner to cool the kitchen … as well as many other plans to improve the property.

She was taking over as the owner of the house, and even began dictating what she wanted. One such demand was a twenty foot container from Holland which would be permanently parked on my back patio.

She told me I had to help her by paying for its shipping, and that she would pay me back later. I knew what that meant – up until then, I had never met an honest person on the island – so I refused her request. We went shopping for all the new things, and each time she took me to a shop, she spoke only Dutch. Without me realising at the time, she had every receipt made out in her name when I handed over the money.

Even the food I bought from supermarkets was considered 'food for the house' in her eyes, and she began helping herself. She took whatever she wanted down to the beach to share with her friends. That was the typical culture on the island: whatever you had was automatically taken as if it were there for the taking, just like my time in Venezuela!

After having the girl in my house for a week, and being tired of how she was speaking to me, I had had enough. One morning, she started shouting at me because a couple of my friends had visited me the night before. She told me she would not stand for people visiting the house, so I reminded her of who owned the place and kicked her out.

That night, she went back to my house with some of her friends and emptied the place of everything I had bought, including things that came with the house.

The next day, a friend picked me up, and we went to the electrical and water companies to transfer the bills into my name. I didn't want the waitress cutting me off.

The gas company was closed by the time I got there, so the waitress who had already visited was able to cancel the contract and get the deposit back for the bottles which I had paid for. She also went to my house insurance company and tried to cancel my house insurance and get the money from that too! Fortunately, they refused her.

When she moved out of my house, she stole all the warranties for the new air conditioners and other appliances and also stole the original deeds to my house. It took a threat to bring the police to the Spanish tapas restaurant where she worked for her to return them.

A few weeks later, I signed contracts to work in Kazakhstan. I was worried about the house being left empty because crime was escalating dramatically on the island. Out of pure desperation, I agreed to rent the two spare bedrooms to two young girls, one from Surinam and the other from the Dominican Republic.

They had lived on the island for several years. Not to be ripped off yet again, I had the same real estate agent write up a formal rental contract that allowed the girls to rent their rooms for a very small fee per month.

I knew it was a mistake but I just wanted someone living there to prevent thieves from breaking in whilst I was away.

Anyway, the girls moved in that weekend. I explained that my only rule was that no men were allowed in the house. Naturally, they helped themselves to everything in my fridge, freezer, and cupboards.

I was flying to Kazakhstan soon, so I didn't let it bother me too much; I'd be gone, and they'd have to shop for themselves. I made the girls sign the rental contract and figured the formal approach to be a better solution.

I was later to learn whilst away in Kazakhstan that the Colombian real estate agent never bothered to collect the signed contract, nor did she bother to collect the monthly rent or ensure that utilities were being paid. Actually, the real estate agent never visited my house at all.

Before leaving for Kazakhstan, I paid a Dutch marine to be my caretaker. He was paid to go to my house every week to ensure everything was okay. The very weekend I flew out, the two girls had a big party. My house was still full of men sleeping on my sofa and chairs the next morning when my caretaker walked in.

He threw all the men out and gave the girls a strong warning, but people on that island don't care about warnings. They live for the moment just like the majority of Latin Americans did. I also had a lady drive past my house every morning, on her way home from working at a hotel all night. She sent me emails explaining that there was a different car in my drive every morning.

The girls never did paid any rent, or any of the utilities, and they were eventually kicked out. My electric bill was incredible because they had every air conditioner on twenty-four hours per day. All my frozen foods and cleaning liquids were taken as well; I suppose they stole them for their families.

During my time in Kazakhstan, I had Colombian builders in my house renovating it. All was going well until they began laying new floor tiles throughout and broke through the bathroom floor. When they did so, they were greeted by millions of cockroaches. They escaped from under the tiles and ran up the bathroom walls and across the ceiling. Lisa was there supervising for me at the time and ran out of the house screaming. Lisa would regularly visit to take photos and later email them to me so I could see the progress.

The cockroaches were living under the house because all the waste water pipes had totally corroded. No wastewater was getting to the septic tank alongside the house. The surveyor had failed to find that problem; he didn't even wonder why the septic tank hadn't needed emptying for several years. The wastewater had eaten deep into the walls, so those had to be completely removed and rebuilt.

While all this was going on, a Colombian electrician, who had already rewired my house and been paid in full for doing so, wormed his way back into my house to rewire it again for a second fee. As I was off the island, he had told my caretaker that I had asked him to return!

The first time, he had just fitted a breaker box and pretended to rewire the house. The second time, he lied to my caretaker and said it was the second part that he'd come to finish. Therefore, he got paid twice for doing the same job.

Something else the islanders liked to do was visit. When they visited, just like when I lived in Puerto Ordaz, they came empty-handed. Once they had consumed every beer in my fridge, they'd leave and visit someone else. In the beginning, I needed to put up with a lot just to get to know people and find my way around the island.

Later, when I was in a position to stop all that, I was totally ignored by the islanders … unless I invited them for freebies, which they never refused.

In the bars, they adopted the Latin American culture and got familiar with tourists and invited them to other bars. If the tourist agreed to go, they'd telephone and bring more of their friends, and the tourist would need to foot the entire bill. The islanders never had any money on them, or so they claimed. They'd order take away food and drinks to supply their entire families and have it added to the bill!

When I first got there, I needed to be driven around because I had no idea where to go for things. Each time, I was forced to fill their petrol tanks, tip the pump attendant ten dollars, and feed them before getting dropped off at home.

I knew I was being financially milked, but I didn't have much of a choice at that time, it was the island way!

Chapter 22
Kazakhstan

In September of 2009, I flew to Kazakhstan to start working with Chris again, as he'd made sure I had the contract as his senior quality assurance engineer. I hadn't seen Chris since working with him in Nigeria back in 2004. I still had outstanding issues on the island, however … and a few more horrifying surprises in store for me on a scale I could never have imagined possible.

Kazakhstan was a very hostile environment to work. We were warned not to walk around alone and never to use the local taxis. Former colleagues had taken local taxis and been taken down backstreets where thugs would be waiting to beat them up. Several were medically evacuated with fractured skulls, broken ribs etc. I never dreamed that I, too, would fall victim to an attempted murder.

My worst fears were confirmed when I got back to the island on the 31st January 2010. It was clear that I'd been ripped off by the caretaker.

The first time I use the shower, the water quickly filled the drain pipe and flooded out of the bathroom and out the back of the house. The new wastewater drainpipe didn't lead to the outside septic tank. Instead, it was buried under concrete.

The Colombian electrician had robbed me of everything I'd

bought, including clothes, shoes, Mont Blanc pens, DVDs, Ray Bans, tools, and even my bedroom door keys together with $5,200 dollars of holiday cash. He had also stolen a Bible written in English, which the Gideons had given me when I was just ten years old.

It was a nice start to the carnival month. Not even the island police could help because the Colombian electrician had somehow heard they were on their way to visit his place and moved all my things he'd stolen out.

The carnival festivities were in full swing, and they were leading up to the carnival's grand parade on the 14th of February. I had waited a long time to see it, so I was excited. *This time,* I thought, *nothing will go wrong.* Not!

I'd stuck it out in Kazakhstan for five long months to ensure I would see my first carnival, which would surely be worth the wait. I followed my caretaker's instructions regarding the grand parade day. I stayed in my house, ready to be collected in the morning before all the roads were closed off around the island's capital.

Anyway, after taking it easy by staying home for four nights and declining the Friday night/Saturday morning pyjama parade, to ensure I wouldn't be tired for the grand parade, I was wide awake and rested for the big day.

I got up early that Sunday morning. My camera was fully charged, and I ate a good breakfast to soak up the day's beer intake and ready to be collected, as promised by my caretaker. *What could possibly go wrong?* I thought.

After waiting a couple of hours to be picked up, and calling my caretaker several times to ask when he was coming, I dozed off on the sofa. I woke up a couple of hours later and quickly called all the local taxi companies, but they all told me the same thing: "You've left it too late." All the roads were already blocked off for the grand parade, and there was no hope of getting anywhere near the carnival unless I was prepared to walk for hours.

Therefore, I spent the entire carnival grand parade day home alone with no food or drinks. I just kept imagining all that I was missing. With nothing else to do, I decided to walk to the nearest Chinese supermarket, which was a twenty-five minute walk away. In the heat, however, it felt like hours. Of course, nobody thought to warn me that all the shops would be closed until Tuesday. *Even more good news,* I thought, *I can lose even more weight than I've already lost due to the renovation problems and robbery.* The island did have its advantages, I supposed.

By Monday I was starving, but nobody was picking up their mobiles because they were asleep the entire day after partying until five or six o'clock in the morning. Eventually, a friend, Marina, called me to ask how I was doing.

She spoke the usual: Spanish, Dutch, English, and Papiamento. She was horrified that I had spent the day alone at home with nothing to eat, and she immediately rushed over with some traditional island home cooking.

Marina was always the first to come to my aid and solve any problem I encountered on the island.

Marina worked permanent nights at the reception of a beach resort hotel that was just a three minute walk from the beach and close to all the most popular bars and restaurants.

Later that day, Lisa woke up from the carnival asking where the hell I was on Sunday. She was angry that I hadn't been at the roadside to take photos of her leading the grand parade.

When I told her that my caretaker hadn't picked me up as promised, she went crazy. Lisa is a professional Latin dancer, and as I've mentioned, dances for an island dance group. They entertain tourists by performing on stage at hotels, and are very popular.

The Friday before the carnival, we had spent all day shopping for materials such as ostrich feathers for her blue and silver costume. She wanted me to take a lot of photos of her while she and her dance group were leading the entire grand parade. Because her group was the first along the road, my job would have been very easy … if I had made it there.

I spent the following two weeks winding down from all the bad news and horror I had discovered when I first arrived on the island. I deliberately kept myself away from all the people who had ripped me off and let me down. I stopped all building work, and just took things easy.

Marina continued to help me as always, and she even drove me around so I would be spared the heavy taxi fares, plus she'd keep me company whenever she could, so it wasn't too bad in the end.

During this period of time, I met some locals at a bar near my house. It was nice to be far away from the tourist area.

They were horrified to hear how much trouble I'd had with my house just up the road and what my house renovations had cost me. It seemed that, from that point onwards, things would be easier, and certainly a lot cheaper.

In June of 2010, my mother visited the island for the first time, and it was my first incident-free visit. Having a better imagination than I had, she explained what she'd do to my house if it were hers. So the next three months of my life were filled with local builders again.

I arranged to have a very high wall built across the back of my place, mainly for security reasons. I wanted vented blocks to allow the breeze to come through. In the front, I requested a mix of walls and fancy railings with a rolling gate.

Work had just started when I left the island to return to

Kazakhstan, so I relied on photos being emailed to me so I could control the payments. Just before leaving to Kazakhstan, I had rented the spare back bedroom to a Dutch marine and his young Colombian wife. The couple were about to have their first child so I thought they'd be a good choice after the two girls I'd previously made such a mistake with.

During the construction, they called me to let me know that many Colombians had moved into my house.

Apparently, the new tenant had invited his friends over from Amsterdam for free holidays, and his Colombian wife had done the same with her family. My builders had told me there were people sleeping outside on my swing, on my sofas, and even on the floor.

I got them out after giving them thirty days' notice as per the rental agreement, which I respected and they kindly left the place in a disgusting condition. They also failed to pay all the utility bills and stole everything they could carry, just like the two girls had done before.

As a temporary solution, I invited two local people to house sit, rent free, out of pure desperation. I will call them Haitian and Ronnie. All they had to do was pay the utilities. This proved to be the biggest mistake of my life, which almost cost me my life, which fuelled my inspiration to write my story.

Haitian was from Haiti, and didn't have any friends, which I found strange, as she had lived on the island for twenty-five years. Ronnie was a very inadequate islander and alcoholic, who had not completed his schooling.

I didn't know at the time that Haitian was a voodoo priestess and practised voodoo daily. People I had never met were invited to my house in my absence to pay her to carry out voodoo ceremonies. I had no idea that was going on while I was working in Kazakhstan.

During September of 2010, events occurred that changed my plans in a way I never imagined possible. On September 25th in Atyrau, Kazakhstan, the resident security guard knocked on my door at 6.50pm to present his friend.

All his friend could say in English was, "Want lady." I told him no and closed my door on the both of them.

I continued to get ready to go to a wedding party that night, but ten minutes later, I heard a noise coming from my living room. I looked around my bedroom door and found the same young Kazakh man in my apartment with a young girl. I ordered them to leave immediately, but he was extremely persistent and wouldn't leave.

My camera was sitting on my kitchen table, as was some money, and my gold Rolex, which he kept looking at.

I could not turn my back on them and go to my apartment telephone at the far end of the room to call reception, due to my things on the table.

He insisted I keep the girl, and he still wouldn't leave. Finally, he agreed to leave after I took his name and phone number. Of course, his name was false and the number was from a stolen mobile phone, as the police later told me.

After they had left, I finished getting ready and went to the wedding. After just two hours at the wedding party, I began to feel very sleepy for some reason, and I decided to leave much earlier than planned. I arrived at my apartment at around eleven o'clock at night.

I left my camera on my kitchen table, took off my Rolex, and left it at the side of my bed. I woke up early on the Sunday morning, and both my Rolex and Nikon pocket camera were missing.

I told the receptionist and called my company's security. My security was very quick off the mark and came to my apartment to view the security video footage from the closed circuit television cameras. Unfortunately, they had already removed the discs.

They arranged an identity parade with the Kazakh police so I could point out the guard who had brought his friend to my apartment, but he wasn't among the men. Apparently, they'd already fired all fourteen guards who worked that Saturday night, so I couldn't identify the guilty guard.

On Tuesday, along with a licensed translator and a security company representative, I went to the local police station. The building was in a terrible state, a leftover from Russian times.

The entire incident had been hidden from investigation, and I didn't have any hope of recovering my losses. Both the Kazakh police and my company's security did what they could, but the cover-up made it impossible to make any progress.

I was introduced to a lawyer who accompanied me and continued to represent me throughout the proceedings. Her name was Antonina, and I had no idea at the time that she was about to turn my whole world upside down and inside out.

Antonina and I soon began living together. Because we had become involved with each other, Antonina explained that she could no longer represent me as my lawyer. She claimed that it was not professional, and it wouldn't look very good in court.

Antonina recommended two male lawyers whom she'd known for many years. Evidently, they both had well proven track records. In the background of all the enquiries, Antonina was still leading the process, but the two new lawyers were representing me. Antonina had an unusual amount of power in her country, but the alarm bells came too late. She had the local press and television cameras go to the apartment block to put on national television as she conducted her initial investigations.

Later, I discovered that the receptionist was also in on the robbery. She had entered a fake girl's name in the visitor's book at the reception by using correction fluid and covering someone else's name. Therefore, it looked like I was at home the entire evening entertaining someone I'd never met.

The police assumed that the girl who I'd never met must have been the thief. Because I was at the wedding party all evening, it was easy to prove that it was also a part of the cover-up.

Because I was a European working in Kazakhstan, I didn't have the normal Kazakh police working on the case. Instead, I had an internal affairs police investigator, who was very keen to do all he could to help, especially for some extra $$$s.

He came to the quick conclusion that because my residence had deliberately hidden the security camera footage, fired all guards who had worked the night of my robbery, and added a false visitor to the visitor's book, they were clearly covering up the whole incident and therefore responsible. I guess it didn't take a genius to work that out.

Under Kazakh law, my residence's administration had to compensate me for the full replacement value of both my watch and camera. Antonina, together with the internal affairs police, launched a full criminal investigation.

Three more Kazakh police investigators came to my apartment to interview the deputy director of the company who owned the apartments and the administration manager. The president's daughter was the main owner, so they didn't want any bad publicity.

The actual director wasn't in Atyrau that day, so his deputy had to answer all the questions. Antonina questioned him with regard to the missing security camera footage, and he explained that the technician had accidentally switched off the cameras for the entire weekend. Supposedly, they only realised on Monday, after my things had been taken, that nothing had been recorded.

The police took the staffing logbook so they could find out which guards were on duty that night. After a few weeks, they were able to find the guilty guard who had been fired in a distant village. They brought him to the police headquarters in Atyrau and kept him detained until I was able to visit whilst he was questioned.

I'd never seen the guard before because he was always on duty at the rear of the building, at the entrance of the car park. Apparently, the usual reception guard needed to take his break, so he had someone stand in for him just as I was returning from the wedding party, somewhat drugged!

He noticed the gold watch when I walked past him to the elevator. I was with a friend from Uzbekistan who worked at a local hospital. She had accompanied me to the wedding party and just wanted to see me get home safely.

Actually, she left my apartment after just five minutes, but she decided not to return home. Instead, she hung around for a while for the drug she had slipped into my drink to take its full effect. She had spent quite some time talking to the security guard regarding my watch, long enough for me to be fast asleep. After that, she returned to my apartment, together with the security guard, to take my watch and camera.

Once she and the guard had my things, she wasted no time leaving Atyrau and returned to a town called Aksai, which was near the southern Russian border. The police needed to interview her because she was the last person to be seen with me while I still had my watch. This delayed the investigation by a few weeks, until they were able to locate her and bring her back to Atyrau.

When she finally returned to Atyrau, the police took her into custody in their headquarters for questioning. She was detained in a prison cell in between questioning for a full week. For a while, she claimed she was innocent, but after several days, she admitted that she had organised the robbery with the apartment security guard and receptionist.

The receptionist was also involved, as she had entered the false visitor name in the guest book that evening and lent them a master key so they could get into my apartment.

After the receptionist saw the police visit and revisit the building, she took ten days off. Later, she became sick and quit her job. She was not seen there again.

I was advised to leave my apartment and move to a hotel near my office where I would be safer. I moved to the hotel just behind my office, so I was only at risk for the five minute walk to the office. Each day I walked to and from the office, I felt it might be my last.

During that time, I had been calling Haitian and listened to her warnings. When I asked her how she knew all that was going on, she explained that it was what she did. It was only then that I discovered she was a voodoo priestess.

I made the mistake of telling Antonina about Haitian and what she was doing in my house. That caused Antonina to want to speak to Haitian practically every night of the week, despite what it was costing me. Conversations lasted for a ridiculous length of time, and soon Antonina demanded that I give Haitian everything she needed.

Haitian was renting a small bar just down the road from my house, which is where I had the misfortune of meeting her. One night, Antonina called her, and Haitian was in a terrible state. She claimed that someone had broken into her bar and stolen all her stock. She needed to borrow two thousand dollars from me, which she promised to return when she made it back.

Antonina demanded I help her so I sent the money, but I really was not comfortable with the decision. Just four weeks later, Haitian begged me for another two thousand dollars. She said that if she didn't pay the Chinese owner the overdue rent, she would lose the bar.

I thought about the request and sent another two thousand dollars. I figured that, if she lost the bar, I would never see my original two thousand dollars.

As it all worked out, Haitian had to leave the bar because the Chinese owner had obtained legal support to evict her. Haitian promised to return my second loan if it wasn't accepted for her rent payment, but of course, being the same as the other island types, I never saw that money again.

Because Haitian was now out of work and Ronnie was only earning a low salary working as a barman in a beach hotel, they asked for even more money. They claimed they couldn't afford to pay the utility bills each month, and I later learnt why.

In the beginning of January 2011, it was time for me to take a break from the stress and hostilities I was enduring in Kazakhstan and return back to the island. Antonina began performing and wouldn't allow me to go alone, and told me she would have me stopped at the airport if I didn't take her with me.

Antonina couldn't be reasoned with and demanded to go on holiday with me and see my house for the first time. Her real reason was to meet Haitian, as she was unnaturally fascinated with voodoo. There was a lot of paperwork required for her one night stay in Amsterdam and her longer stay on the island.

She needed to fly to Astana to visit the Netherlands Embassy to get both visas required to accompany me. The visas took five days to be issued so she needed to stay in a nearby hotel at additional expense.

Finally, she was granted the two visas, and I used my company's travel department to buy the flights.

All seemed to be going normally until the day came for us to fly out of the country. The problems began when we encountered the Kazakh border police in Atyrau airport.

The previous year, Antonina had her handbag stolen while a man held a knife to her throat. In her police report she had reported that her bag had contained her passport. Later, she had found her passport but forgot to inform the authorities. In the meantime, they had cancelled her original passport.

At Atyrau airport, the border police found that her passport had been cancelled in their computer system and did not permit her to leave for the flight to Amsterdam. After all the expense getting her the two visas, I decided that I would also stay behind until she'd sorted out her passport problem. I should have continued without her!

We had our luggage removed from the aircraft, and we were escorted behind the scenes with the Kazakh border police. They kept us there for another two hours until we'd hand written statements in triplicate, just like in the internal affairs police station.

There was no alternative; we had to get a new passport for Antonina before I could take my much-needed holiday. The complications were just about to begin. In Kazakhstan, as Antonina was in possession of a supposedly stolen passport, it wasn't going to be easy applying for a replacement.

She had to take a nine hour drive to Aksai in northern Kazakhstan, very near the Russian border, to apply for a new passport. Several people had to be bribed because her not stolen passport had caused so much confusion as it had been cancelled, but was still in her possession. It cost over two thousand dollars in bribes to get her a new passport that would allow her to fly a week later.

When we finally got through the border control police a week later, it was a great relief, or so I thought.

Without any reason, Antonina started performing the minute we boarded the flight to Amsterdam. Upon arrival in Amsterdam, she became worse. The minute we got into our hotel room, she started screaming at me to open my laptop and sign into Skype before I could even take off my coat.

Once she had spent two long hours talking to her mother, daughter, brother, and others, she closed the computer and started threatening me with the Kazakh KGB. She demanded my mobile phone so she could have the KGB in Amsterdam collect her and fly her home. I was convinced she was going insane. That was just the start of her unusual behaviour for having a Caribbean holiday.

The next day was wasted with shopping all over Amsterdam for her entire family. She made me buy so much that I had to buy two extra suitcases to carry the lot to the island, and later back to Kazakhstan. If I refused to buy something, she would start screaming in the middle of the street for all to see.

The next day, we flew from Amsterdam to the heat and sunshine of the Caribbean, which I hoped would improve her behaviour. I could not have been more wrong. I bought myself a new laptop in the airport so I could leave it in my island house, to save myself from carrying my old laptop back and forth through airports each time. As events worked out, I never got to use that new computer.

Haitian and Ronnie, who were still housesitting, were both at the airport waiting for us. They didn't have a car, so all four of us, along with four suitcases had to squeeze into the same taxi.

The minute Antonina saw my Caribbean hideaway she became even more crazed. Haitian stirred up as many problems as she could until things became completely out of control. It was a holiday from hell, a holiday I could never have imagined possible.

I rented a car so I could take Antonina around the island and show her how beautiful the place was. I also let Haitian and Ronnie use it so they could go out and give us a little time to ourselves. That didn't work. Even with the car keys on the table, Haitian refused to leave my house.

I became so desperate to get them out of my house, even for just a few nights that I even offered to pay for a hotel and give them daily spending money. But Haitian still refused to go. I could not get her out, not even for a couple of hours.

What it boiled down to was that Haitian was protecting her free lodging by doing everything she could to split Antonina and me up. That way, they would always need to housesit and never leave my house. I certainly didn't have any plans to marry the crazed Kazakh, but just needed to be patient until the court case for my watch was over and leave Kazakhstan permanently.

Because Haitian was a voodoo priestess, my tiled floor was always a mess with candle wax. I could feel a strong presence in the house almost every night before I was finally introduced to the spirit. He liked to be called Brave, but he is better known in voodoo books as Elohim.

I was surprised to learn that Antonina was very much into voodoo, and she encouraged Haitian to continue performing voodoo ceremonies, despite my strongest objections. I became an outcast in my own home even though they were all living off my back. I even took them all deep sea fishing, which was also a waste of time and money, but at least the opportunity meant I was out of the house.

Antonina kept promising me that when I was back in her country, she would create a very big problem for me. At the time, I ignored all her threats and laughed them off. I wasn't doing anything wrong or behaving in a bad way so I couldn't think of anything she could possibly do to cause me a problem.

During my holiday from hell, my mother came for a day visit. She was on holiday cruising the Caribbean and arrived on her cruise ship that stopped off at the island as part of the tour to other island destinations.

Antonina insisted in joining me when I went to collect my mother from the port terminal for her five hour stop-off, to make sure I didn't have the opportunity to explain all that was being done to me. My mother arrived on time at nine o'clock in the morning, so we first drove her back to my house, where Haitian and Ronnie remained, to continue depriving me of any privacy.

It was impossible for me to talk to my mother about the events that were taking place all day, every day. That was frustrating to say the least. I wasn't even left alone in the kitchen to make my mother a soft drink.

I went outside with my mother thinking I might have the opportunity to talk freely with her, but that was also a waste of time: Antonina, Haitian, and Ronnie followed us out.

While we were sitting outside on my veranda, a wild pigeon flew in and perched itself on my outdoor swing. The swing was large and could seat three people. It had a canopy above to shade its occupants or shelter them from the rain.

The pigeon landed on top of the canopy and looked like it was quite at home. While there, it kept looking at us the whole time. After about half an hour, Antonina reached up to the bird, picked it off the canopy, and brought it to meet everyone.

The bird remained completely calm and undisturbed while we each took a turn to stroke it. We put it on my green table below the kitchen window, and we gave it some bread and a little bowl of water. It wasn't hungry or thirsty; it just watched our every movement.

Because my mother only had five hours on the island, we couldn't spend any longer at my house. We returned to the capital, just a twenty-five minute drive away.

On my mother's first visit to the island back in June 2010, she had bought some wooden ornaments, which were made in the Amazon rainforest from the mopa mopa tree. She was very fond of her last purchases, and she wanted to return to the shop to buy some more. Of course, we were not permitted to go alone as Antonina insisted on tagging along with us.

By the time we had parked and my mother had been to the shop, we only had enough time to stop for something to eat before taking her back to her cruise ship.

That was the last I would see of my mother until April 2012, due to my overseas work schedule and life. It took a serious medical problem to stop me in my tracks, but when I next saw my mother, she was there to help as usual. The moment we waved goodbye and walked back to the car and out of sight, Antonina started performing again. She was in a worse state of hatred and jealously after she had met my mother.

Back in Kazakhstan, she had an eight year old daughter who was sadly retarded and was desperate to try for another child. After several abortions during a previous relationship with a Lebanese man she had suffered damages, making another pregnancy life-threatening.

She didn't want to listen to any of the advice the medical profession had given her in the past and wanted to be checked using voodoo. Of course Haitian was only too keen to oblige and made the necessary arrangements for Brave to visit to carry out the procedure. Apparently, she claimed that Brave was studying medicine.

The next afternoon Haitian called Brave and he arrived in the house just moments later. His energy caused two plastic parrots to start singing as they were designed to do whenever their motion sensor picked up movement. It was certainly clear that something had entered the room, as there wasn't anyone near the parrots at the time.

Brave possessed Haitian's body and Antonina was instructed to fully extend her right arm so Brave could take a blood test. To my total disbelief, and before my very eyes a little squirt of blood spurted out of Antonina's vein. Haitian swabbed the tiny little perforation before instructing Antonina to stand in front of her while she (Brave) examined her. Brave always used Haitian to communicate and needed to push his hands into Antonina's abdomen to feel his way around.

After a short time he made his diagnosis and explained that if she ever tried to have a child, it would either kill her, or the child would be badly deformed. Apparently, a previous pregnancy had resulted outside her womb, which resulted in half of her reproductive system being removed on her right side.

Antonina wouldn't accept any of the facts and insisted that Brave helped her. Brave explained that he'd need to call on other spirits who were better qualified, and who may have been able to make some internal changes to reduce the risks if she did become pregnant.

Brave always had his price in return for his help and needed some kind of offering, before he would begin to help. His preferred offerings were normally of a macabre nature and his favourite included blood. Due to all that was going on I offered myself, which he immediately refused. He claimed that I was already a member of his temple, so I couldn't be considered.

Brave didn't like material items either, but all I could think of to offer was a gold bracelet that I'd bought in Istanbul the previous year, while I was auditing a shipbuilder there. I couldn't think of anything else, so Brave finally accepted my gift.

Later that very afternoon, at around six o'clock, Antonina became very sick. She claimed that she was having terrible, unbearable pains in her abdomen and couldn't handle it any longer. She was crying with the pain and began begging for it to stop. Strangely, Haitian ran to us shouting that her father had just called her. She explained that her father had picked up what was going on during one of his voodoo ceremonies in Haiti, which Brave had told him about.

He explained it all had to stop immediately or Antonina wouldn't survive the spiritual treatment she was receiving. Haitian quickly prepared some coloured beads, some herbs and wrapped them in paper along with my gold bracelet. I asked why my bracelet, as it certainly wasn't cheap. She said it had to leave the house as quickly as possible or my house would be cursed forever! *Typical,* I thought, *I lose again due to all the damn voodoo nonsense going on.*

Haitian, together with me, had to drive to the ocean just down the road from my house to an area where we wouldn't be seen by anyone. Haitian instructed me to go to the water's edge, turn my back on the ocean and throw the package over my shoulder and return back to the car without looking back.

This I did and returned back to the house. Antonina was already feeling some relief so I guessed the spirits had left her alone. She then started on me, promising that she'd make serious problems for me back in Kazakhstan, so I went out into my garden to smoke a cigar. The moment Antonina saw me sitting outside she came rushing out screaming and shouting, telling me to return back inside. This I did, as I knew the entire road would be listening to her performance.

This was the final straw for me and I told Haitian that it was the last time she was going to listen to Antonina. I added that there was not to be any more voodoo ceremonies performed in my house, but I somehow knew that my demands would be ignored; they always were.

Haitian and Ronnie continued to worry that my so-called girlfriend would ruin their convenient free living situation so they needed to accelerate the current problems they'd worked so hard to create. It was blatantly clear to me that the voodoo, lies, and harassment were never going to stop until I was either dead or a single man again.

In total defiance to my demands, Haitian had convinced Antonina to attend yet another voodoo ritual that was supposed to protect us all. A ceremony that would also prevent anyone else doing voodoo against us.

I, as always, objected strongly to the ceremony but I was aggressively outnumbered. In the meantime, Haitian had already arranged for her cousin from Haiti, who was already on the island, to visit my house to help perform the ceremony.

Haitian had also purchased a white dove, a cockerel and a large sack of mixed plants, chemicals and perfumes, which were needed to conduct the ceremony.

The following afternoon, her cousin who was a voodoo priest arrived at two o'clock and immediately began arranging plastic bowls, candles, plants etc., while we changed into clothes which could never be used again once the ceremony was over.

Antonina was given the white dove to hold while I was handed the cockerel. I was still not showing any interest in the event and continued to protest. My words fell on deaf ears as the ceremony was explained to Antonina who was fascinated in all that was going on.

Four illustrations representing the spirits that were to be invited were placed on the tiled floor in front of the priest and the candles were lit; blue for me and red for Antonina.

Various coloured liquids and fragrances were poured over the leaves in each of our plastic bowls and mixed together. Antonina was the first to be bathed in the mixture after first being covered with talcum powder, and that was where the Dove played its part. It was dipped into the bowl to allow its white feathers to soak up the liquid before being used as a type of sponge to drip the liquid all over Antonina.

The floor tiles were awash with the green liquid as the procedure was repeated time and time again.

After Antonina's ritual was completed, the priest stood up and came to where I was sitting. He took the cockerel from me and began by sprinkling my chest and shoulders with talcum powder just as they'd done to Antonina.

Next, he held the cockerel firmly by its back legs and dipped it into the green liquid in my bowl. With the liquid dripping all over the floor, he gently touched the bird against me, beginning with my shoulders, then chest and eventually my head, each time dipping the bird back into the bowl to soak up more of the liquid. When some of the liquid entered my eyes, it felt like acid, which lasted for another thirty minutes until the burning sensation had worn off.

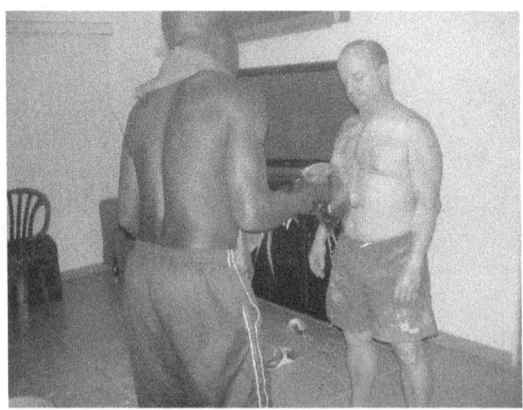

The cockerel was returned to me as I was made to sit back down. Voodoo chanting continued for another twenty minutes and towards the end, I felt a kind of choking feeling in my throat. The choking feeling lasted for about two minutes until it suddenly stopped. During all this time, the bird stared into my eyes, not moving or flinching at all. The moment my choking sensation finished, the bird looked away for the first time.

It was at that moment the priest got up and took the cockerel from me and immediately twisted its head off before I could do anything to prevent it. To my surprise, there wasn't a single drop of blood from the headless cockerel. It didn't struggle, nor flap its wings. Its headless body didn't react in any way, but just lay still on the tiled floor a few feet away from where its head was dropped.

I asked what the choking sensation was while the cockerel seemingly stared into my eyes. Haitian didn't want to give any explanations at the time, but later told me it was my spirit. She added that nobody could do voodoo to me again as my spirit had been moved into the cockerel and that the cockerel's spirit was set free in the sacrifice.

Sick and tired of all the nonsense, I told Haitian that the ceremony was the last to be performed in my house and if she didn't like it, she should find somewhere else to live.

Fortunately the dove's life was spared, and the bird was released outside the front of my house directly after the ceremony was finished.

Like after all Haitian's previous voodoo ceremonies, the plastic bowls, clothes, towels and dead chicken were taken to a quiet place close by where nobody could see and dumped. I could only imagine the tens of thousands of plastic bowls that must be dumped in the waste ground back in Haitian's own country.

Haitian continued to occupy my house twenty-four hours per day and spent her time just eating and sleeping. I did not have my house to myself for a single minute. Haitian ate a huge fried meal five times per day, and then went to bed to sleep it off. Her inadequate boyfriend would be out of the house for the majority of the day working at his hotel bar. This suited him, as he was petrified of her voodoo ceremonies and especially of Brave, who didn't like him.

My house was always filled with the smell of fried garlic and onions because that was the base for everything Haitian cooked; she didn't know any other ways to prepare food. If I ever tried to sit outside to smoke one of my Cuban cigars, Antonina would again come out and start screaming at me for the entire street to hear, so I became a prisoner in my own house … some holiday I was having.

So many times I wanted to go out and do the usual things people do whilst on holiday: go out for a beer, eat out, or visit friends on the island, but I was denied everything. I couldn't wait for the two weeks to come to an end so I could put some distance between Antonina and my house sitters, and try to recover some earnings I'd lost due to all of them.

There wasn't anything I could do to evict Haitian and Ronnie because on the island, and under Dutch law, it was illegal to make anyone homeless. It didn't matter whether they were misbehaving or homeless before moving in, so I needed to think up a plan to change the situation and permanently remove them all from my life, and permanently.

I began to think about resigning from my job in Kazakhstan once I'd been compensated for the theft of my watch, which would just leave Haitian and Ronnie to deal with upon my return.
The strangest thing was the pigeon which had arrived during my mother's visit came back regularly just to see what was going on. It used to stand on my table and just look at me. It was totally relaxed and I could pick it up any time I wanted.

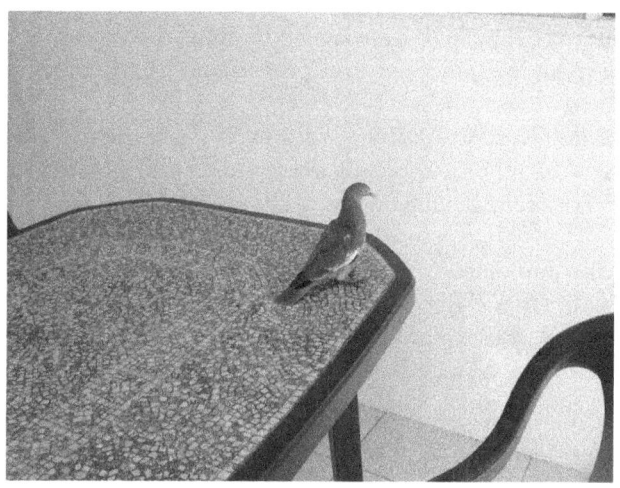

Each new day, my holiday became worse and worse until the two weeks were finally at an end. Brave had continued to visit and kept reminding me that I should not return back to Kazakhstan. He repeated his warning that death was waiting for me on Tuesday March 15th and I should keep away from my hotel room door, especially around ten past six in the evening.

Brave assured me that he would be with me on the night to help prevent my death, but I was so sick and tired of voodoo by this time I didn't pay much attention to him.

When the time came to haul all the suitcases back to the airport, I knew it would take a few months to make back part of the money I had just wasted.

We eventually arrived in Kazakhstan without stopping over in Amsterdam because I was damned if I was going on any more thankless shopping trips. My plan was to finally attend the court hearing in Atyrau for the theft of my Rolex and avoid Antonina for the rest of my life. Then for my own safety, I would leave the country and never return.

Thinking my agonising days would soon be over, I was yet

again very mistaken. Unbeknown to me at the time, they were just about to explode out of all proportion!

Antonina went to visit her family in Aksai the day after we arrived back in Kazakhstan because she couldn't wait to take the two extra suitcases full of presents back to them.

That was quite a relief because I was finally alone and able to relax and try to forget about all that had happened on my holiday from hell. A friend of mine, whom I worked with, visited me in the evenings because he wanted to know all the grim details of my hellish trip.

My temporary relaxation was soon to be cut short. Antonina called me screaming, and she demanded that I open my laptop and sign into Skype so she could see I was alone in my hotel room. I did what she ordered, but seeing me alone with my friend was still not enough for her.

She instructed me to carry my laptop all around my hotel living room, bedroom, and even bathroom so she could see I didn't have any lady visitors with me.

I did what she instructed, but she continued screaming at me and said she didn't believe me. She was threatening me with the police, the KGB, and some of her Kazakh mafia friends. She warned that they would go to my room and arrange it so I would never be seen again.

Andy, listening to all this, offered to let me stay on the sofa in his room for my own protection, but I declined his offer. Antonina returned to Atyrau three days later, and she immediately wanted to speak to Haitian to tell her how terrible I had been behaving. The lies were blatantly obvious, but Haitian enjoyed listening to them and encouraged Antonina to call her at least once per day and give her more stories.

Life, as usual with this Kazakh, was totally out of control. I didn't have any idea what to do. Antonina, Haitian, and Ronnie had wasted thousands of my hard earned dollars, and I needed to make it back before contemplating quitting my job and getting the hell out of Kazakhstan.

Waiting to attend court over my watch was quickly moving to the back of my mind. I began to focus my attention more towards all the danger I was exposed to, which was increasing by the day, and began to take Brave's warning more seriously.

As it happened, that was already a part of Antonina's sick and disturbing plan. It materialised that there wasn't going to be any court hearing over my stolen watch. I discovered that Antonina was a friend of the girl who had organised the robbery and that she'd already been paid off. The two male Kazakh lawyers were just a pretence to make me think the proceedings were going ahead as normal, plus they were out of work at the time and needed money.

I realised I would never recover my losses for paying for the transportation, food, accommodations and day rates for the two lawyers, and began to think about packing my bags and just getting the hell away from the country.

Antonina became increasingly aggressive until the night I told her she could not waste any more money phoning Haitian every day. I was sick of that woman making the hell I was already living in even worse.

That really didn't go down very well. On March 15th, I was on the phone with Haitian in the evening. I explained that, after the enormous cost of my holiday from hell, plus all the damn shopping and the money I had loaned her for her bar, it was time for me to start looking after myself.

I continued to explain that I wanted her and Ronnie permanently out of my house and life as I was disgusted with what they'd caused for me under my own roof, and that I was sick and tired of voodoo when the unforeseen happened.

I didn't see Antonina coming over to the sofa I was sitting on when she attacked me from my left side. She smashed a white soup bowl into the side of my head, just behind my left ear. The bowl shattered under the incredible power of her blow into dozens of smaller pieces.

I felt a terrible stinging and burning sensation, which caused me to drop the telephone and fall back on the sofa with my head resting on a cushion.

I remained conscious, but only just. I felt a hot and cold tingling coming from where Antonina had hit me. I opened my eyes, but I could only see green for several minutes. Suddenly, I felt a strong need to get up and forced myself to do just that before Antonina attempted to try murdering me a second time, but with a large carving knife.

Antonina was immensely and extraordinarily strong for a woman and after an intense struggle, I removed the knife from her and threw it out of the window where it landed in the snow.

The cushion my head had been on was completely saturated with blood and I could feel it continuing to run down my back. Due to the intense struggle, my blood was over the carpet, the coffee table and even sprayed all over the windowpane.

I reached for my mobile phone and started to call my company's emergency number. Antonina screamed across the room that if

I went to hospital, she would call her friends in the KGB, and I would be taken away long before any help arrived, and never seen again!

She told me she would explain that I was attacking her and her daughter. She said I would go to a Kazakh jail, which I would not survive more than a few hours.

Knowing that she really did have such powerful contacts, I closed my phone, and quickly made my way to my bedroom, and wedged a chair under the door handle for added safety. I took the above photo as evidence of what she'd done to me, should I need it, and wondered how I could survive the rest of the night.

Wedging the chair behind my door handle didn't work. The crazed Kazakh kicked and kicked the door until she had smashed her way through it. She was holding yet another knife, this time a bread knife, and she tried to stab me to death yet again. She was slashing the air with the knife, trying to cut me. I struggled with her a second time, while my blood was squirting all over the white bedroom walls until I managed to take the knife off her.

I was sure by that time that I wasn't going to survive the night. Antonina returned to the living room, and after a few minutes, I started to hear thumping sounds. I looked out of the bedroom and saw her throwing herself at the kitchen table trying to hurt herself so she could blame me.

When she looked at me, I could tell she had hurt herself, but there weren't any marks on her, which was a relief. After that, she called a medical team to come to her aid because her heart problem had started again. Her heart problem must surely have saved my life that night.

A paramedic team arrived and took her away for observation. I was finally alone and safe, at least for the rest of the night, or so I thought.

At four o'clock in the morning, I was woken up with a loud banging at my door. *What could possibly be happening now?* I thought. I ignored all the knocking and banging in case it was Antonina returning to complete her murder attempt. The banging grew louder so I went to the door and looked through the peephole only to see two Kazakh men. At first, I thought they might have been the KGB who'd come to take me away. I asked through the door who it was and they said they were my company's security. I opened the door to find two rather skinny Kazakh men. They claimed there had been an official and documented complaint made about me by a Kazakh woman called Antonina.

I couldn't take any more, so I told the Kazakhs to get out of my room. I didn't want more problems from them. They refused to go and made me accompany them to their office. There, they interrogated me and made me take a breathalyser test because Antonina had told them I was very drunk and had tried to kill her and her daughter!

Fortunately for me, I hadn't been drinking anything and passed the test without any sign of alcohol, which convinced them that her story was certainly not true, if only the part about being drunk.

They could see the blood still seeping from my fractured skull; it completely covered the back of my T-shirt and had soaked into my jeans.

I told the security staff to take the shattered pieces of the soup bowl so they could take Antonina's fingerprints. I figured she couldn't make her story stick with only her fingerprints on the shattered pieces, but in my absence someone had already been to my room and removed all the fragments before the staff could retrieve the evidence.

I then realised that the KGB were now involved because I couldn't imagine anyone else being able to get into my room to remove all the evidence.

The sun was already beginning to rise, and I had just an hour to clean myself up and make it to the office. I couldn't stop the bleeding, so I tried to cover it up with a thermal neck tube I used in the severe cold weather.

I arrived at the office, but instead of taking off my coat as usual, I kept it on to conceal the continuing blood flow. I walked over to where Chris was sitting. He didn't notice the look on my face as I approached him.

I went straight to his desk so he could see what Antonina had done to me. The look on his face was one of shock and horror when I partially opened the collar of my coat and pulled down my neck tube, which was already soaked in blood by that time. He said I had to go to hospital immediately, but I told him I couldn't due to Antonina's threat.

I explained to Chris that I needed to leave the country as quickly as possible because I would not survive much longer. I was supposed to give thirty contractual days' notice to terminate my contract, but Chris explained to the senior manager that there was no time to waste because my life was in imminent danger.

I was booked on the early morning flight the very next day. I didn't have much time to pack, so I didn't bother and left all my things behind. I only took my laptop, passport and wallet. My stress level was on an all-time high as I wondered whether I'd be disturbed again. I was worried that Antonina would find out I was leaving the country and block my exit or whether the KGB would pick me up. I couldn't get any sleep, even though the night before was so horrifying, but kept thinking that soon my nightmare would be over. I went to the hotel reception and settled all outstanding bills, including the cost for a new bedroom door, so I wouldn't have any issues when I checked out.

I joined a group of other colleagues in the lobby at 4.30am

that were also taking the same flight. Our bus arrived on time, and just half an hour later I was at the airport with my one-way ticket out of Kazakhstan.

To ensure some support getting through the airport border police, most of whom were Antonina's friends, I arranged for a representative from my Kazakh agent to meet me at the entrance of the airport. My agency was also my sponsor and visa holder, so it was in their own interests to escort me through the airport and ensure I got away. I also asked the representative to wait until I had successfully passed through the border police before leaving.

It was probably the most nerve-racking time of my entire life because Antonina's uncle was the chief of the border control police for the entire country, and I didn't know what she had told him.

Luckily for me, my friend Andy Taylor was also on the same flight. I asked him to pass through the security and border police just after me in case I was detained.

That way, if the KGB had been informed and waiting for me, Andy would be there as a witness and could alert my company that I had been taken and hadn't succeeded to leave the country.

If Antonina knew about my escape plans, she would most certainly have instructed the border police, the Kazakh KGB and also her uncle to prevent me from leaving the damn country. If they had picked me up, she'd have me held behind the scenes until she could arrange for her KGB friends to take care of me - permanently!

I think the speed with which I left Kazakhstan was what spared my life, as Antonina didn't have the chance to make any arrangements.

I kept a very low profile as I neared the border control police. I didn't want the head of the police recognising me, as he was a friend of Antonina and also her brother who used to work with him. When it eventually came to my turn, I sheepishly walked up to the kiosk to have my passport processed. I kept my head down and hoped that my collar would help to hide my face as I went to the police.

Once I was successfully through the border control, I walked as far into the departure gate as possible so I would not be clearly visible. Andy, who was following close behind me, deliberately stood between the border police and me for additional cover.

It had been snowing hard and I was worried in case they would cancel, postpone or delay the flight. After the longest nerve-racking hour of my entire life, it was finally announced that we should proceed through the gate. A battered, old Russian bus was waiting outside the door to take us to the aircraft. It was at minus forty-eight degrees centigrade so everyone else was wrapped up in much the same way I was, but for a different reason.

Still needing to carefully conceal the deep wound to the side of my head, I followed all the other passengers and approached the doors with the freezing cold wind howling past outside. The police sergeant, Antonina's friend and ex-colleague of Antonina's KGB brother, spotted me just as I was passing through the doors.

I thought, *this is it, this is the end of me; they've got me, and there is nowhere for me to run.* He had a startled look on his face because he had seen me entering the country only a few days before with Antonina.

While keeping an eye on me he immediately took out his mobile phone and started looking for a number to call. Surely, he was calling Antonina to ask why I was leaving so soon after arriving, I thought. I can only imagine that he couldn't get a dial tone or an answer from her phone, so he had no other choice other than to let me proceed to board the aircraft.

Once I was safely seated on the aircraft, my heart continued pounding heavily due to my continuing worry about being taken off the aircraft. I was sure the policeman would still be trying to call Antonina for instructions. Due to the runway being covered in snow and ice, the aircraft needed to make one slow pass down it so its engines could clear it away while controlling its speed with its brakes on.

The entire aircraft was shaking with the powerful thrust from its engines while it cleared the snow. This made my escape to freedom even more intense. The aircraft could have been ordered to return at any second, if the policeman had succeeded to make contact with Antonina.

After what had felt like hours, the aircraft finally left the ground and I could, at last, begin to relax for the very first time after so many months of hell. I finally started to believe that my nightmare was over and began to wipe the memories of Antonina and Kazakhstan from my mind for good.

As far as I was aware at the time, the only cloud left on the horizon was the fact that Haitian and Ronnie would be waiting at my house when I arrived home. I began wondering how they would react after seeing me so soon after all the hell they had caused for me under my own roof. I wondered which excuse they would use to try to lessen the bad atmosphere. I wondered what they would try without the support from a crazed Kazakh psychopath.

I didn't have the time to call my house sitters to announce my sudden return to the island. That was fine with me because I didn't intend to give them any warning in any case. As far as they were concerned, they finally had my house to themselves and would never see me again. They would claim it as their own, as planned if Antonina had succeeded in murdering me, per the local island law.

I arrived in Amsterdam airport after sleeping for most of the flight. I was totally exhausted from the lack of sleep from the recent events, and I had lost a lot of blood. I spent the night recuperating in my usual hotel across from the central railway station in Amsterdam before continuing to the Caribbean the next day.

I stayed in the hotel which happened to be the same place where Antonina created so many problems for me just three weeks before. The second time around felt like heaven, which I had just avoided visiting earlier than planned! I felt like I had won against all the odds, like I had survived the impossible and that I was still alive to tell the tale, which inspired what you're now reading.

I went to visit some friends of mine near the hotel, as I knew I could always find them at my favourite Irish bar. Sure enough, they were all there. They were surprised to see me again so soon, and they were delighted to see me without the strange Kazakh woman who had blatantly refused to be introduced to them just three weeks before, which had been very embarrassing at the time.

I showed them the gash to the side of my head, which was still weeping blood because I hadn't had any stitches. They were all horrified after I explained how I got the wound. I didn't feel like explaining all the latest events because I was so desperate to put everything behind me, and permanently.

On the way back to the hotel I bought a large box of tissue paper and covered a part of the hotel pillow to protect the starched white cotton case from my blood and went to bed very early. I was still quite weak from all the stress and lack of sleep, and I needed a relaxing start to the next day's long haul flight back to the island. I was quietly excited that the next day would be the renaissance of a new kind of life. A life I had always dreamed of having.

It was no surprise that I fell asleep the moment my head touched the pillow. I didn't wake up until eight o'clock the following morning, and I felt better than I had felt for several months.

I arrived at the check-in desk in Schiphol airport with three hours to waste. I enjoyed walking around the airport with the thought that I didn't have to buy anything for anyone.

The duty-free area felt so different and relaxing. I casually made my way in the direction of the business class lounge, and I realised that I was standing right outside the Rolex shop where I had bought my watch back in 2006.

I looked at the watches on display and wondered whether I would ever dare to replace my beloved watch in the future. I already knew the answer, which was yes, if only to reinforce my private defiance for those who had taken my last one and caused me to meet Antonina.

I arrived at my departure gate in good time, and I couldn't help thinking about what had passed through my mind when I proceeded towards the departure gate the day before. The second approach did feel like a renaissance. I walked slowly and reminisced about the horror I had just been through, all the while trying to conceal the big smile that was trying to spread across my face.

I sat down in the very same seat number that I had sat in just three weeks before. And much to my surprise, the seat next to me, where Antonina had sat before, remained empty for the entire flight.

Reality set in and I began to believe that I really had survived. Shortly afterwards, I was served a complimentary glass of champagne, and I made myself comfortable for the ten hour flight ahead.

Soon, I was airborne and wondering when I would next touch down on European soil. Then I started thinking about what reaction my troublesome house sitters would have when I returned unexpectedly, and very much alive!

I decided not to start thinking about what lay ahead until the time came. Instead, I tried concentrating on relaxing and enjoying the view from the upper deck of the Boeing 747-400.

The skies were clear and blue as I passed over the United Kingdom. We were at cruising altitude by the time we passed over

Wales, so I couldn't see the place where my mother lived. *She's probably worrying herself half to death,* I thought. I had called her from Amsterdam to let her know I had slipped through the Kazakh authorities and avoided the KGB so at least she knew I had survived the murder attempts.

The flight felt completely different for some reason. Maybe it was because of all that had recently happened to me, or the thought that I had left Kazakhstan for good, and was free to look for my next overseas location to work.

During the flight, I began to think about ways to evict Haitian and Ronnie so I'd have my house to myself again. I figured that I'd have to pay them to leave, but that didn't work when I offered them a few nights in a hotel on my last visit. I began to consider selling my property, as that would certainly solve the problem, as the law couldn't stop me selling, which would succeed in getting Haitian and Ronnie out of my house.

Chapter 23
Back to the Caribbean

My flight touched down half an hour early on the island, and for the very first time, I wasn't really happy about it.

I had my usual window seat during my flight back from Amsterdam, so it wasn't difficult to keep the wound to the left side of my head out of sight from the flight attendant and other passengers.

I was the first to pass through the island's customs control. Due to the Caribbean heat, I carried my jacket over my arm, not thinking about my wound. As I handed over my passport at the immigration desk, I was given a strange look and asked if I was okay. I realised what the policewoman had noticed and said I was fine and would get checked later in the day at the hospital. I passed through all the people waiting at arrivals, and fortunately, I wasn't recognised by anyone for once.

I passed through the gate and out into the heat and sunshine. There, I lit my first cigarette since the business class lounge in Amsterdam. I could see the long queue of taxis a few yards away, and I began to imagine my reception when I got back to my house just a twenty minute drive away.

Reality brought me back to earth firmly when I walked over to the line of taxis and jumped into the one in the front of the queue. The driver, Tristan, was a friend of mine, and I hadn't seen him on my previous visit. He wouldn't have had any idea what had been going on the last time I was there or what had been done to me.

When Tristan noticed the deep wound to the side of my head he was shocked to say the least and asked what the hell was going on with me. I began to explain why I needed to return so soon, which fascinated him. He was totally dumbfounded and suggested we go for a beer before he took me back to my house. He explained that I would be better prepared that way.

We stopped off at a Chinese bar called the 'Hoi Sing', which was managed by a Chinese family. I always visited them when I was left to my own devices. The Chinese manager was in bed and sleeping as usual as he worked the evening shift.

I was glad he wasn't awake, because I was in no mood for an audience. Tristan had planned to finish work early that day to take a rest, so it suited him to sit and listen to the most amazing story he had ever heard from a friend. I was sure everything I told him would be all over the island by the next day, so I was careful with regard to the details I gave him.

After a couple of hours, it was time for Tristan to drop me off at my house. He wouldn't accept any payment because I'd paid our bar bill and entertained him like he'd never been entertained in his life. I knew he couldn't wait to get home and tell his wife all that had been said.

The front door to my house wasn't locked, so I let myself straight in. I was expecting to catch Haitian sitting on my sofa in front of lit candles. I was right, as it happened, and she nearly fell off my sofa when she looked up and saw me standing there. She was busy performing a voodoo ritual for someone she knew, or maybe a ritual to bring more trouble into my life.

"Oh my precious brother," she screamed as she rushed towards me to hug me. "I thought I'd never see you again," she cried. The false and nervous tears were running down her face.

I said with a serious look on my face, "With no thanks to *anyone*, I am alive, and back to stay for a while, or at least until my next overseas contract." She immediately began examining the side of my head, which was still in a rough shape and went to get some antiseptic cream and a dressing.

She said that death was waiting for me at my hotel room door the night Antonina tried to murder me. Because I avoided going through the door, I had survived. I told her to stop her nonsense and to shut up.

Strangely, she knew all about the white soup bowl that Antonina had smashed into my skull. She explained that Brave Elohim had been with me to protect me, and that it was Brave who had caused the soup bowl to shatter into pieces so it couldn't be used again. I told Haitian I didn't want to see or listen to any more voodoo; I just wanted to relax and return to a normal life.

Later that night, Ronnie came back from the hotel bar. It was clear he put on a false and forced smile on his face. The disappointment that I was alive was clearly obvious. I couldn't stand the fake and uncomfortable atmosphere, so I freshened up, put a dressing over my wound to conceal it and took a taxi to the capital. I wanted to get away from them and talk to a few locals I knew while listening to typical Caribbean music played for the tourists.

The next day, I got up late in the morning. As I walked out of my bedroom, I found Haitian sitting at my dining table. She and Ronnie always chose to eat and talk right outside my bedroom. It was a constant reminder that I didn't have any privacy in my own home.

She was using the new laptop I had bought three weeks before. She was listening to music when, suddenly, my bathroom door slammed shut at the other end of the room. It closed with enough force to shatter the opaque glass in it, but miraculously nothing broke.

All the doors and windows were closed, so I had a good idea what or who had entered my house. I asked Haitian if she was expecting anyone, but she didn't answer me. Just seconds later, she shrieked and jumped up from her chair, almost turning my heavy dining table over. My new laptop flew across the table and almost landed on the floor.

I knew exactly what was happening, and then she came over to me with an all too familiar expression on her face. Haitian was no longer Haitian; it was Brave. As impossible as it sounds, there is no mistaking the difference between the two in terms of their expressions, voices or mannerisms.

Brave approached me with his usual greeting with his arms crossed for a sometimes painful two handed handshake. I had to cross my arms and also join the two handed handshake. Brave's handshakes were normally a painful experience to say the least, but not this time.

Brave welcomed me back with a warm expression on his face. He was happy to see me alive after warning me about what would happen on March 15th and he was pleased that I had survived certain death.

Brave claimed the fame for protecting me that night, and he also declared that he was responsible for ensuring that the soup bowl shattered when Antonina smashed it into my head. He told me to take his advice seriously the next time he gave it. I asked why he couldn't have stopped the bowl hitting me but he just smiled back and didn't answer my question.

Brave didn't stay long. He examined my wound and left after just ten minutes, and Haitian became her usual, obese self again. Every time Brave used her to communicate with me, she was left lifeless. She always used his visits as an excuse to go back to bed.

Two nights later, Brave returned as himself at the usual time of one o'clock in the morning. There was no doubting Brave's presence, he always made it very clear that he was passing by to check out my house. On such nights, I heard noises that eventually woke me up. The sounds became annoying, and I usually walked outside my bedroom and into my living room to see what all the commotion was about.

The moment I walked out of my bedroom, I instantly felt his presence. After some time, I could locate exactly where in my living room he was. As unreal as it sounds, it was very real for me.

In the living room, the pair of plastic parrots were singing. They belonged to Haitian, and they had a motion sensor so whenever someone walked past, the damn things would start singing.

This night, the parrots were continuously singing, so I took the batteries out of them. To my total disbelief, the parrots continued to sing after I had removed their batteries. Consequently, I carried them outside and trashed them.

I got angry and opened a bottle of Gold Label whisky, which my mother had given me when she last visited. I proceeded to sip glass after glass of it without getting any benefit whatsoever. Brave loved whisky, and he had the ability to take the full effect from me.

Without using Haitian's body to communicate to me, I got an unmistakable feeling that my problems were far from over. It felt like I was being sent a warning, and as it turned out, my instincts were right.

Two days later, Antonina called me from Kazakhstan. She was crying on the phone, saying she was so in love with me and so sorry for trying to murder me. I guess Brave did have something to warn me about after all.

I told her that I never wanted to hear from her again and that I would block her from calling and emailing me, which is exactly what I did. It was no surprise that that didn't work; she still had Haitian's number!

Antonina called Haitian, and as expected, Haitian took her phone call in private so I couldn't listen to the conversation. Haitian was still intent on protecting her free accommodation, and she needed Antonina's help to continue destroying my life until she had succeeded.

Haitian promised Antonina that she would talk to me and repair all that they had done to me. I knew by the way Haitian came to me with a pathetic look on her face what she was about. I turned my back and went outside to wait for a taxi to town.

After my holiday from hell, I was not going to accept any more bullshit, especially from a voodoo priestess with a hidden agenda.

The island has many strange laws. One of them states that if somebody can prove that they had taken care of a house where the owner had died, they automatically became the new owner.

Haitian saw the phone call from Antonina as another opportunity to make my life totally impossible all over again and she encouraged Antonina to return to the island.

Though I wouldn't deal with the crazed Kazakh, Haitian maintained contact with her whilst smiling sweetly and calling me precious for some pathetic reason.

Three weeks later, Haitian warned me that Antonina was returning to the island to visit us. I told her to stop her nonsense; it was impossible for Antonina to get a visa without being sponsored by someone living on the island.
Unbeknown to me, Haitian had helped sponsor Antonina's second visa. Also, the woman who worked in the travel agency in Kazakhstan still had my credit card details to debit for Antonina's trip back!

A week later, Haitian informed me that Antonina was returning to the island to make everything right. Naturally, I went ballistic. I couldn't believe what was happening to me all over again! I remembered the hell I had endured the last time … and the murder attempt. I felt that I was no longer strong enough to go through any more of it.

There was no way in hell I was going to allow her back into my life. I asked Haitian how she knew Antonina was returning to try to destroy my life yet again.

Haitian, the evil woman that she was, lied. She claimed she didn't know the details. I, however, knew exactly what had been going on behind my back. Haitian was so obsessed with getting rid of me permanently that she wasn't going to stop at anything until she'd succeeded.

Eventually, I started to believe that Antonina had acquired another visa and was returning back to the island. I unblocked Antonina on Skype to tell her she was not welcome in my life or on the island or in my house after her last visit.

Using Skype, I could see her in a hotel room in Astana, the capital of Kazakhstan, as she waited for the Dutch embassy to grant her a visa. I heard her room telephone ring, and I knew it was a man from another room who required servicing.

She told me she had to go to the hotel's reception to pay the room charge from the previous night, but I knew that was a lie. Bills aren't settled until it's time to check out.

She didn't think I could hear her customer entering her room or telling her customer not to say anything because she was talking with me via Skype.

I certainly did hear everything because her bed was very squeaky, not to mention hearing her speaking words of encouragement to her customer. After a very noisy hour, I shouted through my laptop to turn the lights on immediately. Naturally, she took her time doing that.

She had covered herself with one of the bed sheets, but she failed to instruct her client who had just finished using her to keep the hell out of sight of the laptop's camera. I could see a skinny Russian man in the background putting his clothes back on. I told her again to forget ever returning to the island.

Unsurprisingly, the next day Haitian informed me that Antonina would be arriving on the island in two days' time. When I asked her how the hell she knew, she just put on the usual pathetic expression and said the spirits had told her.

Two days later, Haitian and her boyfriend went to a beach to see a festival going on there. They told me Antonina was arriving on the Amsterdam flight and that they would drop me off to welcome her!

I still didn't believe a word she had said, but I agreed to go to the airport to prove them wrong. I really shouldn't have done so.

The flight came in on time, and I waited for half an hour before turning towards the taxi rank only to see Antonina! I could not understand how she had been granted a visa. My nightmare was about to continue on a grander scale than ever before.

I asked her where she was going to stay because I wasn't letting her anywhere near my house, or myself for that matter. Antonina followed me to my taxi and threatened me with the police, just as she had done in Kazakhstan.

I totally ignored her and proceeded to get into a taxi to go back home. I realised that Haitian was the instigator of my continued hell, and that she had gone to the beach with her inadequate boyfriend to stay out of the way.

When I arrived at my house, Antonina was full of apologies

about the attempted murder, but I wasn't having any of it. I went straight to my bed with the intention of pulling Haitian aside the next morning to ask her what the hell she had been doing behind my back.

Of course, Haitian denied everything, and of course, Haitian protected Antonina … just like before. The next morning, I wanted to go downtown to buy some more Cuban cigars, and Antonina insisted on joining me, or she would arrange for the KGB to go to the island and make a big problem for me. I just laughed in her face.

Naturally, I was way past caring at that point. I just laughed at all of her threats. I kept thinking to myself, *What the hell made me deserve it all?* I hadn't done anything wrong to anyone, unlike the three of them.

I took a taxi downtown and went directly to the cigar shop in the Renaissance Mall to buy my favourite brand of cigar: Cohiba Siglo #VI. Because I received a warm welcome in the cigar shop, Antonina started to perform again and in front of everyone.

Before things got too out of control, I cancelled my plans for visiting other venues and took another taxi straight home. That was just the beginning. Soon after we returned to the house, Haitian and Ronnie arrived and started to make things much worse.

Of course, they sided with Antonina, as always. She made sure she had Antonina all to herself, but I didn't care, I just went to my bedroom and watched TV. After a while, I realised that the house was quiet, and I ventured out of my room to see why.
To my surprise, the place was empty. I was all alone to soak up the peace and tranquillity. It didn't last long: Haitian and Ronnie returned just half an hour later looking quite pleased with themselves.

I didn't see Antonina anywhere, and I asked where she was. Haitian said she had helped protect me and dropped Antonina off at a nearby hotel where she would be well taken care of.

She wouldn't tell me which hotel because she claimed it was better that way. She hadn't considered the fact that if anything happened to Antonina, she would be held responsible as her sponsor.

After two days, I demanded to know where she was. Haitian told me which hotel, and off we went. I had never seen the hotel before even though it was just a ten minute walk away. Haitian and Ronnie had lived there for many months because the cockroach-infested rooms were only ten dollars per night.

It was also where all the island refinery workers chose to stay due to its low cost. The hotel was full of illegal Venezuelan and Colombian men, and no women ... except Antonina.

Of course, Haitian and Ronnie had shown Antonina around when they dropped her off. The bar was the first place they showed her so she could be seen by all the workers as being a lonely woman staying there. We found Antonina's room and went straight in just as a Venezuelan man was leaving. It looked like she had not had any sleep since arriving.

Naturally, she refused to leave with us because she was making money from all the Latin Americans there. We went back to the reception and threatened the guy working there. I told the man at the reception that I would have the police raid the place if he did not help me by kicking Antonina out, as most of the workers staying there were illegal on the island. He agreed to help.
She came back to my house so I could get her visa revoked in the morning and have her deported before she could cause any more problems.

In the morning, I left for the authority's office to cancel her visa. I planned to go to the police for help after that. That plan also got spoiled because Haitian knew what I was going to do and advised Antonina to stay with me.

When we got to the capital, I tried to buy her a coffee, but she just continued walking. Because I had not invited her back to the island, and because I never wanted to see her again, I stopped trying to reason with her. Instead, I walked off in the opposite direction and took a taxi straight home.

I should have grabbed the opportunity and continued to the authorities, but my mind was scrambled with all the stress that was rising by the minute.

An hour later Antonina, called me and asked where the hell I was. I calmly replied, "At home, where else?" I actually had my house to myself because Haitian was out, as she wasn't expecting me to return for several hours.

Thirty minutes later, Antonina turned up in a taxi. She walked straight into my house to collect her things because she had already made a deal with the taxi driver that she would see him all right if he helped her.

I encouraged her to get the hell out of my house by throwing her little case out of my front door. I thought that would be the end of the hell I was living in. But I couldn't have been more wrong!

An hour later, the police visited me. They demanded to know why I had brought a poor Kazakh lady all the way from her country only to abuse her and sell her off to the highest bidder.

I couldn't control my emotions any longer; I just started laughing at the police for believing Antonina. I invited the two policewomen into my house and showed them the photos of what Antonina had done to my head. I also showed them my fresh scar.

Thankfully, the two shocked policewomen believed my story and arrested Antonina and put her in jail. At least I finally had something genuine to laugh about. What a relief that was.

It was a Saturday, and Antonina was detained along with all the hookers from Colombia and Venezuela who had overstayed, until she was deported that Wednesday. Antonina wrote and registered an official statement that I had brought her all the way to the island to murder her. Fortunately, and luckily for me I wasn't the one who had sponsored her return!

That was the last I ever heard of the crazed psychopathic Kazakh woman.

After she left, I really started to believe that my nightmare was finally over, but I still had Haitian and Ronnie to deal with.

I couldn't face leaving my house until a week later, but I finally decided to take a taxi to the tapas bar next to the hotel I had originally stayed in three years earlier. I sat at the bar talking to a bank manager friend of mine while enjoying my favourite brand of Cuban cigar, when a local woman entered the bar with a man I assumed was her boyfriend.

Because I was sitting near the corner of the bar, she made eye contact while rearranging her bra in a very obvious manner with her blouse half open for the entire world to see. That should have been my cue to go somewhere else. She had agreed to go for a drink with the Spanish guy just so she could have free drinks while she looked for a bigger catch.

My first thought was that she looked like a hooker. Unbeknown to me, she was a professional hooker who also worked as a salesperson for a very expensive Italian men's clothing shop on the corner of the Renaissance Mall.

She picked up on my conversation with my friend regarding where the best place was to buy good quality trousers, and she confidently butted into our conversation. She sat right next to me and explained where the shop she worked was.

I could see which direction it was going because the guy she had walked in with was now being blatantly ignored. I was fresh meat.

Nevertheless, I had already been at the tapas bar for at least four hours, and I wasn't fit to stay for another four so I made my excuses and left.

Three days later, I received a missed call from a number that wasn't associated with any name in my phone. I broke my cardinal rule and called the number back. I don't know what possessed me to do that. If I called every missed call I'd received on the island, I would have been bankrupt.

A woman answered my call, and I asked who she was. She replied, "It's me, Inez. Don't you remember me?"

I was being completely honest when I told her I didn't know anyone called Inez. She explained that she'd spoken to me in the tapas bar on the previous Saturday.

I began to remember talking to some woman, but I still didn't remember any Inez. I wish I'd never returned that call because another nightmare was about to begin.

She persuaded me to visit the Italian men's clothing shop where she was a sales assistant to show me the quality of the trousers they stocked. She added that they had a tailoring service to turn them up for short-legged men like myself. That last point piqued my interest because I didn't know where to go on the island to get trousers turned up so off I went.

I found the clothing shop just where I had pictured it from her description, on the corner of the Renaissance Mall. It was located right where taxis dropped people off. The shop was nicely laid out, and a shop assistant quickly approached me.

"Now do you remember me?" the assistant asked. "No," I answered. I really didn't remember her face at all. "I'm Inez. I was talking to you on Saturday night," she said.

I had to be honest and admit that all I remembered from the bar was seeing a woman struggling with her little silicon bags in her bra.

She seemed to react very well to that, and she took me by my hand as part of her personal treatment to score a new customer and walked me deeper into the shop.

Actually, she looked totally ridiculous in her free issue, company supplied uniform. It was ridiculously tight, at least two sizes too small. She was wearing four or five inch heels, which made it look like she was wearing stilts under her trousers as you could see the outline of her heels a few inches up her trouser legs.

She began by showing me the trousers they had in stock. After some sales talk, she persuaded me to buy a couple of pairs before leaving half an hour later.

I needed to return two days later to collect my new trousers. I was horrified to find that, contrary to what she'd told me to secure the sale, they were dry clean only, just like so many I already had, tailor made in South Korea. Therefore, I hadn't actually gained a thing.

Not to miss an opportunity, she started flirting with me and asked which hotel I was staying in. It seemed like a well-practised speech. She was quite taken aback when she learnt that I had been living on the island for the past three years.

After further interrogation, she uncovered the fact that I was a manager in the oil and gas business and was off the island more than on it. *The thought of house sitting is clearly on her mind*, I thought.

She persuaded me to take her out to dinner, which I did, but on my own terms. She wanted seafood, and I wanted a sixteen-ounce rib-eye steak, so steak it was going to be whether she turned up or not. I really didn't care.

I met her in a cigar bar just across the road from the restaurant that owned it. Amazingly enough, she arrived at exactly six o'clock in the evening, as planned. I was impressed, but that only lasted for about two seconds.

After she had said hello to the barman, bar manager, and waitress, she finally came over to me. Meanwhile, I was just sitting there patiently, waiting to be the last to be greeted.

She sat at the bar next to me and her very first words were, "Look at me. I'm totally naked from my waist down." I didn't react at all because it was perfectly clear from the moment she entered that she wasn't wearing anything, or at the most, something as skimpy as a G-string. Her dress was so short, she looked like a perfect hooker, and I was already starting to feel uncomfortable having her sitting next to me. I really didn't want people seeing me with this new floozy.

I'd only seen such short dresses on the street girls who came over from Colombia and Venezuela to make as much money as possible from visiting tourists. Inez was no different.

The barman, whom I had known for a long time, had known her a lot longer, and he had seen this forty-year-old hooker with hundreds of tourists over the years. He wasn't such a good friend because he didn't tell me to drop her as soon as possible. He was Colombian, so he probably assumed I wanted to have my wicked way with her before leaving her as hundreds or even thousands had done before me.

We finished our drinks and crossed the road to the steak house. All their steaks were always of the finest quality and came from Argentina. The steaks were all grain-fed Angus beef. It was my favourite venue when I wanted a steak. The staff knew me very well because I went there two to three times per week, usually for lunch when I knew it would be quiet.

It was no surprise that the staff had all seen Inez before, but with a different man each time. I noticed the manageress's expression when she saw that Inez was with me this time, and she probably wondered what the hell I was doing with her or where I had been to have met her.

The waiter came to take our order, and after he had patiently waited for Inez to finally decide what she wanted, he turned to me. I simply told him I'd have my usual order, including the wine. He nodded, said, "Muy bien señor," and went away to get the wine. Inez said, "Oh my God, he knows exactly what you want! You've been here before?" I replied, "Just a few times."

Moments later, he returned with a large bottle of chilled sparkling water together with a bottle of Saint Émilion Grand Cru. Once Inez tasted the wine, she commented on how nice it was and asked where it came from. I told her it came from Bordeaux, and she asked, "Where's that?" I thought, *I'd be better off ordering sangria for this old floozy.*

An American friend, whom I hadn't seen for three years, was on the island making use of his timeshare with his wife. He had arranged to meet me that very same night in the tourist area on a beach pier. I explained to Inez that once we'd finished, I'd drop her off wherever she wanted to go because I had to meet a friend on the pier. She told me she wanted to go with me. That certainly wasn't quite what I had in mind because I wanted to catch up on things with my friend and didn't want anyone seeing her with me.

After finishing my conch (sea snail) and sixteen ounce rib-eye, we took a taxi to the beach pier to meet my friend.

Inez explained that she had a Colombian mother and an island father who had jumped ship when her mother became pregnant. Such events were quite normal on the island. Sadly, her mother passed away when she was only seven years old, and her uncle had brought her up.

We arrived at the beach pier, and sure enough, my friend was waiting for me at the bar. It was really great to see him again, and we sat at the bar catching up on all that had happened since we'd last met. Inez kept herself amused by dancing alone in a style better suited for the red light district. It was becoming increasingly embarrassing to be associated with her that night with her dress barely covering her backside. Looking like a street hooker was certainly the distinct impression she wanted to give every man around her.

We couldn't believe the free show she was putting on while she danced alone in the middle of the dance area, so we both deliberately faced the bar. That way, whenever she looked in our direction, she wouldn't have the audience or interest she was working so hard to get.

We called for the bill and made our way to the main road to drink and chat in another bar. The bar was situated halfway down a street full of bars and restaurants about a ten minute walk away.

Seconds later, I heard a shout. Inez was busy trying to catch up with us, struggling with her ridiculous red plastic high heels in the sand. "Where're we going next?" she questioned. But she should have asked, "Why are you leaving me behind?"

Clearly, Inez was not the type to give up easily, and she tagged along even though she was being ignored.

We sat at the bar and ordered a couple of beers. Inez ordered a glass of Old Par whisky for herself before I had the chance to ask what she wanted.

My friend and I continued to chat about each other's lives, and he was shocked to hear about all the problems Antonina, Haitian, and Ronnie had caused me in my own house and that under the Dutch law, I couldn't kick them out. He also couldn't believe my miraculous escape from Kazakhstan.

I didn't see him again for several months. Instead, I met other frequent visitors to the island who also couldn't sell their timeshares either; so continued visiting the island just to make the best use of them.

I didn't see Inez until the following weekend. Word had got around to her that I was having a barbecue at the house. She hadn't been invited for obvious reasons, but that didn't make any difference to her.

Because so many people she knew had been invited, she didn't want to miss out. She was actually the first to arrive, and she was dressed in a skimpy white bikini and very little else and asked where my pool was. I didn't have a pool at that time, even though I was getting quotes from various contractors.

Fortunately, soon after her arrival, other guests started arriving, so that took the pressure off me. Only half the number of guests arrived, which was normal on the island. Consequently, there was far too much meat, but nothing went to waste as the Venezuelans stole as much of it as they could.

Nobody thought to tell me they were making frequent trips to their cars carrying cases of beer and meat packed in take-away boxes they'd found in my kitchen cupboards. Once I knew Venezuelans had shown up, I couldn't go out of my house as I needed to guard my few remaining ornaments which I'd collected from all over the world.

I'd asked my Venezuelan cleaner to the barbecue along with her three daughters, as I knew she started work in the Hoi Sing bar at four o'clock so couldn't stay long. I hadn't planned on them bringing their boyfriends with them, which I knew would mean trouble.

The islanders never wasted a text message or a quick phone call out of common courtesy to inform they couldn't make it, so I could gauge the number of people coming; that wasn't their problem. Instead I wasted a lot of money preparing enough for everyone just in case they did arrive. I later asked myself why I bothered.

After quite a pleasant afternoon and evening, the last stragglers left. There was still no sign of Inez making plans to go home. After Inez passed on her last chance to get a free lift home, I began to wonder if I'd be nobbled yet again for the cost of a taxi.

It was soon apparent that going home couldn't have been further from her mind. Inez automatically assumed she could stay the night, even though I hadn't made any suggestions in that direction.

Inez was in full party mode, but with nobody left to entertain, she suggested that we go down the road to the fisherman's bar, built half over the ocean.

We arrived just in time to catch last orders at the bar. We walked down the small wooden pier and sat down at a table on the very end of it. It was quiet and with a very beautiful atmosphere sitting in the moon light over the Caribbean, only listening to the waves gently lapping against the shore rocks.

We chatted for a while, and most of the conversation was about places to go on the island and what I did for a living. At that point, she told me she had an eighteen-year-old son who had been brought up by his father.

Inez was certainly not the motherly type, and having a son would have seriously cramped her style. Because the bar had closed, we ended up returning to my place. Inez continued to drink, but she only had me to entertain.

We were in my bedroom watching a pop concert on TV, which provided a little privacy from Haitian and Ronnie who were guaranteed to break up any private little meeting. For all I knew, they were probably eating just outside my bedroom door to listen, as they had done so many times before, to check if I was alone or not.

Inez automatically stripped down to her skimpy white bikini and proceeded to dance provocatively in front of the TV. She was topless, but I just sat on the edge of my bed wondering whether she'd ever suggest calling for a taxi. The suggestion never came. Her intentions were quite obvious: she wasn't planning on going anywhere else that night.

Once the concert finally ended, it was sleep time, which is exactly what I did. Inez stripped naked and cuddled up to me with the hope that something would become of it, but it wasn't going to happen, and nor was I interested or awake enough to last any longer to make love to such a well-tenderised body.

To my dismay, she stayed for the rest of the weekend, until the Monday lunchtime, as she wasn't due to work until one o'clock in the afternoon. I really didn't enjoy this floozy's company, as she was so opinionated and confident. I can only admit that as I was lonely, I felt something was better than nothing, so I allowed her to stay. I felt that it was clear that nobody in their right mind wanted her, in any case.

On the Sunday, we took a friend's taxi down to the local village to have lunch in a bar. The steak and steamed shrimp were well known in the area.

Before leaving, Inez produced a pair of shorts, which probably would have been too small for a Barbie doll, but she somehow managed to squeeze into them. With her shorts and red plastic high heels on, she looked like the perfect hooker.

After we ate, we waited outside the bar for my friendly taxi driver to take us back home. Due to her obvious appearance, three cars pulled over to ask how much she charged per hour. Rather than being insulted, she found the questions hilarious. She even said to me, "Look at me, I look like a hooker."

Unbeknown to me at the time, Inez regularly walked the streets of the red light district working as a street hooker for additional income. She had spent nights in every hotel on the island, each time with a different client.

The following week, she told me the most outrageous stories about her time in the brothels. She had stripped naked on stage in front of a full male audience and pole danced naked alongside the other hookers. I learnt that Inez was a lesbian, but men paid more.

To keep in with the various brothel managers, she made her customers pay the bar the usual one hundred dollar bar fine, because she was taking customers away from the hookers working the bar.

When Inez became a regular visitor to my house, probably because no one else wanted her, Haitian got involved again. Despite explaining some of the things Haitian had done before, Inez seemed to play into Haitian's hands as if she enjoyed it.

Inez also had her sick, exhibitionist eyes on Haitian's obese boyfriend. She would rush into the kitchen in the morning, the moment she heard Ronnie, wearing only one of my short T-shirts and nothing else. She caught Ronnie's attention by knocking something on the floor and bent at the waist to pick it up. I caught her several times, which infuriated her while she was busy giving a free show to see how he'd react.

By the time I joined them in the kitchen, Ronnie's face was the colour of a bright red tomato. As I entered the kitchen Inez protested angrily at my presence because she could no longer perform. I reminded her that it was my house and my kitchen, but as always, the islanders lacked any kind of respect and would simply ignore such comments.

Now, Haitian had an additional motive to cause trouble, as she had done so many times before. At every opportunity, Haitian interrupted conversations I was having with Inez by butting in and speaking in Papiamento to Inez. She knew I didn't understand a word of it.

Naturally, I protested and instructed that only English be spoken under my roof, but I was always ignored. Several weeks went by, and just like before, the situation worsened until someone had to go.

I had been out of work for four long months, but I still didn't have any privacy in my house. One day, an agency from the United Kingdom called me. It was regarding another contract in Nigeria, which I was interested in because there hadn't been many other enquiries up until then.

The only worry was what Inez would inevitably get up to whilst I was away, as if I cared. The contract rotation was twenty-eight days on and twenty-eight days off, so there was a lot of flying to do.

I told Inez she could continue living in my house, which she refused because it would have cramped her style with Haitian and Ronnie there. Instead, she chose to return to living in her Colombian friend's house on the north part of the island. There, she could continue to pick up tourists for her own financial gain, just as she always had before meeting me in the tapas restaurant a few months before.

So it was back to Nigeria in July of 2011. I was a little apprehensive after previous exploits in the country, but I felt that the island wasn't exactly being kind to me either.

Chapter 24
Return to Nigeria

Nigeria is a country full of surprises, and I'm not just referring to the wonderful choice of characters living there. Even though I already had so many experiences there, I still loved the people, and still do to this day.

I arrived at Port Harcourt airport, which looked just as it did years before. With the usual donations for the immigration and customs staff, I got through with all my possessions intact with the aid of a few twenty dollar notes. My armed escort was waiting outside the airport, but I needed to wait for others to clear immigration. It took an hour and a half for the stragglers to be accounted for before we set off to the different places pre-booked to accommodate us on our arrival night.

The next morning, I met some others who were assigned to the swamp I was to be based at and off we went. It had rained most of the night, so the roads were in a terrible condition. It took us over three hours to arrive at the camp where people of many nationalities were busy expanding the upstream oil facilities.

Our accommodation was a typical set-up consisting of rows of narrow containers kept off the ground by concrete footings and all linked up with electrical and telephone cables.

Due to the high malaria and dengue fever risk, doors were

always kept closed, and the small rooms were sprayed on a daily basis.

Power cuts were a regular occurrence when the diesel generator would break down due to dirty fuel blocking the filters. The lack of air conditioning was the main discomfort. If any insect was found inside the trailer, it had to be destroyed before sleep was possible. In swamps, almost everything flying or crawling bites, and some bites could be fatal. Even inside the camp perimeter black mamba snakes were found on a regular basis. They weren't actually black in colour, but instead a light brown colour. They got their name due to the inside of their mouths being totally black.

We averaged fifteen men per month going to hospital with malaria or dengue fever or both! One South African colleague contracted malaria and went downhill very fast. In the Nigerian hospital, they identified seven different types of malaria parasites in his body at the same time. He lost over twenty kilos in two weeks and was lucky to make it through. It amazed me that so many people walked around in short sleeved shirts, shorts and flip-flops given the amount of bloodsucking and biting insects around.

I never bothered to take malaria tablets because there were many side effects. Instead, I preferred to soak myself in insect repellent containing a minimum of 50% Deet in the hope that I would evade being bitten in the first place.

On a previous project, one South African colleague was unlucky enough to get cerebral malaria and died in just ten days in a hospital in London. Cerebral malaria has to be treated the moment you contract it. After just a few days it is already too late to cure, and he had waited too long to seek help.

While working my twenty-eight days on and off rotation, I returned to the island at the end of every four-week visit. Four weeks doesn't sound like long before a four week holiday, but four weeks in a swamp goes very slowly.

Due to flights not lining up, each trip required a night in Amsterdam. Amsterdam was one of the most convenient stopovers and gave me the opportunity to buy things unavailable on the island, or much cheaper than the goods on the island.

During my first trip to Nigeria, I told Haitian that she and her pathetic boyfriend had to get out of my house because I was sick and tired of all her voodoo and troublemaking. I gave her until the end of August to find somewhere else so she would be gone before I returned home.

Of course, even though both Haitian and Ronnie had stayed in my house for over one and a half years rent free, neither of them managed to save a single cent. Instead of using the opportunity to build up some savings, they ate more and used up every spare cent they made.

Respecting the Dutch law, I offered to pay the deposit and first three months' rent for them to move out and rent a new place.

Haitian explained that she could never leave the house because she needed to rent a really big house in order to have space for all her personal possessions. She continued until I agreed to send her three thousand dollars, which she claimed she needed for a new place. She had already had over $20,000 due to the bar she never paid rent for, a car I needed to buy for them, a generous gift to her voodoo-practising father after the Haitian earthquake and many other needs. They were just milking me dry of anything I'd earned.

I sent the money and found my house empty for the first time since I'd bought it. It was certainly empty! Haitian and Ronnie had robbed me of so many things when they'd left, including clothing, the new laptop I had bought in Amsterdam airport with Antonina, my camera's tripod, some rather expensive jackets, all my kitchen's saucepan lids, knives, forks, soup bowls, side and dinner plates. I wasn't left with a full set of anything once they had gone.

That's the thanks I get for helping people out, I thought. It was eight months later that I learned Haitian didn't really rent a place at all. She'd lied to me about needing the three thousand dollars. Instead, she moved into Ronnie's mother's house just two streets behind mine.

There was still a bad atmosphere lingering in the house even though I finally had it to myself. The stale and musty stench in the large back bedroom, where Haitian and Ronnie had slept, was unbearable.

I tried to leave the bedroom door open to allow some fresh air inside, but that permeated the air throughout the rest of the house. If I was expecting visitors, I'd have to close the door and spray air freshener all around the living room. I had to completely redecorate the room because Haitian had spat an orange liquid at the walls during her voodoo ceremonies. I wouldn't allow her to perform voodoo any more in the house, but I knew she would continue in the privacy of her and Ronnie's bedroom. They stuck cheap plastic hooks on the back of my new varnished bedroom door, completely defacing it, and also on the walls.

I had to put the mattress outside to let fresh air work its way through it. Even without the mattress, the room still had a stale, musty smell, which remained for several months, so I redecorated it.

While I was on the island, I wanted to get into my storage room, which also doubled as my workshop, at the back of my house. I went to where I always kept the keys, but they were gone.

I looked everywhere, but to no avail. Out of desperation, I called Haitian who admitted to taking the keys so no one, including myself, could open the door. Apparently, her personal belongings were still being stored there.

I demanded she return my keys immediately because I needed

to get into my workshop to do some things. She refused until I told her I'd cut my lock off because I needed to get in. She arrived in a remarkably short time with the keys, but she stressed that I must keep my store locked and not allow anyone in.

"What a bloody cheek!" I told her. She was not a friend and not renting the space. I also questioned what the hell was the three thousand dollars for if she didn't use it to rent a place? As always, she ignored the question and told me not to touch her things or there would be trouble. I knew what that meant.

I opened my workshop, but I couldn't even get through the door because the entire room was packed full of junk which was no good to anyone. There was a broken old fashioned TV, an old plastic typewriter, dozens of empty washing machine soap bottles, old furred-up aluminium saucepans, and broken bar stools.

I called her and told her she had to collect it all or I would arrange for it to be taken to the island dump. She freaked and threatened me with voodoo if I touched any of it.

With no voodoo and the absence of the smell of garlic and onions being fried five times per day, Inez moved back in. I just wanted to have some company, but I could have chosen better!

On evening I was standing in my living room talking to Inez who was in the bedroom at the time. Without any warning and for no apparent reason, I found myself lying on the floor where I was just standing in terrible pain. My right knee was badly dislocated and already very swollen. I couldn't understand what could have happened, and neither could Inez. I couldn't make it to the car so Inez called an ambulance to come and collect me.

Almost half an hour had passed before the ambulance arrived. By that time my knee was like the size of a football. The two paramedics secured me onto a stretcher and put me in the ambulance and proceeded to drive off to the central hospital where I'd be treated.

Once in the hospital I was given morphine for the very obvious pain and left to wait until a doctor was available. Soon after being examined, I was sent for an X-ray. The X-ray clearly showed my dislocated knee had half an inch gap between my bones. I waited a little longer, before two doctors returned, and together put my knee back into place. Next, I had to have a cast wrapped around my knee. Actually, the cast began at my ankle and continued up the entire length of my leg to my hip.

With my new purple cast I couldn't drive any more. Inez could therefore have full use of my car until my cast could be removed. I was told the cast needed to stay on for at least six weeks, but as I was soon to fly back to Nigeria, the cast had to be removed after just ten days.

I was determined the cast wasn't going to impair my holiday and managed to keep mobile with the use of crutches and taxis. Getting up and down steps was the most difficult manoeuvre, not to mention getting on a deep sea fishing boat! I had previously charted the boat and invited a good friend who was also a bar owner to accompany me on a deep sea fishing trip. Such trips were certainly not cheap in the Caribbean so I didn't want to lose my deposit, nor let down the boat owner who I had fished with so many times in the past.

I arrived at the quayside where my thirty-seven foot charter was moored at six o'clock in the morning on a terrible day. With torrential rain and gale force winds I worried whether the trip would be cancelled, and also if my friend would even turn up. At 6.15am the captain arrived together with his son, who was also his deckhand, and five minutes later my friend beeped his car horn as he drove past us to look for a place to leave his car.

With help from the captain and my six foot friend from the Dominican Republic, I was helped to board the vessel and into a soaking wet chair so I wouldn't risk falling on the very bouncy ride out of the marina. The storm was one of those freak Caribbean types, which soon passed by. Unfortunately, the rough seas had caused the fish to swim into deeper water so we knew we wouldn't have too much luck until later in the day. The going was very quiet, which was sad for my friend's first fishing experience. Luckily, the boredom wasn't to last.

The storm had loosened a large amount of seaweed from somewhere, which was floating all over the ocean. This became a real nuisance as it fouled our fishing lines, which we constantly had to reel in to clear them. Sometimes, a large piece of seaweed would foul a line causing the ratchet on the reel to slip and making us all jump, thinking we had a fish on.

The floating seaweed did have some very good advantages though. Some species of fish liked to shelter beneath it and feed on it at the same time. This was especially the case with dorado, which some people like to call dolphin fish for some unknown reason. They don't have any resemblance to dolphins.

In the Caribbean, they were mostly referred to as mahi mahi. With mahi mahi you could distinguish the males from the females as the females had smaller, more rounded heads than the male's larger, squarer heads. Mahi mahi like to jump out of the water once they are hooked as if they are dancing and usually gave a good performance. They are as tasty as they are beautiful with their turquoise appearance.

In the afternoon, my captain noticed a large area of seaweed in the distance and headed in its direction to pass as close as he could alongside it without risking our lines getting fouled again. As we began to pass the weed, the action started.

Suddenly, bang: one of the two rods on the port side was hit and the reel immediately started to spin; a second later, bang again and the second rod on the port side was hooked up too, then again from the rod on the starboard side which was almost bent double. The captain instantly pushed both the turbo diesel engine throttles hard down for a few seconds which hurled the boat forward at a rate of knots to ensure we all had tight lines and firm hook ups.

With the very loud roar from both engines, and a large plume of smoke from both their exhausts, *game on*, I thought as I was handed the starboard rod by the deckhand. My friend was handed the second from the port side and the deckhand took the third.

I couldn't assume the normal fighting position, which required both legs to be in a bent position on the footboard sticking out from the base of the revolving chair. Much of the fighting power was gained through the legs and lumbar region to get the necessary leverage to 'pump' the fish to retrieve the lost line from the fish's initial few runs.

It wasn't possible to simply reel in a fish of sizable proportions, especially all the while the boat was moving forward to keep the lines tight. Instead, I had my damaged right leg's foot on the deck and my left foot on the footrest, making it rather uncomfortable and difficult to play my fish. My fish was particularly frisky and crossed the deckhand's line. The deckhand noticed what was going on and crouched down and got under my line and stood up again, the other side of it. A minute later he had to repeat the procedure as my fish retuned back to my side again. My fish was trying everything not to end up on a plate.

Fish have the ability to spit out a hook the moment you allow the line to slacken. It is as if they are waiting for the opportunity, much to the frustration of many game fishermen. I particularly liked my choice of fishing boat, as the captain always flattened the barb on all his hooks to allow the fish to discard them easily if ever the line snapped. That was another reason never to allow the line to slacken.

The boat only used 50lb breaking strain line which meant the fishermen couldn't tighten the drag setting on their reels too much, to make the fish get tired sooner. I always set the drag setting on my own reels to 25lb. That meant the fish was pulling away from no more than a 25lb load.

It also meant that the fisherman was also pulling against a 25lb load, even if a fish weighed over 100lbs. If a fish pulled more than 25lbs, the clutch inside the reel would slip, enabling the line on the reel to be stripped until the fish grew tired. For the bigger fish, I used a 'fighting' belt. My fighting belt was about 5" wide, which spread the load around my lumbar region.

It had two narrow belts hanging from its front, which were there to clip onto the two lugs on large game fishing reels. It was a great help when I had a big fish hooked. When it was time for a fish to make another run, I could simply release my rod, leaving my belt to hold it, which gave my arms the chance to rest while I waited for my reel to stop getting stripped and again start pumping back the fish to regain my line. The technique was simple, but very effective.

You needed to smoothly pull the rod back towards you as far as it was comfortable, and then wind the line back onto the reel as you allowed the rod to smoothly fall forwards again. Also, with the boat's continuing forward motion, it was impossible to simply reel the line in normally in any case.

Considering we had had a very poor start to the day, catching nothing by 2.30pm in the afternoon, we returned back to the marina at 4pm with seven mahi mahi, one barracuda and two small tuna fish.

Once back at the marina, the deckhand would skilfully clean the fish and cut them into fillets for me to take what I wanted. I'd always drop some fish off to the seventy-nine year old lady living to the left of my house, and also some for the family living the other side of my house.

I liked to cook mahi mahi by seasoning some flour to cover a piece of fillet and deep fry it for fifteen minutes. If I ever returned with some lunar tailed grouper, I'd always kept them for myself and never gave those away. For me, they are the very best eating fish in the sea. They tasted as though you have cooked them in honey, as they were so sweet. You could identify them by the yellow crescent on the edge of their fins and they would only be a couple of pounds in weight.

While I was enjoying what I could of my time back on the island, it was becoming more and more clear that Inez had very obvious plans for putting my house to good personal use during my four-week trips to Nigeria. She began to receive a constant flow of text messages to her phone, all written in Papiamento so I knew they were from another islander. She used to show me the messages saying they were from the Colombian woman she rented a room from at the north end of the island, who I knew didn't speak Papiamento. From the delight on her face, they were obviously from another man or men.

I knew exactly what she'd get up to the minute I left. What I could never have imagined was that she'd made arrangements for a local man to move in the very same day that I'd flown off the island. When I was flying to Amsterdam, I suddenly had a strong gut-wrenching feeling that someone was with her in my house. As it turned out, my instincts were right.

She also demanded that I keep my rental car on-hire while I was off the island. It was a pleasant little luxury for her because she could drive down to the red light district just ten minutes from my house, to pick up additional customers when the local guy wasn't staying the night.

Before flying off the island, I had bought a listening device from a local island conman. All it needed was a mobile telephone SIM card slotted into it and a power supply. I hid it behind the TV in my bedroom thinking she would never find it, but after just a few days, it was unplugged, and after a few more days, its battery had depleted.

It did last long enough for me to listen to what Inez was doing with several different men in my bedroom. All I had to do was call the SIM's number and listen in. That experience was terribly painful while staying in a trailer in the middle of a West African swamp.

I called Inez just to interrupt her, but she always turned her phone's ringer off when she was busy. When I did manage to call her, she was always very aggressive and didn't want to speak. After that, she would hang up on me.

Like a perfect fool, I informed her of my arrival date. In hindsight, it would have been much better if I had given her a date a week later so I could catch her busy. I could have put it in all the local newspapers.

After flying from Nigeria to France, France to the Netherlands, and Netherlands to the island, I needed to wait over an hour at the island's airport for Inez to finally arrive in my rental car to pick me up.

When she finally arrived, she didn't say, "Hi, darling," or, "How are you?" No kiss, no nothing. Inez was angry I had returned because she couldn't use my house as a whorehouse for another four weeks.

She drove to the Italian clothing shop where she worked and left me to drive myself home. The fuel gauge was lower than empty. I opened the cubbyhole where I always kept some spare cash for parking and petrol, but that had also been emptied.

I got to my place and it was quite a sight. My garden hadn't been touched even though I'd left money for it to be maintained. I had electricity, water, and cable TV bills that hadn't been paid, which I'd also left money for, and my air conditioners had all been left on.

She had left plenty of evidence that there had been some wild nights while I was away. Under my sofa, I found the remains of a broken ashtray which I had bought in Amsterdam, and the base of a wine glass. Under my coffee table, I found the remains of another glass.

All my beer, whisky, and every other type of spirit had all been used up, and there was not a single thing left to eat. Inez had certainly been busy milking my house. Like Haitian and Ronnie, the marine and his young Colombian wife, the two young bar girls, and everyone else on the island who had entered my house, Inez had helped herself, together with her clients, to much more than she/they should have.

Why did I think anyone on the damn island would be different? In the middle bedroom of my house, Inez had stored her fifty-seven pairs of shoes. They were all very high heeled; bright, and multi-coloured, just like the ones all the other hookers wore whilst walking the streets looking for business.

When she returned back that evening, she had a very aggressive attitude towards me. Just like in the past, I was not welcome in my own home because it disrupted the lifestyles of those who used and abused it for their own gain.

She demanded I thank her for keeping my place so clean. I couldn't believe it. I asked her what all the broken glasses were doing under my sofa and coffee table. And then I asked her about the broken ashtray and disgusting sheets left in the washing machine, which I had already carried out and trashed.

Of course, she knew nothing about any of it and denied everything. I told her to get the hell out of my house and my life and go back to the brothels she loved so much. She ignored me because she didn't want to lose her free, private brothel and free rental car that suited her lifestyle so well.

Instead, she attacked me. She scratched my face and dug her acrylic nails into my chest, adding yet another scar to the ones Antonina had left. Inez wanted me to hit her, it was just like when Antonina threw herself at the kitchen table and chairs in Kazakhstan. *History*, I thought, *is repeating itself.*

I crossed my arms and let her get on with it without returning fire so she wouldn't have any excuses to call the police or anyone else, and then went to bed.

The next morning, I did the gentleman bit and made her some fresh coffee, freshly squeezed orange juice, and sandwiches. Meanwhile, I started the car and turned on the air conditioning while she was getting ready so she would be comfortable before she began working in the menswear shop.

I did my usual shopping to restock what Inez's sex clients had been encouraged to help themselves to, including my Cuban cigars! I decided that she was going the same night. I picked her up at eight o'clock in the evening from outside the shop where she worked and drove back towards my house.

Inez, as usual, insisted on driving. I moved over and let her take control. When we approached my house, I told her to stop at my favourite Hoi Sing Chinese bar, which she did, to my amazement.

She parked the car in true island style, right across two parking slots, and got out. In the bar, Inez was unusually friendly towards me, as she must have known I was about to kick her out. She even showed interest in my work instead of quizzing me about my salary to try to find out what I actually earned.

I wasn't being taken in by her desperate attempt to make things right this time. I just ignored her, looking across the bar whilst sucking on my Cohiba. After a while, I turned to her and coldly said, "We're off."

Of course, Inez asked where we were going next, so I turned, looked her straight in the face, and said, "To help you pack."

She ignorantly looked dumbstruck at first and then asked if we were going somewhere? I replied, "Me, no; you, yes." Startled, she asked, "Where am I supposed to go?" I replied, "Anywhere you want so long as it's the hell out of my life."

The three minute drive home was quiet … very quiet.

As we entered my house, I went straight to the kitchen and took out a roll of black plastic garbage bags that she could use to fill with all her nightlife clothing and fifty-seven pairs of high-heeled shoes.

Inez still couldn't believe she was finally being kicked out, but she only had herself to blame, just like Haitian and Ronnie and every other islander who had abused a good thing.

She didn't start packing anything; instead, she poured herself a whisky and sat next to me on the sofa. She tried to make polite conversation, hoping it would all blow over.

After two years of pure unadulterated hell, I was not going to be seduced into changing my mind. I got up and started packing for her, starting with her shoes from the middle bedroom into the black plastic bags.

She figured there was no going back and started to pack her skimpy little clothes from my bedroom drawers into more bags. Unbeknown to me, she took my five-day-old iPad, wedged it against the floor and the wall, and stamped on it. The screen shattered and the frame broke. After that, she put it back where she had found it.

After she had finished packing her clothes, she called her Colombian friend to come to collect her, and re-joined me back on the sofa.

Money, gold, and diamonds meant more to Inez than loyalty, love, and security.

After another twenty minutes, she received a missed call from her mobile. Without saying a word, she rushed out of the front door, jumped into her friend's car, and left.

Fantastic, I thought. For the first time, I was home alone and feeling so good about the sudden silence that I didn't know what to do next.

The following day, I drove into the town to pick up some more Cohiba cigars. I met the same island salesman who had sold me the little listening device.

I started talking to him about having security cameras fitted around my house to deter thieves passing by. He claimed to specialise in security cameras and said he'd come over to show me what he had available.

I'd already received a quote from a professional security company, but it was rather high. My hesitation gave the salesman an excuse to sell me his cameras, which later didn't work. He also sold me a computer and said it was necessary for the cameras to record to. Of course, there were no guarantees or refunds on the island, so I lost again.

The time came when I really needed to use the workshop. It was still full of Haitian's junk, so I began to call her from Nigeria several times a week demanding that she remove it. Every time I called, she promised to have it collected, but I knew she had no intention of losing her free storage space. Several more weeks passed before I told her that if it had not been removed by the Friday, I would have it all taken to the dump.

The Chinese bar owner, who had evicted Haitian from her bar just down the road, said she'd be happy to help me because she knew all I had been through with Haitian. She had experienced so many problems with her previously.

Early that Friday morning, she arrived with her father and one of his Chinese friends who brought his lorry. In no time at all, they had emptied my workshop of everything and even swept the floor clean.

When the bar owner saw the bar stools, she said that they were hers; Haitian had stolen them from her bar when she had been evicted. She left very pleased to have her stools back.

That day was bright and sunny, like most days on the island, with a gentle breeze that took the edge off the thirty-four degree heat. I packed some ice in my cooler bottle and drove down to a nearby beach, which was just twenty minutes away.

Content that I had finally trashed all Haitian's junk and could finally start making use of my workshop, I lay on the beach for the first time in months. I rented a sun lounger. It was so nice to just soak up the sunshine and drink a couple of cold drinks.

This is why I bought a house so far from Europe, I thought. I wondered whether a little bit of sunshine had been worth all the pain, stress and murder attempts.

I drew the conclusion that nothing could be worth all I'd gone through, and I began thinking about what to do with the place. After I'd taken in enough sunlight for the day, I made my way back to a peaceful, quiet house to try to begin enjoying it for the first time. That was what I hoped would be the case, but sadly, I was wrong again.

I had just finished watching a movie and gone to bed when I heard a police siren very close by. It only sounded for a second or two, and then it stopped. A couple of minutes later, it sounded again.

I got out of bed and peered through a gap in my front window blinds. I saw the flashing lights from a police car parked right outside my house.

Opening the front door to see what was going on, I heard the sound of Haitian's voice screaming, "There he is, there he is! He's the one who gave all my things away!" *What the hell is this all about,* I thought and went to unlock my drive gates to meet the police.

Haitian was screaming for the entire street to hear, "This is the man who gave all my things away! Arrest him now! He's got to pay for what he's done!" She continued on and on that I needed to compensate her six thousand dollars.

The police asked me why I'd removed all the woman's things from my store, to which I replied, "Because, after months and months of ordering her to remove it, and after telling her that if she didn't remove her junk from my property I would do it for her, I finally did just that."

The police told me I had no right to remove her things. I replied, "My house, my land, my store. I have every right to remove what doesn't belong there, especially considering the space isn't even rented."

To that, she started screaming yet again. Even Ronnie came forward and pointed his finger at me. He said, "You're in big trouble now, Andy. Real big trouble." I asked him to explain exactly what 'big trouble' I was in.

I knew what he wanted to say, but he couldn't explain to me in front of the police officers. I said it for him: "Voodoo? Is that what you're threatening me with?"

The police looked at them at that point, but she said, "What voodoo? I don't know anything about voodoo." I just started laughing in her face and turned to the police officers and said, "It is because of voodoo and interfering in my life that I kicked his and her ass out of my house and out of my life!"

Haitian freaked again and denied knowing anything about voodoo, so I asked Haitian if she wanted me to show the police officers the photos of her performing a voodoo ceremony for Antonina in my living room.

She looked horrified and said she didn't know what I was talking about. I repeated to the police that I had called her every day since arriving back on the island, including the day before I removed her things, but she still chose to do nothing about it.

Again, she started screaming that I was a liar and had never called her. She was holding her mobile phone in her hand, so I asked her in front of everyone if it was her mobile phone. She admitted that it was, so I asked her how long she had owned the phone. She answered, "You know I've had it since last year. Why do you want to know?"

That was what I was waiting for. I snatched her phone out of her hand, opened her call register, opened 'received calls', and showed the police.

My name was recorded every day for the previous two weeks, and then two to three times per week from Nigeria. "Now do you believe me?" I asked the police. I asked again whether they'd like to see some photos of her performing voodoo in my house, dressed in her white gown and wearing a red sash over her shoulders.

The older of the two police officers said that he didn't believe a crime had been committed, that it was more of a civil problem. He turned to Haitian and advised her to get a lawyer to deal with her things because it wasn't really a police matter.

When the police left, I was again in need of relaxation. After all that commotion, however, I was awake for almost the rest of the night.
No longer thinking I'd ever have any peace on the damn island I began thinking positively about cutting my losses and selling the house and moving on.

The next morning, I was outside washing down my paved drive

to freshen it up and remove all the dust that always got blown in, when Haitian had the nerve to pull up outside my entrance in the car I'd bought. She shouted, "I'm walking on your name. I was up all night burning candles in your ass. Soon, you'll be sorry, soon you'll regret trashing my junk, soon you'll be in so much pain you'll want to die. No doctor will be able to save you. I'm going to make sure you die!" She drove off after that.

I arrived at the house one afternoon a couple of days later and noticed that someone had drawn a strange kind of sign on the white wall adjacent to my entrance. I walked back from my car and noticed someone had also cut three little chunks out of the rendering on the corner of the opposite wall.

I went to open my front door and noticed three deep hammer marks just under my lock. Someone must have hit my door very hard because my doors were new and made of very hard wood. I began to clean and grabbed a bowl of warm, soapy water to wash the sign off my front wall.

After removing the drawing, which had been created using a stick of charcoal, I inspected the rest of my front wall. I found a small piece of folded cardboard that someone had taken the trouble to wedge in between the top of my wall and my white aluminium railings. It had my name written inside it three times.

Later that day, I decided to remove some of the weeds outside my front window because I hadn't done any gardening for a few weeks. Hidden amongst the weeds, I found half a chicken's eggshell that contained a piece of folded paper with my name also written three times.

There was no doubting who had done everything. It was clear that Haitian was continuing with her vindictive, sick, pathetic ways because she was not being allowed to live for free any more.

I called my Colombian handyman and asked him to do a really thorough cleaning around my house. I also asked if his wife wanted to clean the inside.

They spent the whole of the next day cleaning, and they found several more items outside my house that were well hidden. Haitian had also gone to the trouble of planting several items inside the house before she'd left.

I knew I would never be left alone to live a peaceful life, so I called a real estate agent to put my house on the market. On Monday, the sign was erected and photos were taken, but the real estate agent was hardly professional. He never bothered to upload the photos to his website.

Two months later, the sign was collected without warning or explanation, not an email or anything. I called another real estate agent who also erected his sign. He prepared a contract and uploaded the photos onto his website.

Okay, I thought, I'm *finally making a move in the right direction.* I felt quietly confident that there was at least a glimmer of hope that I'd be rid of the place and never need to return to the damn island again.

I continued rotating back and forth between Nigeria and the island until an increasing pain in my abdomen finally stopped me in my tracks. It had started soon after arriving in Nigeria in December, but on the 4th March 2012, I contracted chronic pancreatitis. Pancreatitis is known to be the most painful condition a bodily organ can hand out.

The deep, nagging pain I was suffering from since December 2011 suddenly hit an all-time high, delivering the most incredible agony I could ever have imagined possible.

I can best describe it as having a sword being pushed deep into my pancreas before it was twisted ferociously. At the same time, it felt like a strong hand was squeezing and crushing my pancreas.

I called one of my workers to call the camp doctor because I didn't have his number. In just three minutes, the Nigerian doctor and his nurse arrived at my room. He quickly assessed the amount of pain I was in, and helped me to his clinic where he could take better care of me. I couldn't straighten up and was curled up as I slowly managed to walk to his clinic. It was a short walk but still took me ten minutes. Both the doctor and nurse helped to support me while we gradually made the short trip.

He began by inserting a needle into my vein and connected a paracetamol drip to help reduce my pain. He continued to make several other checks to diagnose my problem. He said I needed to go to Port Harcourt where they had a better equipped clinic, so arrangements were made for a driver and an armed escort to take me there in the morning.

The next day, my armed escort, together with a mobile police escort, arrived to safely move me to Port Harcourt. Upon arrival, I was met by a South African doctor and taken directly to a bed where they changed my intravenous needle and connected me to a new paracetamol drip. I never found out why a new doctor insisted on replacing a perfectly positioned intravenous needle to one of their own?

Nothing by mouth was her first instruction, and that was the way it went for the next three days until I became stable enough to be flown out of Nigeria.

A Nigerian doctor accompanied me all the way to Paris and administered morphine at regular intervals during the flight. Because the flight tickets arrived very late, we only had an hour to make the two-hour drive to the airport in Port Harcourt.

While under the influence of morphine, I called Christopher, a Nigerian airport security friend, to inform him I was on my way because I was dying. He was horrified when he heard the ambulance sirens. He ran around the airport informing all his colleagues that his brother was in trouble, and that they should take out all the stops so I could make the flight.

He did such a thorough job in fact, that they even prevented the Air France check-in desk from closing. Plus, the air traffic control would not allow the flight to leave until I'd boarded.

As amazing as it sounds, my Nigerian security friend did quite a spectacular job holding up a fully loaded aircraft until I was on board. At the time, they were building an extension to the airport and the usual entrance was blocked off with traffic cones. Christopher even moved the cones and waited outside to catch the attention of the ambulance and guide it right outside the airports doors.

He made me give my passport to my doctor to get my boarding card while he personally escorted me straight through passport control without my passport. We went straight through the body and hand luggage scanners, through the departure gate and straight onto the flight, while my boarding pass followed behind with my doctor.

None of the Nigerians expected to take a dash from me this time out. They were all too worried about my critical condition and didn't try to ask me for anything! They were absolutely wonderful with their support and understanding.

I can only assume that the passengers who had been kept waiting had been informed that the delay was due to a medical emergency. When I entered the aircraft, everyone started clapping. My doctor arrived a short time after me, and the Nigerian air traffic control finally gave the all clear to take off.

Once in the air with the fasten seat belt sign turned off, we started looking for a place to hang my drip. Amie, the Air France flight attendant, rigged up two coat hangers from the overhead lockers which did a fine job.

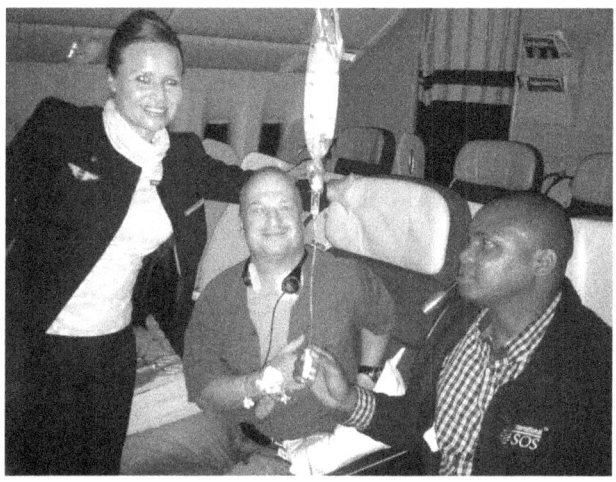

Because we were flying business class, the food menu was soon distributed. My wonderful doctor reminded me: "Nil by mouth!" It was my fourth day without food, so I had to put my menu back in the slot in the back of the seat in front of me and continue to endure the intense hunger pains I was having. The hunger pains were one thing, but the intense pains my pancreas was handing out were really something different.

The flight eventually landed in Paris after a one hour stop at Lagos. My doctor was busy putting all his equipment back in his bags while I struggled to put my jacket on with the needle in my arm. I'd passed my paracetamol bag through my sleeve, but with the intense pain, it was difficult to twist my body around to get into the rest of my jacket.

Many people stood in a queue watching me struggle until a Nigerian lady asked whether she could help. *Wow,* I thought, *at least there is one person with a heart.*

My accompanying doctor arranged for a wheelchair to meet us at the door of the plane, which had the added advantage of being fast-tracked to the immigration authorities. If it wasn't for the shorter route, it would have been a very long walk, and another hour spent in a queue.

An ambulance had also been arranged for my arrival, and it was waiting for me right outside the entrance. It took me to a hospital in the centre of Paris under blue lights and sirens where they confirmed the original Nigerian doctor's diagnosis that I was suffering from chronic pancreatitis.

The hospital didn't specialise in pancreas problems, so later that night after having a CT scan I was driven by taxi to another hospital in the centre of Paris. That hospital had France's top pancreas surgeon who could better deal with my problem.

The next day, they gave me an endoscopy and threaded a stent (tube) into my main pancreas duct, as they found it was blocked. They also gave me a CT scan. Once the results were available, the hospital decided that what I needed was beyond their capabilities, and I was discharged after five nights.

With the stent fitted, my health insurance flew me back to my point of origin, so I ended up back in the Caribbean. Unfortunately, the stent must have moved by the time I arrived on the island, because I was in the most intense agony once again. The next day, I went back to the airport to book a flight to Wales because during all this time, my mother had discovered a facility specialising in pancreas problems just forty minutes from her house, which was in Morriston Hospital outside Swansea.

It took seven days to get a seat on a flight out from the island because it was high season and all flights were fully booked. One morning at 4am I was hit with the most intense agony. I called the island conman, who lived just up the road, and thankfully he arrived outside my door in just five minutes, to take me to the new hospital in the village just down the road. I slowly walked to his car doubled up in agony, bent over and clutching my abdomen.

We arrived at the hospital just ten minutes later. I was crying with the pain. As soon as the Colombian duty doctor was told I had chronic pancreatitis she administered morphine and a paracetamol drip. She told me not to worry as they could carry out an operation right away! I knew that there were very few surgeons in the world who could carry out the Beger procedure, which I needed so I declined her kind offer. Once the morphine and paracetamol had taken effect I returned home with a prescription of oral morphine and tramadol painkilling capsules.

A few days later I departed the island and had deliberately overdosed on all the medication so I would look fit to fly. I was already flying as I entered the airport, but I knew it was only a temporary relief from what was to come once it had begun to wear off.

I finally arrived in Amsterdam airport and needed to wait another six hours before taking the one hour flight to Cardiff in Wales. I couldn't show anyone the intense agony I was enduring, as they wouldn't have allowed me to board the flight to Wales. I received some concerned looks due to my grey colour as I passed through the usual scanner before entering the departure gate, but I put on a false smile and was allowed to proceed.

Once in the air, I requested to be met with a wheelchair at Cardiff airport, as I knew I could no longer walk. When I was asked why, I explained that I was no longer capable of walking another step due to having chronic pancreatitis, and I was returning home for an operation. I'd waited long enough before requesting so I knew the flight wouldn't turn around due to a medical emergency.

The only chance I had of surviving was to make it to Morriston Hospital. The flight attendant understood and made the requested arrangements before we landed. By the time I landed in Cardiff, I was basically on my last legs and fading fast, leaning forward and could no longer sit back in my seat. I was supported while walking down the steps at the aircraft's door, as I was in a terrible state once we'd landed, and met by a man with the wheelchair. Time became everything and I was fast-tracked through the airport until I finally passed through the little arrivals area. It felt comforting to be back home on my own turf!

Chapter 25
Hospitalised

Soon, I left the arrivals area, where my sister was already waiting for me. It was the first time I'd seen her for several years, but it was a comfort to know that family are always around when you needed them the most.

The airport assistant pushed me all the way to my sister's car, and off we went. Due to the state I was in, my sister drove me directly to Morriston Hospital's casualty wing. My colour was so grey by this time and I could barely talk due to the agony I was enduring.

In the accident and emergency arrivals room, I was taken in by wheelchair pushed by my sister and seen immediately. A nurse asked whether I knew what my problem was, and I managed to squeeze out the word 'pancreatitis'. A doctor was informed and he immediately ordered morphine, which seemed to be routine when treating someone with pancreatitis.

I heard the nurse attending to me tell my sister that I wasn't going anywhere for a few days. Not long after, arrangements were made to admit me to Ward G, where I was to remain for the following two weeks.

I was administered a daily regimen of painkillers and a fat-free, light diet that was designed to be pancreas friendly. Basically, I ate baby food. It was in Morriston Hospital that I finally learnt what a complex and important organ the pancreas was. Apart from manufacturing digestive enzymes, it also manufactured insulin. As my pancreatic duct was blocked, my pancreas was basically eating itself every time it produced digestive enzymes.

After two weeks I was discharged with a large prescription of drugs that would last four weeks, until my much-needed operation. The normal waiting time for my operation was six months, which I certainly would not have survived, so I had to go privately. Four weeks later, I returned to Morriston Hospital to get prepared for what is known as the Beger procedure.

Emotions were running rather high while I lay there alone in a different part of the ward, waiting for the surgery I would undergo in the morning. All I kept thinking about was the 67% survival rate after such a massive operation.

I was confident that, with my luck, I would be among the 33% that didn't make it, but I was damned if I was going to give up without a fight! I kept thinking of what Haitian had promised me, and that I didn't want her to have the satisfaction that she'd succeeded in killing me.

At half past five the next morning, after a sleepless night, a nurse came to my bed and told me that I needed to shower and prepare for surgery. That shower felt very different. I felt like I was showering without any feelings or emotions. I felt like I was showering for the very last time. I felt so terribly alone.

I returned back to my bed in a kind of semi-shock, not really aware of my surroundings anymore. Soon after, the anaesthetist booked to take care of my pain and sleep administration visited me to explain the forthcoming procedure and the risks associated with having an epidural needle inserted high up inside my spinal column.

He was extremely detailed in his explanations, which added

the fear of God to how I was already feeling. He produced a document that I needed to sign my authorisation to continue. It cleared him of any responsibility in the event that my body did not perform in the right manner.

In less than an hour, my surgeon came to my bedside to inform me that, because there had been a serious accident, there was not a free bed available for me in the high dependency unit for post-surgery care. *Just my luck,* I thought as I began to dress again for the journey home.

I was picked up a couple of hours later by my mother for the second time, along with another big prescription of drugs to help with my discomfort and taken back to my sister's house. A couple of days later, I received a second surgery date for a month later. I repeated the very same procedure a month later, but everything felt different. After all the same activities as the previous month, my surgeon greeted me, instead of the anaesthetist.

He informed me that there had been another big accident, and my overdue operation had been cancelled yet again! I told him I was not leaving, as I knew inside I was not able to fight for life much longer, and off he went to see what he could do to change things.

After a half hour, a nurse came to my bed, accompanied by a porter, to take me down to the operating theatre. I owe my life to that surgeon in Morriston Hospital, Swansea and will never forget that he put his neck out to save my life. This is the reason why I was able to write Andy's Story, and no other.

Before entering the theatre, I was pushed into a room where I met the very same anaesthetist who had visited me before. He was already in surgical green, and prepared me for surgery in a room just outside the operating theatre. He started by numbing my spine where he was about to insert the epidural needle.

Next came a shock: I felt an extremely sharp pain as the epidural touched a nerve that was not yet numbed. The anaesthetist gave me another numbing injection and repeated the process several more times until the epidural had been inserted all the way up my spine. He then taped it firmly in place and made me lie back on the bed.

While he was carefully positioning the needle, a male nurse pushed gently against my shoulders to stop me pushing forward when I felt each stabbing pain. *This gives a new meaning of being stabbed in the back,* I thought. He was also professionally and genuinely sympathetic with what I was going through and very comforting and reassuring.

The anaesthetist then placed a mask over my mouth and nose and encouraged me to breathe in the oxygen, as he put it, which had a slightly sweet smell about it. I pulled it away from my face and laughingly said it's not just oxygen, smiled and placed it back in position on my face and inhaled deeply. The next thing I knew, I was waking up in the evening in the high dependency unit with tubes coming out all over my body.

I had four tubes coming out of my neck, two coming out of my left arm, one coming out of my right arm, a catheter, two drains coming out of my lower abdomen, and a tube that had been inserted into my nose and down into my stomach.

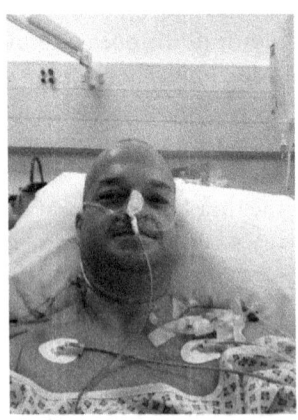

I was assigned a dedicated nurse to watch over me, as well as a doctor. Soon after waking up, my mother arrived to see how I was doing after the ten hour procedure. With all the medication being pumped into me, I was feeling somewhat comfortable considering I just had my stomach, pancreas, gall bladder, and several feet of small intestine worked on.

Life seemed to have a totally new meaning after that. A woman in the next cubicle was not so lucky. After a team spent over an hour and a half trying to resuscitate her after a similar operation, she passed away. It made me feel so guilty to be alive. I was thinking, she must have a husband and children and I hadn't, so why her and not me? I would have taken her place without thinking if only it were possible.

After what I'd seen, I persuaded the high dependency unit to let them have my bed for someone else more in need than I was. After three nights, they transferred me back to Ward G. I was in a different part of the ward this time, close to its reception so they could keep a close eye on me. The nursing staff were amazing there, and they did everything they could to make me feel comfortable.

Soon after arriving in the ward, they came to remove my catheter and asked whether a young student nurse could remove it, as it would be her first time, which I agreed to. Expecting a little discomfort, I waited for the pain. Fortunately, the pain I was expecting didn't come. Instead, it was all over in just a couple of seconds.

Because I still hadn't been reconnected to the morphine machine, I decided to go for a walk, get some fresh outside air, and smoke a cigarette. I was rather light-headed, and it took me about ten minutes to walk down the long corridor before taking the elevator to the ground floor, buy a newspaper from the shop at the hospital entrance and finally get outside.

I continually kept holding my stomach area throughout the walk. After a couple of puffs on the cigarette, I became really faint and giddy. Luckily, I had a wall to fall against. After that, I made my way back to Ward G.

Very soon, an incredible pain beset me where they had done the amazing operation. It grew worse and worse, which caused me to take little tiny steps as I slowly returned the way I'd come. After almost half an hour, I made it back to my bed. Seconds later, one of the nurses appeared and helped me back onto my bed just in time before I passed out with the pain. She wondered where the hell I had been.

She asked where I had got the newspaper from which was under my arm, and I replied, "The shop at the hospital entrance." I received my first reprimanding and was told in no uncertain terms that I was not to walk anywhere. The nurse added that walking around could result in my insides becoming outsides as I was only clipped together.

Once I was hooked back up to the morphine machine and tinkering with my iPad out, things began to feel more normal again. My mother visited me every afternoon, and my sister every evening. I was well taken care of. The nursing staff in Ward G continued to do all they could for all the patients to help raise morale, and they were simply amazing.

One unfortunate old man was admitted to my ward after having a severe heart attack at the age of ninety-six. He lay on his bed all day, completely still and unable to talk. I often wondered whether he was aware of his surroundings or whether he could hear people talking around him. His tongue was hanging out of the side of his mouth, and it was a deep purple colour.

Five days after my surgery, I became increasingly aware of my pain level rising. It became stronger by the minute until I could not move or speak. I couldn't even turn and reach for the attention buzzer to call for help. I eventually managed to get the attention of an eighty-six-year-old man in the next bed, and he used his buzzer to call for help.

Every time a nurse came to see what was wrong, the ninety-six year old heart attack victim saw the nurse and started making all kinds of noises. He stole the show every time, leaving me completely ignored.

My pain soon became unbearable, and I wanted to die. A few times, I got lucky and a nurse came to my bed and checked my equipment. She said it appeared to be working fine, but something was certainly not fine because I could no longer take any more pain, a fact I made clear for everyone in my ward. Finally, a young anaesthetist came to see what was wrong.

I had a button attached to the morphine machine that I could press for extra doses of morphine in between the pre-set dosages.
It didn't matter how many times the button was pressed, the machine was set to not give any doses more frequently than five minutes. The young anaesthetist noticed that I had pressed the button over four thousand times, so he realised that there was something seriously wrong.

He asked me whether I could lean forward so he could check my epidural needle, but all the pain had made me too weak to move. Two nurses helped me bend forward causing more agony so he could lift up my T-shirt and check my needle.

As soon as he could see my back, he immediately gave the instruction to bring a portable dose administrator because my epidural needle had moved out of position and was not able to block my pain at all.

The ward sister came quickly to my bed to apologise for all my intense pain, and she offered to have another epidural needle fitted. After remembering what it felt like when it was originally fitted, I declined her kind offer and chose to go with the portable unit to see whether it could do the same job.

Actually, the portable unit was not anything like as effective as the epidural block, but I was so well used to being in agony by that time, I basically didn't care anymore and at least I could see the needle in my arm rather than having a needle up inside my spine. The added advantage was that the new unit had wheels, which meant I could be mobile again! As a child, I could never keep still for long, much to my mother's dismay!

An hour later, equipped with my new portable machine, I headed down the corridor to buy a newspaper and pop outside for a quick smoke. The nurses began to give me a break because they knew it was better for my circulation to be mobile a few times per day.

On my seventh day in the ward, two physiotherapists visited me.

They told me I needed to accompany them for a short walk, and they'd be each side of me in case I wobbled. Much to their surprise, I asked whether we were going outside. They explained that that wouldn't be possible until a few more days of practice, and that they would just take me as far as the main corridor.

When I explained that I went down to the end of it a few times per day, took the elevator down to the ground floor, and went outside the main entrance, they just looked at each other in total disbelief.

So off we went with my morphine machine by my side in the direction of the shop to buy another newspaper. Halfway to the shop, the two ladies said that I'd gone far enough for one day and that it was time to return to my bed.

Okay, I thought, *I won't be a problem patient.* I did what I was told and returned to my bed and remained there for a few minutes until after they had gone *and the coast was clear.* Shortly after, I went for a newspaper for the eighty-six-year-old gentleman in the next bed and a quick smoke for myself.

My surgeon visited me most days to check on my progress.

His entourage always accompanied him. He was pleased to see me progressing in the right direction, better and better every day.

Due to a shortage of hospital beds, I volunteered to give up my bed just nine days after surgery and continue my recovery at my sister's home. I guess we all make mistakes, but that was a big one. I nearly undid all my surgeon's handiwork … and nearly succeeded in killing myself.

I did not know which foods I should avoid or which I should never eat again, nor had I been prescribed an amazing medicine called Creon. Creon is a pancreas enzyme that I needed to take every time I ate food. I chose to have smoked salmon with Philadelphia cream cheese and brown bread and butter.

Because it was so soon after being stitched back together, my pancreas was not able to cope with all the fat and grease, and I became very sick that night. I was awake most of the night with stomach pains that became progressively worse. I had terrible indigestion, until the pain became impossible to deal with.

My sister had already left for work in the morning as she owned the Mumbles Beauty Clinic, so I was alone to cope as best as I could. The best I could do, however, was not enough. All I managed to do was get down the stairs and find a phone to call my mother.

When she picked up the phone, I couldn't speak. She couldn't hear anything coming from my end until I forced one word out of my mouth: "Help." She immediately feared the worst, dropped everything, and drove over to my sister's house. She found me curled up into a ball on the floor of the living room in terrible agony, clutching my stomach.

She helped me half to my feet so I could make it to her car, but I was still curled up. I was able to walk a little, and slowly made my way to her car. A few minutes later, after avoiding most of the holes and bumps in the road we arrived at my mother's house where she could take care of me. Every bump in the road, which we couldn't avoid, was like being shot.

My condition deteriorated rapidly. Soon, I was in the bathroom vomiting bright yellow bile. I was in intense agony every time my newly stitched stomach muscles went into spasms.

Eventually, after the yellow bile was depleted a dark green fluid was thrown out. At that point, there was absolutely nothing left in my stomach to bring up, but that was only the beginning of my pain.

I continued to deteriorate until I ended up kneeling on the living room carpet with my arms on the sofa. The pain was similar to the pain I experienced when my epidural needle had shifted out of place.

My mother called the hospital, and the reception at Ward G told her to dial 999 and ask for an ambulance because I was in a very dangerous condition. I remember thinking that it was the second time in my life that my mother had called an ambulance for me.

The ambulance was called, but it had to leave from Morriston Hospital, which was quite a long drive away.

The ambulance controllers, true professionals in South Wales, also alerted the quick response vehicle, which arrived in just ten minutes. The paramedic entered my mother's house and found me in the same position I was in when the ambulance was alerted. He couldn't move me in the condition I was in until he had reduced my pain.

He began to give me gas, which was a safe option with no side effects for anyone, but it didn't help. He tried to push an intravenous needle into my arm, which took several attempts because my veins had learnt to hide from needles after my time in hospital.

Eventually, the ambulance arrived with two more paramedics to take me back to hospital. I was helped to my feet, but I was still curled up and not feeling any better. The paramedics surrounded me in case I fell as we made our way to the ambulance.

Those guys were fantastic. They were also very understanding and sympathetic to the discomfort I was enduring. They were fully familiar with what the pancreas can hand out. In the ambulance, the quick response paramedic was able to get an intravenous needle into my arm and hook me up to a liquid paracetamol drip. After that, they securely strapped me in for the ride back to the hospital, which I'd only left twenty-four hours before.

My mother called my sister, and she immediately cancelled all her afternoon appointments at her beauty salon so she was able to drive back to the hospital to see me.

When my ambulance arrived back at Morriston Hospital and the paramedics were busy wheeling my body into the accident and emergency room, both my mother and sister were already there.

Naturally, they were terribly concerned that I was suffering almost uncontrollably, and they were asked to move aside so I could be wheeled back into the hospital. I was wheeled into a cubicle that was freezing cold, and a Filipino nurse soon attended to me.

The first thing she did was hook up another bag of liquid paracetamol to help ease my pain. After that, she covered me with a blanket because I was shivering so much. Six hours later, I was admitted to Ward G for two more nights so I could stabilise. After I was discharged, I went back one week later because my surgeon wanted to check on my progress. After that, I returned to the Caribbean at the end of the week.

The island customs stopped me at the baggage scanner and

asked why I had so much medicine in my bag. I wasn't feeling up to giving a long, drawn-out explanation, so I just lifted up my T-shirt to reveal my new scar. He motioned for me to pass through the gate without any further ado.

I arrived at my house twenty minutes later, which looked fine from the outside. When I entered it, I was shocked to see mosquito curtains had been pinned around the entrance to my bedroom.

The conman who was watching over my house for me had turned it into a showroom where he could sell his imported mosquito curtains from China. The plan was for the two of us to share the profits 50/50.

He bought them for three dollars each, and he told me he was selling them for just ten dollars each. After paying the import duty, we were left with five and a half dollars to split between us ... or so I was told.

I pulled the trashy net off my bedroom doorframe because it was always in the way when I went through it. It left holes all around my new doorframe. I told him I did not want my house used as a showroom for the general public to enter, and I warned him not to do it again. After checking my personal items left in my bedroom drawers, I discovered many things had been stolen.

The salesman encouraged the general public to pass through the net fixed around my bedroom door so they could see how it closed automatically behind them due to its magnetic strips. There was no way of telling who had taken all the gold and money I kept in my room, but that wasn't of any concern to the conman as long as he secured new sales. For all I knew, he might have taken my things himself.

The next day, I was disturbed by a loud knock on my door. An islander was returning to buy another mosquito curtain. I told him the salesman wasn't around, but I would look for a curtain. I found one in the back bedroom, along with hundreds more like it.

I asked him how much he paid before because I wasn't sure what to charge, and he held out forty dollars. That was a surprise since my so-called partner had told me 50% of each curtain was not quite three dollars.

After checking my emails, I discovered I had been accepted for a six-month contract in Delft, Holland and needed to fly there in just two weeks. I immediately started making arrangements to ship all my personal possessions back to the United Kingdom, and sold off as much of it as I could, including my beloved fishing gear!

Nobody on that island ever seemed to have money, so I had no choice other than to let people take things with the promise that they'd pay me as soon as they had enough money. Of course, the outcome was obvious and I never received a cent.

So six weeks after my operation I was off to work again, just a few months earlier than advised.

Chapter 26
The Netherlands

I arrived in Amsterdam on the 27th of July 2012, which was a Friday morning and took my time getting to my usual hotel in the centre of the city, opposite the central railway station where Antonina had joined me before. I'd used the same hotel for many years whenever flight connections forced me to.

They had recently renovated part of the old building, and I was lucky enough to get a new room. I went to sleep early that night, and I spent the next day wandering around looking in shop windows before taking a train south to Delft on the Sunday, which just happened to be my 50th birthday. A birthday I wasn't expecting to reach.

Just an hour later, I arrived in Delft. I was grateful that it was a warm and sunny day. The taxi driver recommended places to spend the day, and it was a good start to the new location.

I found a nice bar where I could sit outside to enjoy the sunshine called the Café De Engel, lit a Cohiba, and sipped a cold Dutch beer. It all felt very relaxing until I heard a voice that was deliberately loud enough for me to hear.

The voice said, "I bet he's English, with a pint and a cigar." I reacted by saying, "Welsh, actually." I smiled and continued gazing out across the town square.

The man introduced himself as Jack, a bricklayer from Northampton. He explained that he had been working in Delft and around that area for almost five years. He proceeded to recommend all the popular places to eat and drink.

One of his younger Dutch friends turned up, Gordy, and they started taking me from one place to another, which was not a bad start for my first day in Delft.

I woke up the next morning feeling a little worse for wear considering I was not to drink alcohol for the rest of my life, and took a taxi to the office where I would spend the next six months working as the project quality manager.

The project was still in its front-end engineering design phase, so there was plenty to do, including writing procedures for the project staff to follow. I was only working from Monday to Friday, so I had every weekend to enjoy and absorb the ambience of Delft. I noticed numerous tourists of differing nationalities visiting the quaint little town.

Due to the rather limited choice in my hotel's restaurant, I chose to eat out every day by walking five minutes to the town square. The first bar I passed was called Café Koepoort, which meant 'cow gate' in Dutch. It was the original entrance to the square, where they had driven the cows through on market day hundreds of years before.

The owner was a truly amazing lady called Sonja. Sonja and the other Dutch regulars in her bar became like family for me. Considering the pressure of so much work in the office, Sonja's bar was a relaxing retreat.

Not long after I arrived in Delft, my so-called island salesman friend offered to help me find a courier to ship my remaining cargo back to the United Kingdom. I knew only too well by then that when an islander offered to help, it was not going to be free.

He quoted me $1,900 dollars to ship my cargo using a local

island courier. He also sent me the company's salesman's name, email address, and phone number. That way I could check to ensure that the quote was genuine. Not.

He also added that it was the last chance to ship anything back to Europe, the next opportunity would be six months later! As if!

Of course, the deal had already been agreed upon, along with commissions and a few hundred dollars extra, but I wasn't accepting it.

My so-called local friend reacted very badly to my refusal after he, "Had gone to so much trouble to help me." He told me to arrange my own courier. My cases were to stay in the house for several more weeks until a Dutch friend helped me find a professional courier who eventually shipped my things.

That wasn't before the conman went through all my things, helping himself to whatever he wanted. Some of the items he took were quite valuable and impossible to replace, especially all of my instruments I used for piping and welding inspection. He probably sold those to the island oil refinery workers because they'd be no good for anything else.

His next email included the utilities bill for the previous month, which also horrified me. I couldn't understand why my electricity bills were always double the normal cost when he was looking after my house than when I lived in it.

A few weeks later, I discovered the reason.

My very good Dutch friend Jan emailed me to ask whether he could buy two small wooden tables from me. His wife had seen them in my living room when they had collected a stereo system they'd bought.

I told him he could have the tables for free, all he had to do was collect them. I gave him the salesman's mobile number so he could make sure the house was open when he arrived, so off he went.

That evening, he emailed me to confirm he had the tables, but he explained how shocked he was when he arrived at the house. The front door was left wide open, and when he walked inside, he saw that all my air conditioners were on full blast.

Also, the damn Chinese mosquito curtains had been refitted onto my bedroom doorframe … and all the other bedroom doorframes. He even put up a curtain on the back door.

My dining room table was completely covered with hundreds of curtains, and my living room was full of boxes. The salesman had turned my house into a showroom and warehouse where the general public could check out the merchandise before buying it.

It was great for the salesman: a rent-free showroom with free electricity. He boasted to my friend that he and his girlfriend spent their free days at the house. There, they got their washing done using the stock of powder and completed other tasks at my expense.

Because my house was on the market, I called my real estate agent and had him visit my house to have the salesman remove everything. I wanted the conman kicked out, and I wanted the keys taken away from him.

The conman sent me thirty-seven abusive emails that weekend, but I didn't bother answering any of them.

Jan found a courier who would fly my cargo back to the UK for just $535, proving the conman's quote was totally ridiculous. I don't know what I would have done if it weren't for my Dutch friend. He did so much to help me. If only I had met him a few years earlier!

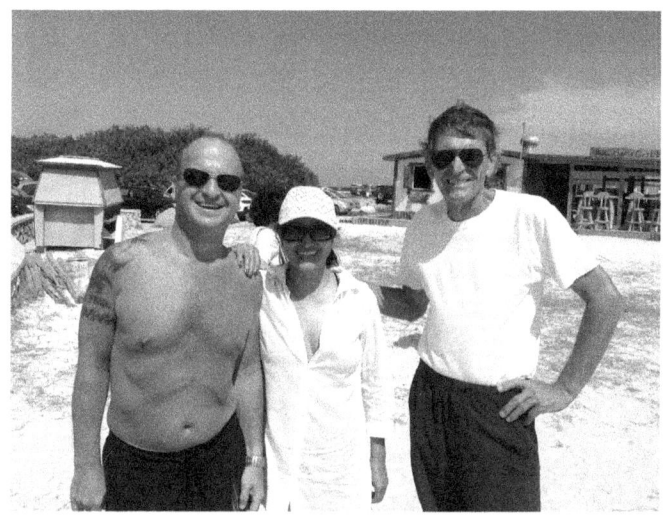

After working a few weeks and trying to achieve as much as possible to bring the project deliverables up to date, I had finally worked myself half to death. I was not supposed to return to work for a few months, so just six weeks after my operation was way too soon.

One Saturday morning, I was wandering around the town square area in Delft watching a brass band playing whilst talking on the phone to my mother. I started to lose the feeling in my left hand, with which I was holding my phone.

After a short time, my entire arm began to go numb. Then my right arm began to feel the same. I was now using both hands to hold my phone because it began to feel heavier by the minute. I started experiencing pins and needles all over my back, and my legs became heavy to move.

I finally made it to a bench seat in the town square, so I took the weight off my feet whilst continuing to talk to my mother. She was getting increasingly worried as I described what was happening to me.

My arms became too heavy to hold my phone to my ear, so I said goodbye to my mother. I told her I would call her back later.

I felt weaker by the minute, and I ended up lying down on the bench. At that point, I began sweating intensely all over my body. I ended up completely soaked. I decided I couldn't stay there indefinitely, so I slowly sat up and gazed across the square. I saw the first bar I went to, where I had met Jack on my birthday.

I slowly stood up, but I felt very giddy. I was walking all over the place like a drunken man. People were looking at me wondering what was wrong with me.

I managed to get to the bar, but I almost fell on top of the outside tables whilst passing them to enter the premises. At the bar, I sat on a stool. The barman came over to me and asked whether I was feeling okay.

I told him I wasn't feeling very well, and he gave me a glass of water. He called the owner who had recently recovered from a cancer operation himself. He tried to call an ambulance, but due to the brass band's performance, all the streets were closed off.

I called a local Dutch friend called Myrthe, but she told me she was out of town coaching hockey and could not get to me. I next called Jack. He was free, and he came straight to the bar to meet me.

In the meantime, Myrthe called Sonja, and she dropped what she was doing to find me. Following the bar owner's directions, she managed to drive reasonably close to the bar. Both Jack and the bar owner walked with me by walking on either side of me in case I fell one way or the other.

Ten minutes later, Sonja arrived and drove me to the Delft hospital. They kept me there until the next morning when I felt fine again and went home.

A strange visitor landed outside my hospital bed window while I lay there alone. It reminded me of the pigeon outside my house back on the island, the day my mother had visited me. It was a little freaky, as even when I walked down the hospital ward's corridor to the television room, the feathery visitor walked along the outside wall until it could look at me again.

The next day, I went back to Sonja's bar in the afternoon to thank her for helping me the day before, but she wasn't there. Instead, Myrthe was there along with a carrier bag she had filled with a new razor, toothbrush, toothpaste, other toiletries, and a new pair of pyjamas. She was about to bring it all to me while I was in the hospital as she knew I didn't have anyone else to help me. That was so typical of the thoughtful and wonderful people in Delft.

I moved out of the hotel and into an apartment because the company I was working for said it was cheaper for them. It was a good move because it gave me the opportunity to cook for my local Dutch friends and invite them over from time to time.

The Dutch encouraged me to learn the local customs, and near Christmas, on the 5th of December, they all came over to my apartment with very nice food that they had prepared the night before. They came with little presents, which they'd wrapped up ready to play a 'Sinta Claus', or 'Sinterklaas', patron saint of children, game after we had finished eating.

In the Netherlands, 'Sinterklaas' came before Santa Claus and added to the build up to Christmas. As usual my wonderful Delft friends helped me clean up before they left. 'Sinterklaas' was a very exciting time for children and on the previous weekend, 'Sinterklaas' had ridden a white horse through the streets of Delft. Everyone in Delft was out that day and had lined the streets in readiness to watch 'Sinterklaas' riding by. It was so busy that day, and the atmosphere in the beautiful little town was electric.

During December, I'd arranged to spend Christmas back in Thailand. I hadn't been to Thailand for five years and I often wondered how Wi was doing. We had kept in occasional email and telephone contact since I'd left the country and Wi always stressed how worried she was when I told her what was going on in my life, so I booked flights and a hotel room in Bangkok and off I went.

Wi was waiting for me at the airport to welcome me back, but where I didn't know. After walking around for an hour I found a kiosk which was to help tourists. A very nice Thai gentleman had been watching me looking around and offered to help me. As my mobile phone didn't work there he used his phone to call Wi.

Wi answered her phone and explained that she thought she'd seen me walking past her several times, but she remembered me as short and fat, not short and slim, so didn't approach me. I told her to go to exit gate number three which I was close to, so she met me a few seconds later. Wi looked exactly the same as I remembered her five years before.

She was amazed how much weight I had lost due to my pancreas problem and told me that she couldn't call me 'Baby Pig' any more. Actually, due to my pancreas and new diet, I had lost twenty-eight kilos so some good came out of it. It also rendered me as a non-smoker, much to Wi's delight, but I would still have the occasional beer from time to time; but not too often.

It was also the perfect opportunity to meet up with Neil, or should I say Alan #3?

We hadn't met for four years so Neil and I had a lot to talk about. It was also a great opportunity to show Neil my favourite restaurant in Bangkok. It was probably the only place Neil hadn't already been to in Bangkok. It was a seafood market as well as a restaurant and located half way down Soi 24, off Sukhumvit Road.

We had the taxi stop before we entered Soi 24 so we could walk the rest of the way. Actually, I had forgotten how far down the Soi the restaurant actually was and it felt like forever until we could finally see its huge street sign.

You could simply buy your choice of fresh seafood from all around the world and take it home, or have it cooked any way you fancied and eat there. It was the restaurant's proud boast that if it swims they'd have it! You couldn't possibly miss the street sign either.

It was my original plan to fly north to meet her family again as her father wanted to show me how my cows were doing. I had bought five cows back when I worked in Kuala Lumpur, but they had increased since then to over thirty so Wi's father was very proud of all he had done while taking care of them. My time in Bangkok went very quickly so I didn't make it up there. Sad, really, as I hadn't seen them since my Thai wedding day.

Instead, we spent my short visit in downtown Bangkok and exercising Wi's little dog, Booboo. She had rescued him from Thai children in the street near her place. They were throwing the newly born puppy up into the air and watching it land on the ground. Wi ran over and rescued the poor little puppy, its eyes still closed, and taken it home to try to bring him up herself.

Wi fed him milk through a syringe and he managed to survive. She took extra special care of him and called him Booboo. Wi also made monthly trips to the local veterinary for Booboo to be checked over and have his injections to protect him from getting heartworm, which is prolific in hot countries.

I promised that I'd see her father on my next visit, which would be in July 2013.

My work in Delft was extended until the end of January 2013, which suited me fine because I was busy looking for another contract back overseas. I definitely didn't want a lapse in work after being out of commission for almost five months in 2012 due to my pancreas.

I was happy to leave my job there as it released me so I could return to an overseas location, but deeply saddened with the thought of when I would next see my Dutch friends.

On my last night in Delft, my friends had arranged a farewell party in Sonja's bar. Myrthe had gone to the trouble of cooking very nice Indonesian food for all to eat as part of the get-together. Unbeknown to me at the time, they had secretly got together on the Sunday afternoon prior to my departure to make some team photos, which they had framed behind glass and presented, to me on the night. They had even attached two pairs of little wooden Dutch 'clogs' to hang down over the front of the frame!

To add to my rather emotional farewell, Sonja's mother and father also joined the party. They were such lovely people and Sonja's father was a famous glass blower, and his products were well known in Holland and extremely valuable. Her father came over to me and began to explain that during his manufacturing career he had only ever made one dolphin.

During his detailed explanation, it was clear that the one and only dolphin he had ever made was a prized possession of his. With no further ado, he carefully un-wrapped the package he was holding and presented me with his dolphin. I felt quite choked to receive such a beautiful keepsake from Delft and it will be something I will always keep on display, but in a very safe place.

After a few weeks I secured a new contract back in the Middle East.

Chapter 27
Kurdistan

In April of 2013 I went to Kurdistan, an oil and gas rich region of northern Iraq. My first impression was how nice the people were in Kurdistan, quite comparable to Europeans. Erbil can proudly boast to having the oldest city in the world, the 'Citadel', which dates back over six thousand years and was under restoration at the time to bring it back to its former glory.

Erbil was a peaceful city and there weren't any real security issues for several months. That said, as an expat in a foreign country with a history which included war, I didn't advertise my presence anywhere. I avoided trips to the popular souks and other attractions. Instead, I travelled to and from the office every day and only made a brief visit to a nearby hotel on a Friday night with a couple of Dutch colleagues.

Sadly, things did seem to hot up as Al Qaeda moved up north, as there wasn't much more they could destroy down south in Baghdad and other areas. It was a sudden reminder when five car bombs exploded not far from the office I worked. Two of the car bombs were disguised as ambulances, which I felt was extremely distasteful, but the insurgents didn't seem to have any limits. A convoy of crude oil tankers were also stopped and their drivers beheaded on the roadside by their fellow Muslims. We could only imagine if we had also been stopped.

Fortunately it didn't last long and there were no more instances until a shoot-out down the road in Kirkuk, which was televised live on Kurdish TV. The Kurdish people were not about to entertain any more mistreatment after what they'd already been through years earlier. The Peshmerga, who were their original freedom fighters and now their official national guard, managed to kill all twelve of the insurgents in a long street fight, which they'd televised for all to see.

After working for four months it was time for me to have a break. I hadn't seen Wi since December so I decided to return back to Bangkok to see how she and little Booboo were doing. I arrived just a week before my birthday and rented a room in the same hotel as the last time, as small dogs were allowed to stay. Naturally, we needed to use the service lift so the other guests wouldn't see Booboo, but that was fine. So Booboo was also on holiday.

We had made arrangements for Wi's father to fly down and join us for my two week visit. I hadn't seen him since our wedding day and wanted to see how the seventy-six-year-old was doing. He enjoyed his stay, as there were so many new experiences for him, even though it was in his own country.

He hadn't eaten sushi before, nor pizza, curry or Italian food, so every day we'd take him somewhere different. A Thai friend arranged for us to go on a day fishing trip just outside Bangkok where I managed to catch eight large catfish before giving up exhausted, but Wi's father continued until he'd caught twelve of them.

After a pleasant break, it was back to Kurdistan and business as usual. I decided not to leave it quite so long before taking my next break, but that time was to return to Wales for a couple of weeks and see my mother. As usual, two weeks went very fast and I returned back to work via Dubai, as I needed to have a TV interview with Marine Biz TV.

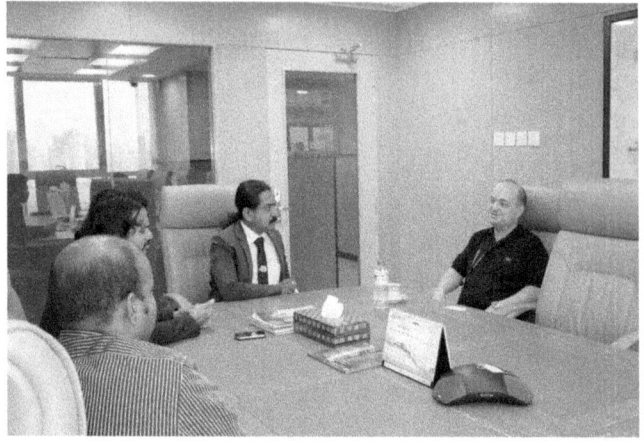

The interview was to create enough footage for a twenty-two minute final cut documentary about my life in the oil and gas industry. There was a lot to discuss and the final outcome was two thirty-minute interviews which the TV company broadcasted all over the world.

The first interview regarded my thoughts on working both onshore and offshore and advice for new recruits thinking to work offshore. The second interview was focused on the murder attempt made on me in Kazakhstan and the dramatic effect voodoo had on me, which changed my plans for continuing my life on the Caribbean island.

The company I was contracted to in Kurdistan was allocated an unlucky 'block' by the ministry of natural resources, so after drilling several oil wells they decided it wasn't going to be a sustainable investment after all and disbanded their team. So it was back to Wales for me until my next overseas contract.

After working seven days a week for nine months, I was feeling tired by then in any case, so it was somewhat a sad result from visiting Iraq, but the much needed rest was welcome. The people were very nice in Kurdistan and all the problems were not their own doing. I sincerely hope that one day, the problems will all come to an end and the country can return to its former glory.

Chapter 28
Malta

After leaving Iraq earlier than planned, I made a visit back to Delft in Holland to visit my Dutch friends. During my two week visit I was receiving many work inquiries so I figured I'd soon be contracted on another overseas contract.

The contracts didn't materialise so in March of 2014, I flew to Malta to stay in Qawra for a month, as it had been nine years since I'd last visited the island. It was a perfect opportunity to rewrite this book as its first edition contained many mistakes from its original American publisher's editorial proof read, which they had had done in the Philippines!

The proof read was disastrous as this manuscript was rewritten in a form of English new to me. There are still mistakes, which I have since missed, but they're hard to pick up on a computer screen.

On my first day, I needed to look for somewhere I could have a traditional English breakfast to start each day. The first place I found was across the road from my hotel called 'Images', which was owned by a half-Maltese, half-English man called Mark with his partner Vanessa from Wales.

Mark was well known on that part of the island and his bar

was famous for its karaoke nights. Mark's proud boast was that he could sing all the well-known songs ever written. I continued to visit 'Images' every morning for a good meal before starting my day. Mark was also a great asset to visiting tourists with organising tourist trips on both the main island, Gozo and even across to Sicily.

On my second day on the island, I found an alluring wine bar, boutique and café called 'Bella Bar' close to my hotel in Qawra, which I also began to visit every day. The venue was perfect with its relaxing background music, fast Wi-Fi and friendly atmosphere. As I sat down, a tall slim lady with a foreign accent began by serving me an Italian coffee, while I opened my laptop. Her name was Livia and she was from Hungary, living on the island together with her Hungarian husband and cat.

Later that day I was introduced to the owner, Susan, who was originally from Glasgow, Scotland. Susan explained that her husband was currently overseas on business in the Philippines, but due to return in a few days. That Sunday, I got to meet him. Susan introduced me to Chris later that afternoon who was originally from Sweden. Despite Chris's jetlag, he chose to spend the rest of the day in their bar and we both had a lot to talk about.

Chris explained in great detail the advantages of living on the island, and I began wondering why I had ever bought a house in the Caribbean, so far from Europe and also from home. I began to think if I'd originally purchased a property in Malta, I would have avoided all the hell I'd been through, meeting Haitian and Ronnie, and all the other deceitful people on that Dutch Caribbean island.

As an added bonus of living in Qawra, there was a spa just across the road called 'Soul Solutions', which was owned by a lady from Dublin in the Republic of Ireland by the name of Tracy. Tracy had a strong character and was most entertaining with her vibrant Irish twang. I'd occasionally visit Tracy's spa to receive revitalising holistic therapy and reflexology, which refreshed me and gave added energy to continue working while on the island.

It's still a slight culture shock being back in the company of genuine and civilised people; such a change from what I'd been used to, especially after some events I should not have survived, which I can finally start to put behind me.

For now, I will continue travelling around the world, visiting and experiencing new cultures, and later write a sequel to better explain what became of Andy.

Thank you!

www.ingramcontent.com/pod-product-compliance
Lightning Source LLC
LaVergne TN
LVHW051108080426
835510LV00018B/1960